YAHWEH TO HELL

Why We Need Jesus Out of Politics!

RICH WOODS

YAHWEH TO HELL
WHY WE NEED JESUS OUT OF POLITICS!

iUniverse books may be ordered through booksellers or by contacting:

iUniverse
1663 Liberty Drive
Bloomington, IN 47403
www.iuniverse.com
1-800-Authors (1-800-288-4677)

ISBN: 978-1-4917-5989-9 (sc)
ISBN: 978-1-4917-5990-5 (hc)
ISBN: 978-1-4917-5988-2 (e)

Library of Congress Control Number: 2015903389

Print information available on the last page.

iUniverse rev. date: 3/13/2015

CONTENTS

To the sun, moon, and stars in my universe—my wife, Jane. I am nothing without her.

ACKNOWLEDGMENTS

→ First and foremost, I would like to thank my inner circle: MJ Mandalay, Cigars & Scotch, Shadow, Joe Conte, and my brilliant, breathtaking wife, Jane. Not one of you is sane, and I would trust you all with my last dollar.

→ Dr. Sheila Ackerlind, who has the academic background to tell me when I am mistaken and who loves me enough to let me down easy.

→ William Hamby, columnist and secular activist, for writing my foreword, and not making me feel like an idiot even though he's a lot smarter than me.

→ Bob Ingle, renown author, radio and TV political analyst, and syndicated columnist who takes the time to offer sage advice when he doesn't have to.

→ Penn Jillette, who, despite his celebrity, has always been gracious to Jane and I.

→ Richard Dawkins, Daniel Dennett, Sam Harris, and the rest of the rational, scientific minds who help us to think differently.

→ My Family, lunatics all.

→ Everyone whom I quote, dead or alive.

→ And lastly, to Hitch. He was like no other.

None of what I do happens without any of you.

FOREWORD

When I was asked to write a foreword for this book, I was both honored and a little flabbergasted. Rich Woods and I go way back, and for all the things upon which we agree, we are something of an odd couple. I'm a bleeding-heart liberal academic, and he's a Jersey workin'-man's man who speaks nostalgically of the old Republican party. I spend a great deal of my time trying to get people to be civil to one another, and Rich can, and often has, derailed the whole thing with more insults per paragraph than high school dropouts per Sarah Palin rally. Okay, that was a bit forced, but they say you should always lead with a joke. Also, I think it's important to honor the tone of what is to follow, even if it's a bit out of my wheelhouse. This is a funny book, and my specialty is meticulous, sober analysis of religion and politics.

Ironically, the fact that I couldn't (and probably wouldn't) write this book is exactly why I'm thrilled to contribute to it. Early on, Rich makes reference to a certain "left-wing douche-baggery" that would take another book to fully rant about. At the risk of stealing his future thunder, I think this is an important idea for us to explore. I'm a liberal, and it is literally my job to advocate for the oppressed. More than many, I know the power of language to oppress. I'm also a white man in America, and with that status comes a great deal of responsibility to temper my speech. I have the power to oppress, and if I am to be moral, I must not use that power.

The thing is—I think we liberals sometimes get caught up in the spirit of an idea without examining how things actually work on the ground. We understand that it can be harmful to call someone names, so we vow never to call anyone names. We see that bullying harms children, so we make sure that nobody can ever say we stood in a bully pulpit. To our empathetic and pacifist minds, if life can be lived without ever being mean to someone else, it is a better life.

Sometimes, we take that idea too far. The power of language doesn't exist in a vacuum. To oppress with language, there must be a power imbalance. To the point, it's why it's okay for a black person to call me a "cracker," and yet I must never utter the word that must never be uttered. It's why we don't have "White History Month." When language oppresses, it is always spoken by the oppressors. Certainly, when the oppressed employ mean, condescending, or spiteful language toward the oppressors, they are being mean, condescending, or spiteful, and this is a moral decision with which they must come to grips. But we must recognize that this is different in kind from "keeping people down" with language.

As I write this foreword, America is yet again in the midst of a divisive race discussion. There are still nightly protests in Ferguson, Missouri, after a white policeman shot a young, unarmed black man under highly suspicious circumstances. Just last week, a grand jury member allegedly leaked the news that there is not enough evidence to even charge the officer. This may or may not turn out to be true, but unfortunately, it's completely plausible. If another white cop gets away with murdering another black man, it will just be business as usual in America.

The reason I bring up Ferguson and race relations is that I think there's a useful comparison. Quite simply, there is nothing that any black resident in Ferguson can say, publicly or privately, that will unfairly diminish the power of the police to discriminate against black people or murder them with impunity. The reason, of course, is that the police have the power, and the (mostly white) judicial system lets them keep it. Hurtful words don't matter when they come from the powerless. "Oh, you called me a bad name. I'm so hurt. Anyway, I've got a round of golf to play. Watch your back! Wouldn't want you to get arrested for something as trivial as insulting someone in charge …"

Hopefully, this illustrates that "offensive" language doesn't always have the same meaning or power as oppressive language that uses the same words. More hopefully, it explains why the following offensive, often tasteless, derisive, condescending book should be read from front to back—not with a sense of outrage at the delivery but rather with the knowledge that the nonreligious in America are very much powerless against the onslaught of Dominionist religious leaders. These powerful men and women can render an opponent hopelessly unelectable with the utterance of one word: "atheist." Recent polling shows that atheists are less trusted than Muslims in an America that has been at war with Muslims for decades. For all the GOP bloviating about President Obama's (nonexistent) Muslim background, it's actually more likely that we'll have a Muslim president than an atheist one. That's how powerless atheists are in America to effect political change. If an atheist goes on a book-length rant and the language offends? Well, it's one thing to be offended, and that's fine, but it's another to accuse the author of wielding his pen as a weapon of oppression. Quite the contrary is true.

Today's America is absurd. We are the laughingstock of civilized nations. We are the only nation in which it is politically advantageous to not only deny science but to brazenly flaunt "opinions" that are patently false by any sane measure of reality. It has often been said of American Democrats like me that we are too nice. We refuse to take a hard stand, it is said, and our concern for other people's feelings gets in the way of actual political accomplishment. Perhaps Dark Helmet was right when he said, "So, Lone Star, now you see that evil will always triumph because good is dumb." When other people are saying things that most sane people would call stupid, maybe it's time to start calling people stupid.

One of the things that's universally true about humans is that we hate to feel stupid. Rich Woods has taken a direct approach to changing America through aversion therapy. If you're on the fence about either Christianity or voting Republican, then I challenge you to make it all the way through this volume. I don't know if I could do it in your position. But do it—not because it's going to be easy but because there's no excuse for being undecided today. Things are too bad, and they're getting worse. It is more important now than ever for voters to control the destiny of our country. If it takes two hundred pages of well-deserved jokes at the expense of right-wing dignity, then this bleeding-heart liberal with douche-bag tendencies thinks that's a great idea.

William Hamby, MSW

CHAPTER 1
Opening Statements
(A Volley Across the Bow)

Is God willing to prevent evil, but not able? Then he is not omnipotent. Is he able, but not willing? Then he is malevolent. Is he both able and willing? Then whence cometh evil? Is he neither nor willing? Then why call him God?

—Greek philosopher Epicurus[1]

---

[1] Great-Quotes.com, *Epicuris*, http://www.great-quotes.com/quote/5538

Mariama is a delicate eight-year-old little girl who lives in sub-Saharan Africa. She loves music, and she loves to dance. When she smiles, it's as if one can see a reflection of hope and wonderment in her face. She is simply beautiful. Her name means "Gift from God."

Mariama has been solely responsible for her younger brother, Sekou, ever since their mother died of AIDS last year. Two years prior, her father had been killed by guerillas in one of many regional skirmishes. She does not sing or dance anymore. Nor does she smile.

Today, Mariama wakens to a view of her village through indistinct eyes, her vision made blurry by hunger, contaminated drinking water, and a lack of access to doctors. Both Mariama and Sekou are among the fifteen million children who will die from starvation this year, which averages out to a little more than forty thousand dead kids per day. That is about the average stadium attendance for a New York Yankees home game.

Dead.

There are so many children like Mariama and Sekou that they will become mere statistics, which will make their painful deaths easier to rationalize from the comfort of middle-class American suburbia. Empathic disconnect is simply a matter of clicking the remote control and adjusting the central air-conditioning. The only life Mariama has ever known is rife with suffering and the excruciating pain that accords an empty stomach. Every day, she turns her gaze skyward and asks God for help. The Christian missionaries who gave her a brand-new Bible to hold had taught all about a loving Jesus and how he died for our sins. Ask, and he will answer.

She prays, "Please, Lord, can we please have something to eat today? It's been weeks. My little brother and I are hungry. A piece of bread, anything. The pain is too much to bear."

Finally, after years of hearing Mariama's silent prayers, the all-loving, all-powerful Judeo-Christian God Yahweh gives his answer. "Sorry, kid, I'd love to help. But I'm kind of busy right now. You see, little Billy in Topeka has been a good boy, and he needs a new bicycle. Perhaps if your begging sufficiently appeases my ego, I'll allow you to die soon. That's when all the fun happens, anyway. The buffet up here is top-notch. There will be plenty to eat after you enter the kingdom of heaven, so long as you remain faithful to me. In the meantime, just keep reading your Bible until I get back to you."

Fortunately, the Mariama in this story doesn't really exist. Unfortunately, there are millions of others just like her who do. Small, vulnerable, and frail—the meek—many of whom have been taught about the Christian God and will not inherit the earth; rather, they will become a part of it. Ashes to ashes. They pray to the same Yahweh that American Christian children do. Yet today, forty thousand children in Asia, South America, and Africa, just like my fictitious Mariama, will die after having suffered for months or even years.

It was the same yesterday. It will be the same tomorrow.

Champagne

A man has free choice to the extent that he is rational.

—Saint Thomas Aquinas[2]

Most atheists, including myself, will not claim to be absolutely certain, without any doubt, whether or not there is actually any sort of a supreme being. Most nonbelievers are reasonably sure, at least to the extent that their rational minds do not allow them to conclude that there is any such thing as fairies, or that Kirk Cameron has anything but an extremely slim chance of ever winning the Nobel Prize for science. There is no evidence to suggest the existence of any gods, whether they be Zeus, Thor, Mithras, or the Judeo-Christian Yahweh.

---

2   Christian Classics Ethereal Library, *St. Thomas Aquinas,* http://www.ccel.org/ ccel/aquinas.

Moreover, the biblical god is no less of an absurdity than any of the thousands of other gods that have been dismissed over the ages. It is well past the time that America should dismiss the fairy tales we've been raised to believe. The Judeo-Christian God can only be believed if one is psychotically delusional, willfully ignorant, or credulous.

Now, if you're still reading, thank you. I realize that I may have just insulted you. The above assertion might seem harsh. But if you hang in, I believe that, by the end of this book, you will either agree or prove the above assertion to be true.

It's been my experience that many who accord theism haven't given their own beliefs their due diligence, and if shown the facts, they'd feel foolish for having made many of their religious affirmations. As such, I hope to encourage an honest introspection and allow people to reexamine what they claim to believe. I will not do so with a temperance toward political correctness. Certainly that will tug on the short hairs of some people. If you can't take being poked fun at, this ain't the book for you.

While it's not my specific goal to offend anyone, simply by writing this book I most assuredly will. To be honest, I really don't give a shit. The truth can hurt. Especially when the truth involves coming to the realization that you may not be as smart or as decent of a person as you think.

Religious bigotry and ignorance offends *me* every day. The tax-exempt status of the church offends me even more. So if you're *offended* by blasphemy—and not by children starving to death—then truly, in my heart of hearts, I sincerely hope that you fall face-first into a deep fryer.

Many theists, after stubbornly holding onto the religion they were raised with, will eventually become embarrassed for having allowed themselves to fall prey to anti-intellectual dogma. Indeed, what holds many back from braving free thought is the feeling of foolishness that accords having been exposed as committing willful acts of idiocy and admitting that you've been duped. There is no twelve-step program for religious gullibility.

The way to see by faith is to shut the eye of reason.

—Benjamin Franklin[3]

It is also in the spirit of honesty that I confess that I am a little annoyed that I feel compelled to write this book in the first place. I feel no such compulsion to author a manuscript about the lack of validity of astrology and the criminal deception that those who peddle such nonsense are guilty of. The difference being, of course, is that astrologers, psychics, and other purposely deceptive con artists aren't trying to impose their will on the rest of society through legislation. To my knowledge, there are no candidates for public office who answer to astrology lobbies.

In a sane world, organized groups of atheists—as a sociopolitical response to American theocracy—wouldn't even exist. But we don't live in a sane world. We live in a world where the president of the most powerful nation on the planet must publically display his allegiance to an invisible, ethereal dictator, lest the voting masses react adversely and elect someone who will. As such, America leads the world in science denial and, not so coincidentally, idiots.

Men who believe absurdities will commit atrocities.

—Voltaire[4]

The thing is—although no rational person believes in a devil either, there is most assuredly such a thing as evil. Although "magical thinking" is a wicked premise that all religion operates from, American Christianity has given rise to a particularly mean-spirited, ignorant, compassionless sociopolitical paradigm. It allows decent people to disconnect from empathy and rationalize violations of human rights.

---

[3] BrainyQuote.com, *Benjamin Franklin*, http://www.brainyquote.com/quotes/quotes/b/benjaminfr151613.html

[4] Ibid., *Voltaire*, http://www.brainyquote.com/quotes/quotes/v/voltaire118641.html

As such, there is an ideological storm brewing on the horizon of our nation that I believe to have an epicenter of intrinsic malevolence, and I feel morally compelled to fight against it. This sociological malignancy suppresses knowledge, encourages ignorance, and dumbs down the populace by teaching lies and superstition as if they were facts.

This evil goes by the name "Dominionist Christianity."

Part of me would like to temper my language so as to appear more open-minded and perhaps reach a broader audience. However, that would be tantamount to politically correct bullshit on my part. When faced with the pure, unadulterated ignorance that evangelical Christianity inspires, I have found that the most effective way to counter that type of vile pathology is to give it the disrespect it deserves. Being polite to bigots as a means to reach compromise is like negotiating with a rabid badger. It gives respect where none is deserved, and it allows for the perception of ignorance as a valid point of view.

The great enemy of the truth is very often not the lie—deliberate, contrived, and dishonest—but the myth—persistent, persuasive, and unrealistic.

—John F. Kennedy[5]

As such, my verbiage might be considered a tad flippant by some folks. To which I suggest that they get the hell over it. If my use of colorful language offends, yet you are able to rationalize that thousands of innocent people will have died needless, agonizing deaths by the time you finish this chapter simply because it was "God's will," then perhaps you might want to reassess your moral priorities. Because they suck.

Frankly, there is no way to rationally engage those who have abandoned logic and acumen, or who mask their cruelty and lack of empathy under the guise of carrying out the will of an invisible, omnipotent, petty egomaniac

---

5   BrainyQuote.com, *John F. Kennedy,* http://www.brainyquote.com/quotes/quotes/j/johnfkenn125157.html

who demands that we worship him while he dispenses pain and suffering on a sadistic whim. There is no reasoning with anyone who believes that a supreme being demands that we engage in bigotry toward one another. I would no sooner accommodate such insipid, intellectually devoid animus from members of the Ku Klux Klan than I would from people espousing similar ideals in the name of Christian fundamentalism. Just because a sectarian jerk has a cross hanging around his or her neck, that does not absolve him or her from being exposed.

Dickheads are dickheads.

Labels

When I do good, I feel good. When I do bad, I feel bad. That's my religion.

—Abe Lincoln[6], top-hat enthusiast and vampire hunter

Now, I realize that most of the nation identifies with some form of Christianity and that most people do *not* consider themselves to be "evil" or even dickheads. I get that, and they (or you) are correct. Most people who refer to themselves as "Christian" certainly are *not* evil, nor are they dickheads. I, for one, believe that the percentage of people who have malicious intentions to be a minority within American Christianity.

But even those who themselves are not abhorrent, whack-job fundamentalists encourage religious hate and bigotry merely by including those fringe believers under the label of "Christian." While that's probably not the intention of most Christians, the sheer numbers of the Christian majority are what give their lunatic fringe so much sociopolitical influence. In case you hadn't noticed, no one really gives a damn what Shintoists think about birth control.

As such, those with sensibilities based on fairness and empathy try to contribute reason to the national discourse in response to the wickedness

---

[6] BrainyQuote.com, *Abraham Lincoln*, http://www.brainyquote.com/quotes/quotes/a/abrahamlin106095.html

of evangelical irrationality. While I have yet to experience any religion that doesn't fly in the face of reason (and before I'm done here, I'll have some fun at the expense of various religious superstitions), I tend to focus on the perfidy inherent in American Christianity. I do so mainly because—as a resident of the United States—I find that the majority of people who reside here in the United States identify themselves as Christians. A book about Jainism written for a US-based readership would garner about as much interest as one written about the fascinating variety of storage jars.

Good people will do good things, and bad people will do bad things. But for good people to do bad things, that takes religion.

—Steven Weinberg[7], 1979 Nobel Prize winner in physics

Although many Americans self-identify as Christian out of cultural tradition, and they are, in fact, much more casual about their faith than their evangelical counterparts, their upbringing still holds psychological sway. Many don't realize to what extent their indoctrination still affects them. However, it is the predatory manner in which the evangelical movement manifests itself upon the assailable psyches of a frightened populace, and thus influences national policy, that warrants my claim of "evil."

So it's to the cultural (more casual in their faith) Christians whom I am writing.

Saudi America

The whole problem with the world is that fools and fanatics are always so certain of themselves, but wiser people so full of doubts.

—Bertrand Russell[8]

---

[7] Great-Quotes.com, *Steven Weinberg*, http://www.great-quotes.com/quote/22336

[8] BrainyQuote.com, *Bertrand Russell*, http://www.brainyquote.com/quotes/quotes/b/bertrandru121392.html

I harbor no illusions that I would ever be able to change the minds of evangelicals about their beliefs. I won't even try, as people who are brainwashed into a cultlike astigmatism need professional psychiatric help and possibly medication. That is beyond my area of expertise. Trying to reason with a Christian fundamentalist is like debating with someone who only speaks Chinese about whether Superman can defeat the Hulk in a fight.

My battle with those of faith is not even about their beliefs, per se, but about how the causal effects of fundamentalism impose themselves on others by rationalizing the darker parts of human nature and presenting them as "morality." I think that, when given perspective, most American Christians will be able to recognize the bigoted hypocrisy of the evangelical wing of their own religion. The trick is to get the average Christian to recognize craziness in themselves.

That's kind of what my job is.

> *Religion is excellent stuff for keeping common people quiet.*
> *Religion is what keeps the poor from murdering the rich.*

—Napoleon Bonaparte[9]

There are Islamic theocracies that exist in the Middle East today—entire nations whose laws are predicated on the fundamentalist interpretations of the Koran by religious and political leaders. Surely, most Christian Americans understand that if not for the oppressive religious extremism, these nations would be experiencing more progress, equality, and freedom. If not for the severity and absolutism of Sharia law, the people there would live much different, and dare I say *better* lives.

Moreover, the typical American Christian surely understands that the average Mid-East Muslim is not an extremist who wants to hurt other

9   BrainyQuote.com, *Napoleon Bonaparte*, http://www.brainyquote.com/quotes/quotes/n/napoleonbo136563.html

people. Most Americans realize that the main difference between those born into an Islamic theocracy and us is geographic good fortune. I will go out on a limb and wager that the burka would not be such a hot fashion trend, if not for the religious mandate.

The main sociological dynamic that makes life different in the Middle East, as opposed to the United States, is the political strength of those who would impose a theocracy and not necessarily the religion that the theocracy is based on. Yet there is a concerted effort on the part of Christian fundamentalists in America to mirror the political model of Islamic theocracies by substituting Jesus for Mohammed.

Just tell them that their wildest dreams will come true if they vote for you.

—Napoleon Dynamite[10]

We're seeing today—in contemporary America—a radical sociopolitical movement backed by a well-funded network of politicians, media, and PR people who are hoping to impose their evangelical Christian agenda on the populace. It is nothing short of a direct assault on our constitutional liberties. And the Christian proletariat allows it to happen because evangelicals and themselves technically fall under the same religious banner. Casual Christians easily have their perceptions confounded between what (to them) is a benign belief in a Jesus who preached peace and love and what is in reality an oppressive Christian theocratic worldview.

Many Christian Americans never consider that their religion is as potentially oppressive as those who attacked us on September 11. They ignore some early warning signs—like the intolerant and acerbic language of Christian fundamentalists—because many believe their Christian faith differentiates Americans from these savages. And before long, as people allow themselves to get swept up in a nationalist/Christian frenzy, we hand power over to lunatics in the name of God.

---

[10] Napoleon Dynamite(2004), *Napoleon Dynamite*, http://www.imdb.com/title/tt0374900/quotes

Bah, we all know that a theocracy could never happen here in America. Right.

Dominionism

When fascism comes to America, it will be wrapped
in the flag and carrying the cross.

—Sinclair Lewis[11]

Those not yet brainwashed into a theocratic stupor, and who still possess the ability to count to eleven without taking off a sock, find the prospect of Christian rule in the United States terrifying. We've seen what happens to societies that are under religious rule. Moreover, history has shown us what happens to societies under *Christian* rule. And it ain't pretty.

As it has been throughout history, whenever a small group of obscenely wealthy aristocrats are inclined to gather more wealth and power unto themselves, the most effective method of doing so—without the struggling masses feeling equally compelled to roast them on a spit in the public square—is to leverage themselves by using religion. God has anointed kings and has been making men rich for thousands of years. And the G-man is back at it in contemporary America.

I distrust those people who know so well what God wants them to
do because I notice it always coincides with their own desires.

—Susan B. Anthony[12]

It's amazing how—no matter what Christian theocrats propose—Yahweh's wishes always benefit them. Theirs, and the biblical creator's, biases are harmoniously the same. What a co-inky-dink.

---

[11]   Great-Quotes.com, *Sinclair Lewis*, http://www.great-quotes.com/quote/22434

[12]   BrainyQuote.com, *Susan B. Anthony*, http://www.brainyquote.com/quotes/quotes/s/susanbant403780.html

So naturally, this begs the question: Is it "God's" authority theocrats are acting upon, or their own? Isn't it more than a coincidence that, when God and government are indistinguishable, the wealthy always benefit? And lastly, how fucking stupid are people that they keep buying this tightly coiled, steamy pile of crap?"

Because when gods anoint kings and determines wealth, it always comes at the expense of the proletariat. There has never been a Christian theocracy that accorded a healthy middle class. Never. When religion and government are thrown in the mix together, it creates—without exception—an economy where a disproportionate amount of wealth and power are in the hands of very few.

> *History, I believe, furnishes no example of a priest-ridden*
> *people maintaining a free civil government. This marks the*
> *lowest grade of ignorance of which their civil as well as religious*
> *leaders will always avail themselves for their own purposes.*

—Thomas Jefferson[13] in a letter to Von Humboldt, 1813

Thus the placating rationalization is always the same: Just wait until after we all die. The Judeo-Christian God will dispense postlife justice. Tithe now, benefit later. Think of it like an ethereal IRA. Right.

Which makes it all the more frightening that, despite the socioeconomic history of religion-as-state societies, there are Christian fundamentalist politicians here in America who not only believe that there should be no wall of separation between church and state but who also feel that Christianity should have *dominion* over our foreign and domestic policy. The Christian Dominionist approach to governing is not very different from that of their Islamic counterparts, in that the Dominionists feel that Christianity should be the determining factor in legislation. But Christian Dominionism takes fundamentalism one step further into the ignorance

---

[13]   Goodreads.com, *Thomas Jefferson*, http://www.goodreads.com/
quotes/53249-history-i-believe-furnishes-no-example-of-a-priest-ridden-people

abyss and abides totalitarianism. People who hope to usher in the end of the world want control of our nuclear weapons.

Christian Dominionism in America? What could possibly go wrong?

The Big Red Machine

Despite the First Amendment to the Constitution which states that "Congress shall make no law respecting an establishment of religion," the Christian evangelical lobby still extends major influence into the White House. Christian Dominionists, who advocate a supplanting of our Constitution in favor of biblical law, are replete throughout the United States House of Representatives and Senate and are running candidates for the presidency. If this sounds scary, it should.

In a nation that has had a separation of church and state since its inception, we've been allowing that wall to erode under the guise of Christian morality. Revisionist historians pervert past events to coincide with a Dominionist agenda. The definitions of words and terms are bastardized by political evangelists to mean something other than what they were intended. Fear becomes the primary motivator for political affiliation, and Christian middle-America abides. In the twenty-first century United States, Christianity has become a more powerful political weapon than ever before.

America did not invent human rights. In a very real
sense, human rights invented America.

—Former Democratic President and devout Christian Jimmy Carter[14]

Present-day politics being what it is, Dominionist Christianity is much more closely associated with the Republican Party than it is with the Democrats. The GOP is where the "evangelical lobby" has buttered its

---

[14] BrainyQuote.com, *Jimmy Carter*, http://www.brainyquote.com/quotes/quotes/j/jimmycarte146704.html

bread. So for the sake of this book, I'll most certainly beat up more people who refer to themselves as Republicans than not. But make no mistake; I am affiliated with neither party, and moreover, I believe that the Dominionist Christian co-opting of the GOP is not necessarily a reflection of the party itself. There are still some Republicans who do not adhere to religious fundamentalism, and whom, I hope one day soon, will take the party back.

I hope, but I ain't holding my breath.

If we took away the minimum wage—if conceivably, it was gone— we could potentially virtually wipe out unemployment completely because we would be able to offer jobs at whatever level.

—Christian and guano psychotic, Rep. Michele Bachman[15]

And as I confront the half-truths, misrepresentations, and outright lies that come from the Dominionist Christian influence within the present day GOP and its abiding media affiliates, it is also important to understand that I do so with an almost equal disdain for self-serving liberal propagandists. The thing is, for the sake of this book, the regular bullshit that over-the-top lefties spew is not germane to the topic of Christian Dominionism. Liberal douche-baggery as subject matter would demand that I write a different book.

As such, it is fair to say that Dominionist Christianity in American politics is a *Republican* phenomenon. I am unaware of any Democrats in the twenty-first century who might hope to breach the wall between church and state or impose a Christian theocracy. So when it comes to how Christian Dominionists apply their beliefs to politics, the consistently inconsistent historical perspectives and mad-hatter, fact-deficient ravings come from the right side of the political aisle. And the result has been that

---

[15] Thinkprogress.org, *Michele Bachman*, http://thinkprogress.org/ politics/2011/06/16/246618/bachmann-craziest-quotes/

we are presently more polarized and ignorant than at any time since the Civil War.

There was a time in our not-too-distant past when identifying oneself as an American trumped party affiliation. Republicans and Democrats recognized each other as true Americans, and despite our slight ideological differences, we were also neighbors. There were real enemies, both foreign and domestic, and it sure as hell wasn't the guy mowing his lawn across the street who has a different bumper sticker than you.

You know, back in the day, the Colonial period, you had to be a landowner, a property owner, to be eligible to vote, and I don't think that's a bad idea.

—Conservative political activist, radio host, hardcore Christian, and full-bore douche, Bryan "Fuck the Poor" Fischer[16]

When President Eisenhower was succeeded by President Kennedy, our country wasn't being torn apart like it is with today's cable news outlets convoluting information and distorting national policy. The ideological differences between Democrats and Republicans were not so pronounced that the majority of Americans found themselves philosophically diametric. We weren't so likely to distrust one another. And despite having nuclear weapons pointed at us from just off the coast of Florida, we weren't nearly as frightened.

At least not of each other.

Why So Serious?

The thing is, when religion dictates political ideology, it accords some really crazy—and really stupid—affirmations. I realize that those words might seem disrespectful and intentionally provocative. That's because they are. I do not use words like crazy or stupid lightly or with a cavalier

---

[16] Rightwingwatch.org, *Bryan Fischer*, http://www.rightwingwatch.org/content/ fischer-only-property-owners-should-be-eligible-vote

predisposition to name-call those with whom I disagree. I use these words to describe people who make irrational claims as if they were facts and who lack the cognitive ability to alter their perceptions when shown contradictory evidence.

… So in other words, crazy and stupid.

> *I prayed and prayed and prayed. I'm a man of faith. And when I finally realized that it was God saying that this is what I needed to do, I was like Moses. 'You've got the wrong man, Lord. Are you sure?*

> —2012 Republican presidential candidate, "Rockin' Like a" Herman Cain[17], explaining that God wanted him to run for president … and lose, apparently.

If someone were to claim that he was receiving telepathic instructions from beings beyond the edge of the galaxy to perform a series of irrational, mundane tasks, let's face it, he'd be considered (at best) a little nutty. However, when one asserts that he has received extrasensory guidance from an invisible deity, well that's just a "religious calling." The former to an institution, the latter apparently, to the White House.

Moreover, when said imperceptible divinity gives directives to disregard peer-reviewed facts arrived at via scientific discovery, and to legislate in twenty-first-century America so as to coincide with the Bronze-Age teachings of murderous, slave-owning, women-beating goat herders — because said deity left instructions in a holy book that has been edited and translated over thousands of years—well, that's just people of faith expressing themselves in a "Christian Nation."

Sorry. No it's not. It's fucking crazy. Certifiable, bug-eating, Jodi Arias crazy.

---

17   Contemporarycalvinist.com, *Herman Cain*, http://www. contemporarycalvinist.com/2011_11_01_archive.html

But to make matters worse, when that very same cognitively compromised person is shown irrefutable, peer-reviewed, contradictory evidence to the bat-shit affirmations he has made regarding the age of our planet or the origin of our species, he'll more often than not deny what's in front of his eyes in favor of what he wants to believe. I understand that not everyone can understand genetics, biology, physics, astronomy, or neuroscience. But to make specific claims against the process by which facts are gathered—in the twenty-first century, when we all have benefitted from the advances of these very same scientific disciplines—because they inconveniently contradict a literal interpretation of your holy writ, well, that's not just crazy, it's also fucking stupid.

I think there is a theory, a theory of evolution, and I don't accept it.

—2012 Republican presidential candidate Ron "Idiot's Idea of a Libertarian" Paul[18]

Sorry, I may not possess the articulation skills to convey this willful disregard for reason in a nice, politically correct way. If you're not bright enough to understand science, that's fine. Just don't contravene those who do—without any basis in fact—while you simultaneously benefit from modern conveniences and medicine. I don't know a whole lot about cars, which is why I'd never tell a professional mechanic how to do his job.

But if you're a fundamentalist Christian taking offense to being called crazy and stupid for denying science while professing a literal translation of the Bible—accurate as those labels probably are—I'll offer some religious perspective. There are Islamic fundamentalists who do not believe that fresh water and salt water will mix together, because it says so in the Koran. Really, there are Muslims crazy and stupid enough to actually believe that the reason one can drink from a river, and not from the ocean, is divine intervention. Although science has explained how and why this condition exists—not to mention that if you took a glass and filled it with both

---

18 CBSNEWS.com, *Ron Paul*, http://www.cbsnews.com/news/ ron-paul-i-dont-accept-the-theory-of-evolution

fresh and salt water, that they would mix—the fundamentalist Islamic explanation is "Allah magic." If your vocabulary is failing you, allow me to offer a couple of appropriate adjectives: crazy and stupid.

And it is He who has released (simultaneously) the two seas,
one fresh and sweet and one salty and bitter, and He (Allah)
placed between them a barrier and prohibiting partition.

—Surah 25:53[19]

Crazy and stupid becomes more pronounced in the light of scientific discovery. Water-mixing deniers are not "people of faith"; they are pathologically moronic. However, the same pathology that allows for one to make irrational claims refuting basic chemistry or about conversing with space aliens is what allows for a literal translation of the Bible by Christian fundamentalists. What differentiates between these former examples of faulty synapses and the latter—regarding the negative consequences of lunacy influencing one's decision-making capacity—is that fundamentalist Christians are being elected to our legislature and writing our laws.

As such, with the Dominionist Christian co-opting of the Republican Party, there has been a movement away from reason and toward craziness and stupidity in our political process. The GOP is replete with candidates and elected officials who should—in a sane world—be denounced by the RNC (Republican National Committee) for lacking the basic mental competence to hold public office. But now the Dominionist, lunatic fringe has more influence than those who would otherwise espouse traditional Republican socioeconomic ideals. The Christian right forces otherwise prudent Republicans to capitulate and accept irrational platitudes. The sane members left in the GOP fear for their political lives.

But to make things clear—because partisans get all butt-hurt when you criticize their political affiliation—these crazy and stupid accusations are

---

[19]   WordofAllah.com, *Surah 25:53*, http://www.wordofallah.com/woa_read_eng/
files/assets/basic-html/page717.html

not directed at the Republican Party. Just the opposite. They are directed at Dominionist Christian psychopaths who call themselves Republicans, but who truly are not. The inmates are running the asylum.

It's almost as if, while they were asleep, giant space pods have replaced most of GOP's members with lunatics.

Scooby Don't

Let me tell you, I'm a really smart guy.

—Donald Trump[20]

The thing about people who are crazy and/or stupid, is that they don't realize it. To them, it's a natural state of being. The Son of Sam actually believed that his neighbor's dog was giving him valid advice on whom to murder. Never did it occur to him that he might be delusional. Sarah Palin actually believes that she makes sense when she speaks.

Which is why "crazy and stupid" are subjective experiences. Many fail to realize that their faith makes them advocates for nonsensical, bug-nutty political affirmations. For the Christian fundamentalist, despite the myriad of conclusive evidence to the contrary—while it might seem reasonable to them—literal interpretation of ancient texts as scientifically and historically accurate is no less crazy than getting instructions from a homicidal canine mastermind.

And the Dominionist-led GOP is chock-full of people who suffer from the same psychotic delusion as did David Berkowitz and who are getting instructions from imaginary oracles inside their intellectually attenuated craniums.

---

[20]   ABCNews.go.com, *Donald Trump*, http://abcnews.go.com/Politics/donald-trump-president-trump-weighs-sheen-palin-obama/story?id=13154163&page=2

To offer some more perspective, Sir Isaac Newton didn't really "discover" gravity. He was merely the first person to articulate it in scientific terms. It was more likely discovered by the first caveman to fall out of a tree. As such, we all (kind of) know what gravity is. We might not all understand the physics behind why gravity exists as a force in the universe, but we do know that very few of us can dunk a basketball.

Tide goes in, tide goes out. Never a miscommunication. You can't explain that.

—Bill "Asleep during High School Science Class" O'Reilly[21]

As it happens, there is an explanation for gravity. As has been the case with every other discovery throughout the history of mankind, it turned out to not be magic. Those smart science guys have figured it out. Yet despite the scientific consensus, and how even the dimmest among us understands that there is a thing called gravity that forces many of us to rake leaves in the fall, gravity remains a scientific *theory*.

But to my knowledge, despite the Roman Catholic Church ignorantly having once denounced the theory of gravity as heresy, there are no twenty-first-century gravity deniers. I mean, in today's world of understanding that would be downright silly. Picture if you will, trying to reason with someone crazy and stupid enough to claim that gravity is not a force of nature but rather the result of a giant, invisible man whose will it is to keep things earthbound. Further picture said person obtusely offering as evidence the different rates of plummet for a bowling ball and a feather, while you pull your hair out trying to explain elementary high-school physics.

Objectively, a reasonable person might determine that the hypothetical gravity denier would have to be a mixture of crazy and stupid. Subjectively, said gravity denier believes that his singular insight makes him sane and

---

[21]   Huffingtonpost.com, *Bill O'Reilly*, http://www.huffingtonpost. com/2011/01/06/oreilly-god-causes-tides_n_805262.html

smart. Yet we rational folks who understand physics have peer-reviewed, scientific evidence on our side. We could gather an auditorium filled with physicists and astronomers, and implant the gravity denier's own mom—*Total Recall* style—into their slumbering minds, so that all of these experts in their given fields can explain how and why gravity exists as a force of nature. But if said gravity denier is inclined toward crazy and stupid, there is not a whole lot of reasoning to be had.

The only good is knowledge, and the only evil is ignorance.

—Socrates[22]

However, there are more than just a few fundamentalist Christian GOP members of the Congress and Senate who make biblically based claims that deny peer-reviewed science on a regular basis. Moreover, they legislate according to those very same biblical assertions. They are merely gravity deniers under a different guise.

Rather than abide the twenty-first century, Dominionist Christians embrace the historical and scientific predispositions of the twelfth. And with that Medieval perspective comes all of the according less-than-sane, not-too-bright acumen that allows one to assert mythological authenticity. From young-earth creationists to historical revisionists to moral apologists, lies are told in the face of peer-reviewed facts and evidence. It's akin to believing in monsters and goblins. Therefore, it is incumbent upon those with actual morals, and an inclination toward seeking solutions to complex problems, to expose Christian Dominionists and the scare tactics they use to frighten crazy, stupid people into voting for them.

It was old man Santorum all along—and he'd have gotten away with it, too, if it weren't for those meddling kids.

---

22   Great-quotes.com, *Socrates*, http://www.great-quotes.com/quote/1360474

Not Just, Clarice

I do not feel obliged to believe that the same God who has endowed us with sense, reason, and intellect has intended us to forgo their use.

—Galileo[23]

The problem with Republican, Dominionist Christian science-deniers is not simply that they are less-than-sane and not-too-bright, but that they are willfully and gleefully so. The chances are that they have been shown all of the evidence explaining to them why they are irrationally credulous. They just don't care. They are really into being part of this fraternity of knuckleheads.

There is a stubborn incomprehension that accords religious fundamentalism and science denial in the twenty-first century. One would really have to go out of his way to be that sensationally incognizant. We live in an age where we have actual knowledge achieved through discovery, where prior we had only suppositions and curiosity. Facts, as it turns out, are stubborn things. So when someone says that evolution is "just" a theory, anyone with a basic level of understanding would naturally have to assume that said person is "just" a fucking idiot.

Our ignorance is God; what we know is science.

—Robert Ingersoll[24]

Now, I realize that what Christian fundamentalists mean by "just a theory" is "unproven speculation." And maybe the first time one ignorantly and erroneously blathers about what a scientific theory actually is, we can give him a pass. Everyone has a learning curve. However once the term "scientific theory" is properly defined—and explained in simple enough terms so that even someone who believes that a burning bush

---

[23]   Ibid., *Galileo*, http://www.great-quotes.com/quote/52488

[24]   The Works of Robert G. Ingersoll, *Robert Ingersoll*, Volume 1 - Page 55(1900),

once gave life-coaching instructions can understand—and he still defines it incorrectly, be it out of a lack of desire, or the inability to discern, then said Christian fundamentalist's cognitive process could only be described as ranging somewhere between crazy and stupid.

So here's the skinny, which in deep-fried, extra-cheese, Christian fundamentalist, tea party Republican terms would be about a size sixteen:

A scientific theory is not a random thought that a guy in a lab coat has. Theoretical status within the scientific community is achieved by summarizing a hypothesis or group of hypotheses that have been repeatedly supported with testing. Once enough evidence is accumulated by accredited persons in a given field to support said hypothesis, it moves to the next step, known as a theory. To become a theory, a hypothesis would have to endure rigorous scrutiny from experts and academics in any discipline, as it is part of their job to *discredit* said hypotheses.

This is what's known as "the scientific method." It requires peer review, investigation, analysis, and the auditing of affirmations so as to gather consensus. It has become accepted as the valid explanation of phenomenon, and it is the reason why you didn't have to churn your own butter this morning. The scientific method is also the reason why American parents don't lie awake at night worrying about their children contracting polio.

Indeed, the scientific method—as a means of acquiring knowledge—functions in every aspect of discovery. Unless, of course, it doesn't jibe with a literal translation of religious scripture; then apparently it's "just" a theory. Maybe *Schoolhouse Rock* should have done an "I'm just a Hypothesis" episode.

It is far better to grasp the Universe as it really is than to persist in delusion, however satisfying and reassuring.

—Carl Sagan[25]

---

25 BrainyQuote.com, *Carl Sagan*, http://www.brainyquote.com/quotes/quotes/c/carlsagan133582.html

The perfidy that accords science denial and the libel use of the word "theory" lies in noncomprehension of the scientific method. It's as if Christian fundamentalists believe that Charles Darwin was sitting in his underwear, chugging beer and watching an episode of *Lancelot Link: Secret Chimp* when he came to the realization that the primate in the floral printed dress resembled his Aunt Minerva. Not only did Darwin's findings endure meticulous investigations from the scientific community before he even wrote *On the Origin of Species*; the theory of evolution has—since its inception, and continuing to this day—endured more uncompromising analyses as technology evolves. Not one accredited member of the scientific community—despite the purposefully deceptive, pseudo-scientific claims of Christian fundamentalists—has found contradictory evidence to evolution.

To deny Darwin is akin to denying Newton.

Moreover, with advancements in biology, we have conclusively determined that humans and other mammals have a common genetic ancestry. This part of the theory of evolution—which is the essence of what creationists deny—is a scientific *fact*. In the scientific method, there is a clear distinction between facts, which can be observed and/or measured (like genetics), and theories, which are scientists' explanations and interpretations of said facts. Evolutionary biologists have conclusively determined that humans have existed for (roughly) two hundred thousand years, and we have evolved from more primitive primates. Man was not created from dirt, nor woman from his rib.

These are facts, and they are not negotiable. There is no rational argument to be made for denying evolution. Still, there are elected Republicans who truly believe that about six thousand years ago, Yahweh—in his infinite wisdom—created Adam in his own image in the garden of Eden.

Crazy.

Stupid.

Fact, Faith, Fiction

Facts are stubborn things; and whatever may be our wishes, our inclinations, or the dictates of our passion, they cannot alter the state of facts and evidence.

—John Adams[26]

It has been said that those who don't believe in the Judeo-Christian God have no faith. But that is patently untrue. Everyone has faith in certain things or people. Rational people have trust in subjects that deserve it and in those who have earned it. Nonbelievers simply have the same amount of faith in Yahweh as Christians have in Odin, Krishna, or any of the many other deities they do not believe in. Faith is not a concept confined to the hope that one gets invited an ethereal after-party.

Yet faith is spoken of by Christians as if believing in something without any reason is admirable. Christians speak of religious "faith" as though it makes them something other than delusional. Moreover, Christian fundamentalists speak of faith as if it makes them better people. But in reality, it is both an intellectual surrender and a capitulation to gullibility.

As such, in the attempt to gather like-minded morons to their cause, religious fundamentalists will not only claim to "choose to believe" in whatever fact-deficient drivel rocks their flat world but condescendingly state that you should "have faith" too.

When you understand why you don't believe in other people's gods, you will understand why I don't believe in yours.

—Often attributed to Albert Einstein; though he probably never said it, it is nonetheless sensationally astute

---

26   Ibid., *John Adams*, http://www.brainyquote.com/quotes/quotes/j/johnadams134175.html

But here's the thing about faith: what we believe is *not* a choice. Belief is what the acumen of our life's experience allows us to determine is true. With any other determination, we require evidentiary data. It is simply impossible to decide to believe in something that you know to be fiction. We cannot simply "choose" to believe something that we otherwise wouldn't. If the ability to designate conjecture were true, everyone reading this could "choose" to believe that Allah is the reason why there is mixed water in the Hudson River.

The proper term for making cognitively dissonant affirmations that defy reason, so as to placate one's own sense of idealism, is not "belief." It is "denial." Religious fundamentalists don't choose to believe. They choose to remain ignorant via nonacceptance. So when it comes to earning the favor of an invisible Sky Daddy via fundamentalism, theists make guesses based on geography and speak of faith as if it's absolute truth. In America, Christian fundamentalists legislate the same way.

It's turd-eating nuts.

Just because one allows oneself to make the intellectual concession to proclaim something to be "truth," does not make it so. There are plenty of people who believe that the September 11 attacks were an inside job perpetrated by the George W. Bush administration. They might "believe" that Bush and Cheney ordered simultaneous Michael Corleone-style hits on downtown Manhattan and the Pentagon, but that doesn't detract from the reality that they are idiots making grandiose, absolutist claims about things they are simply guessing at.

As such, anytime someone claims to "know" that there is a god—let alone that a religion is "true"—anyone with the slightest comprehension of natural law would have to assume a psychotic delusion on the claimant's part.

Faith means not wanting to know what is true.

—Friedrich Nietzsche[27]

Which leads us to the bastardization of the word "faith" as it applies to facts. People cannot truly "believe" if their prime motivation is the fear of postlife punishment. That's not what "faith" is. Emotional bullying or putting a supernatural gun to someone's head is not a means of persuasion. Intrinsically, a person can "feel" that there is a god, or even have a childlike, incomprehensive belief that there is a god, but one cannot "know" something that has no corroborating evidence.

We have a right to our own opinions but not a right to our own facts. Truth is always truth, and a lie is always a lie. The way to arrive at both is via empirical evidence. Whether many adult Christians want to admit it or not, they don't believe in God as much as they're horrified of the boogeyman. We have all been conditioned to fear the repercussions of not having faith since our childhoods. Regarding the religious stigma of our upbringings, many of us are still childlike. Truth is more difficult to come by when people are afraid to be honest with themselves about how they feel, and they are overcome by fear and guilt.

Which is why rational people will adjust their views based on new, evidentiary data. Show a sensible person a flying carpet propelled by magic, and, if it survives proper testing and peer-reviewed scrutiny, the credibility of this evidence within the scientific community would warrant proclaiming to the world a new belief in mystic propulsion. Any scientist worth his salt would do so, willingly and happily.

Religious faith is the denial of facts and evidence so that dogma can be sustained—and insulated from the twenty-first century. Christian fundamentalists won't change their minds, no matter how much evidence is in front of them. That is not admirable. It is crazy, and it's stupid.

---

[27]   Ibid., *Friedrich Nietzsche*, ://www.brainyquote.com/quotes/quotes/f/ friedrichn131072.html

This may come as a surprise, but when you go to a magic show, they don't really saw a woman in half.

Republic-Code

You keep using that word. I do not think it means what you think it means.

—Inigo Montoya[28]

Along with the confounding of the meaning of *faith* as it applies to *facts*, there are a myriad of other linguistic bastardizations being disseminated for those inclined toward a less-than-rational approach to governance. Whether or not the evangelical Christian, tea party, Republican voting base is aware of the political cryptography that has been woven into their limited lexicon, is entirely dependent upon each individual's capacity for introspection. However, I would bet dollars to doughnuts that many who have fallen prey to the lyrical musings of conservative entertainment media lack the cognitive ability to make the distinction between annotation and proselytism.

Thus, the context of words and phrases within the Republican talk-o-sphere has been conveniently altered so as to equate to something very different—and sometimes the opposite—of what they were originally intended to mean. But most evangelical Republican voters never understood what these words and phrases meant to begin with.

Political language is designed to make lies sound truthful and murder respectable, and to give an appearance of solidity to pure wind.

—George Orwell[29]

---

[28] The Princess Bride (1987), *Inigo Montoya*,http://www.imdb.com/title/tt0093779/quotes

[29] BrainyQuote.com, *George Orwell*, http://www.brainyquote.com/quotes/quotes/g/georgeorwel141761.html

While Jesus makes terrific bait to hook the Christian fish, it takes more than New Testament propaganda to steer an entire sociopolitical movement. Those who would hope to leverage Jesus as a means to co-opt the Republican Party also have had to convince Republican voters that not only was the son of God a total conservative whose motto was "every man for himself," they also need to usurp traditionally admirable words and phrases and alter their meanings to coincide with the rest of the Dominionist agenda. Thus, an entire sociopolitical language had to be rewritten and introduced into the Republican thesaurus in order to transform the GOP from the party of Eisenhower into corporatist theocrats.

Hence, the tea-vangelical movement was born.

Part of the altering of Republican perception regarding the separation of church and state, and translating that into a socioeconomic movement toward an Orwellian division of wealth, is to modify speech. Woven into the conservative lexicon are misrepresentations of words like "patriotism," "entitlements," "freedom," and "socialism,"—and terms like "class warfare," "free market," and "family values." Within the GOP-geist, all of these expressions mean something entirely different today than they did a half-generation ago.

Indeed, the socioeconomic mechanisms that created the greatest economy and the largest middle class the world has ever seen in the years following World War II, have become vilified as *socialist*, and *anti-American*. The *free market* has been redefined as a collusive, rigged market. *Patriotism* has come to mean having an irrational disdain for government. *Class warfare* is used as a term to blame the poor for being impoverished. *Family values* now means Christian-only values. And in GOP terms, *freedom* equates to earning less, not having health care, and yearning for the bondage of trickle-down economics.

There's class warfare, all right, but it's my class, the rich class, that's making war, and we're winning.

—Billionaire who apparently has a conscience Warren Buffett[30]

Moreover, the *racism* inherent within Dominionist socioeconomics is dismissed as political correctness. Tea partiers consistently wave Confederate flags, display overtly ignorant, culturally biased signs, and champion bigots. Yet tea-vangelicals cavalierly disregard their own bigoted ravings as the free expression of "patriots" as guaranteed by the First Amendment. Saying racist things, in the tea party/GOP, somehow does not equate to racism. Moreover, to refer to a right-wing racist *as* a racist is—in their minds—racist. It's dizzying, I know.

The same can be said about the word "morality." Somewhere along the GOP party line, morality—especially as it applies to Jesus of Nazareth—has come to mean an utter lack of empathy and compassion. Screw the poor. And if the sick can't afford decent health care, well then so be it. As Republican Jesus always used to say, "Fuck 'em."

I've been on food stamps and welfare. Anybody help me out? No.

—Actor, tea party conservative and spectacular imbecile Craig T. Nelson[31] complaining about education and paying taxes on the Fox News Glenn Beck program

As such, a few very wealthy people motivated by their own self-interest have decided that the best way to rally support to their cause was to prey upon the vulnerable, albeit culturally intolerant, psyches of Christian voters. Like many before them who hoped to garner more political power, tea-publicans invoke the name of Jesus for financial gain. Hence, the

---

[30] Good-reads.com, *Warren Buffet*, http://www.goodreads.com/quotes/123058-there-s-class-warfare-all-right-but-it-s-my-class-the

[31] FoxNews.com, *Craig T. Nelson*, http://www.goodreads.com/quotes/123058-there-s-class-warfare-all-right-but-it-s-my-class-the

truly moral enterprise is to fight against an ideology whose ultimate goal is to keep the masses in poverty in favor of a reigning aristocracy. There is a *patriotic, moral* obligation to fight the wicked oppression of religious fundamentalism within our borders.

But to win the hearts and minds of those who revere their chains is never easy. The sadomasochistic premise from which tea party Christians operate—both loving a God who reciprocates love via reward and punishment and admiring their economic oppressors—is a difficult psychological barrier to negotiate. For it seems that the only thing that tea-vangelical voters willfully understand less than their Bible is the United States Constitution.

Abracadabra

The purpose of such meditation (yoga) is to empty oneself. (Satan) is happy to invade the empty vacuum of your soul and possess it.

—Tea party Republican candidate and
minister E.W. "No Yoga" Jackson[32]

Whether less-than-sane, not-too-bright affirmations are arrived at via willful capitulation or faulty synapses means a lot. Some people are just crazy and/or stupid, and there is nothing anyone can do to reason with them. Others make internal rationalizations. For the latter, there is hope. For whatever psychological payoff they receive in being part of an ignorant collective, the rewards for braving free thought are much greater.

I get the appeal of making religious mental concessions. I really do. They allow one to rationalize a bevy of self-indulgent, bigoted predispositions in the name of God and to not see a reflection of a douche-bag staring back in the mirror. That has to be a wonderful perk if you're an asshole. You can

---

[32] Theweek.com, *Minister E.W. Jackson*, http://
theweek.com/article/index/245284/
yoga-lures-in-satan-and-6-other-things-the-gops-ew-jackson-believes

hate fags, but it's okay because Yahweh says that homosexuals are immoral. Christianity is like having a license to not have a conscience.

All one has to do to get into heaven—according to Christian ideology—is to ask God for forgiveness. No matter what kind of sociopath a person may have been, a simple "mea culpa" (and a few "Our Fathers," if you're Catholic), and all will be forgiven. So rape, murder, greed, corruption, or even being a Philadelphia Flyers fan—it's all good, so long as you repent and accept Jesus as your lord and savior before you die. Remorseful rapists and murderers are in. Law-abiding, charitable Jews and atheists are out. Gotcha.

If we confess our sins, He is faithful and righteous to forgive us our sins and to cleanse us from all unrighteousness.

—1 John 1:9[33]

So to follow this logic, if Jeffery Dahmer apologized to Yahweh in his own head at the very end, then he's in heaven today. Gandhi, however, prayed to the wrong god. Tough luck, fella.

Not only will contrite sociopaths be allowed to enter heaven, where the comforts are aplenty, but they'll also get to hobnob with all of the other awesome Christian angels. Then they can wag their fingers at all of those who worshipped incorrectly, did not have the correct amount of faith, or who were born in parts of the world forsaken by the Christian Yahweh while they burn away for eternity in a torturous hell. "Hey, can someone turn up the AC? Fetch me a piña colada and have a few of those six-breasted women feed me frozen grapes."

But you have to really, really, really commit to the believing part, or else the whole deal is off.

---

[33] Holy Bible, *John 3:16*, Holy Bible. New International Version ®, Copyright © 1973, 1978, 1984, 2011 by Biblica, Inc.®

And if this sounds dumb (and it should, because it is), then understand that this is the result of what happens when one accedes to magical thinking. From walking on water, to multiplying loaves and fishes, to a postlife paradise—all of this is the result of physics- and logic-defying precepts performed as miracles by an invisible deity. Jesus, the son of God, and God the father are one and the same. Quickdraw McGraw is El KaBong.

Gee willikers. Jesus is magic.

But here's the thing about massive amounts of people believing crazy/stupid shit and the magical thinking that accords American theism: Christianity infects every aspect of socioeconomics. It is how the extremely wealthy get working-class people to vote against their own best interests. Conning gullible people into believing myths and defying reality is what allows the economically elite few who would benefit from a theocracy to gain enough followers so as to anoint them. And historically, God's political mouthpieces live in obscene luxury, while the masses get less and less. Twenty-first-century Republicans are the party of God. Don't you want eternal life in paradise? Join the GOP. Ugh.

For God so loved the world that he gave his one and only Son, that
whoever believes in him shall not perish but have eternal life.

—John 3:16[34]

Which brings us back to the point made at the beginning of this chapter, which is that religious fundamentalism—and Christian Dominionism in particular—operates from a wicked premise. Theocracy, Christian or otherwise, is evil in the very premise from which it operates. Although it's presented as benevolence, it is designed to separate Americans from their constitutional liberties and their money, while we are all promised a reward in the afterlife.

---

[34]   Ibid.

I just whipped your ass

—Austin 3:16[35]

What makes anyone think that any politician preaching blatantly untrue biblical mythology as science and history could possibly have their best economic or social interests at heart? Theocratic drivel put forth into legislation benefits them and their benefactors, not anyone else. Your reward comes conveniently after you die. Theirs is just as conveniently in the here and now.

Doesn't that seem just a little crazy or stupid? Anyone? Bueller?

Enlightenment is a painful process. It scrutinizes all of our beliefs. It puts everything we hold dear under a microscope. The scientific method places value on truths derived from evidence, rather than superstition. If our beliefs survive these tests, then they are worthy. But if they do not, we must admit that we've held falsehoods dear. And that can be a difficult, if not frightening, admission.

Disregarding myths and superstitions is how humans endeavor to progress. Yet there are more than a few within our political system who believe the Bible word for word as a scientific and historical text. That is not a belief that a sane person has. Which is to say that we have a whole bunch of irrational, unenlightened people making laws in America. As such, the Dominionist perspective is that they hope voters either join them in their dogma and remain in the dark or are fearful enough of the dogma that they dare not challenge it, while they legislate those who would defy their dogma into submission.

---

[35] En.wikipedia.org, *Stone Cold Steve Austin*, http://en.wikipedia.org/wiki/
Stone_Cold_Steve_Austin#Austin_3:16_.281996-1997.29

I believe Jesus Christ is God.

—Sen. Marco "Not Big on Symbolism" Rubio[36]

But the con of fundamentalist Christianity is the basis for the legislation Dominionists need passed in order to further endow themselves, at the expense of everyone else. Jesus is how they get voters to become rubes. They are banking on America's collective gullibility, and thus far, their gamble is paying massive dividends. Because Christian Dominionism is not a means to a religious, or even a spiritual end.

Christian Dominionism is the means to an economic end.

[36] BrainyQuote.com, *Marco Rubio*, http://www.brainyquote.com/quotes/quotes/m/marcorubio592662.html

CHAPTER 2
Fairy Tales

(Mother Goose, Aesop's, and Other, Less-Believable Fables)

It's fair to say that the Bible contains equal amounts of fact, history, and pizza.

—Penn Jillette[37]

[37]   Goodreads.com, *Penn Jillette,* http://www.goodreads.com/
       quotes/36113-it-s-fair-to-say-that-the-bible-contains-equal-amounts

Lost in a religious fundamentalist's translation of scripture is the concept of metaphor.

The lack of comprehension regarding symbolism and use of poetic license within religious storytelling is the main component in determining one's fundamentalism. This is because a person is either unable or unwilling to recognize the difference between allegory and reality. Which is to say that sane people don't read fiction and believe it to be true. Harry Potter did not actually rise from the dead because Dumbledore hid the resurrection stone inside the golden snitch.

The ability, or inability, to interpret scripture metaphorically is the primary difference between the Muslim with whom you discuss the travails of raising teenagers and the one who straps dynamite to his chest and walks into a crowded mall. Similarly, in American terms, that is also the difference between a Christian with whom you are able to amiably interact and the Bible-thumping, evangelicals who'd make you want to stab yourself to get away from. Neither fundamentalist is less crazy than the other.

I know Jesus Christ died for my sins, and that's all I really need to know.

—Ann Coulter[38], speaking about her insatiable thirst for knowledge

A conceptual acceptance of religious scripture, as opposed to a literal one, is also a component of sociological sanity. I doubt that even the Bronze- and Iron Age authors of the Bible expected people to be gullible enough to presume true their tales of magic. Since a literal interpretation of these stories would rely on a belief in magic, a reasonable person would conclude that they were written as parables. They were obviously meant to teach lessons, not to be taken literally.

So, in respect to the rationale it takes to suspend disbelief enough to regard any type of impossibility as having actually occurred via divine

---

[38] BrainyQuote.com, *Ann Coulter*, http://www.brainyquote.com/quotes/quotes/a/anncoulter384470.html

intervention: believing that Jesus magically walked on water is no less loony than believing that capturing a leprechaun will earn you a pot of gold. As such, the understanding of what a metaphor is, and how it is used in telling religious stories, is what essentially allows people to "spiritually" identify with their upbringing, and not be crazy. A cultural Christian can relate to the lessons in the New Testament in the context of symbolism.

Moreover, a sensible collation between scripture and the twenty-first century allows one to not feel an overabundance of guilt for having a libido or have a compulsion to do harm to others in the name of their deity. And while all religion that involves "magic" or other impossibilities is irrational, it's understandable how —through the basic skill of differentiating between fiction and history—most Americans are still able to refer to themselves as Christians and not act like lunatics. Conversely, not being able to do so is why so many religious fundamentalists are extraordinary hypocrites.

So, simply stated, the understanding of the Bible's metaphoric nature is why most cultural Christians are decent human beings—and why Christian fundamentalists are generally assholes.

Them, Not Me

No man ever believes that the Bible means what it says;
he is always convinced that it says what he means.

—George Bernard Shaw[39]

Most people tether to their faith for the moral basics: Do unto others. Judge not. Loose lips sink ships. Try not to be such a dick. The religious connotations of virtue are woven through the American lexicon, and Christians associate them with their faith.

---

[39] Quotesplanet.com, *George Bernard Shaw*, http://www.quotesplanet.com/ quote/14451/

Of course, while Christian evangelists like to claim ownership of basic morality, the truth is that the innate morals we all share are universal. They span various cultures and religions, predate Christianity, and are adhered to by nonbelievers as well. However there are Americans who feel they need the crutch of believing that a two-thousand-year-old, deceased deity is the reason why they don't steal their neighbor's newspaper or go on a murderous rampage. Many Christians have never considered that they might just be decent people, and that empathy and virtue are intrinsic.

That is, unless one is born a sociopath ... like those who would deny poor people food stamps.

However—at least to the extent that most Christians view their evangelical brethren as something less than crazy for believing in stories, that if told in any other context, would earn them a new jacket that ties in the rear— the teachings of any of the Christian religions accords a certain level of indoctrination for everyone it touches. If not outright brainwashing. While cultural Christians may be sane enough to recognize the truth in the origins of our species and our universe, their conditioning has not allowed them to make certain distinctions that, if it were not for the subjectivity regarding their faith, they would be able to make easily.

Cultural or doctrinal conditioning is what prevents many theists (believers) from realizing that members of the fundamentalist wing of any religion, including their own, are Gary-Busey-on-meth nuts. The unlearning of psychologically imprinted superstition is no easy task. And it's a task few too many are willing to endeavor.

If there is no God, why bother to tell the truth? Why not steal?

—Former Nixon speech writer Ben Stein[40], who apparently
needs to rationalize his horrid movie, *Expelled,* as something
other than what it is due to the fear of postlife retribution

---

[40] BrainyQuote.com, *Ben Stein,* http://www.brainyquote.com/quotes/quotes/b/
benstein461315.html

Perfidy and larceny come in many forms, Benny-boy.

Yet to simply disregard people whose psychosis allows them to believe magic and fairy tales over science and history as a "harmless fancy of faith"—simply because one identifies on some level with the same deity—is in itself, not very rational. One needs not be a fashionista to see how ridiculous it is to have a high, exalted pontiff in a pointy hat being transported in a glass box on a golden throne while dispensing medieval moral platitudes. Surely cultural Christians see the delirium it takes to blame natural disasters on gays, or school shootings on women's lib. Yet they abide those who do. It's like saying, "Sure, the hardcore members of my religion are infected with the loony virus, but I'm only a carrier."

Certainly, acknowledging that other forms of mental delusion are potentially harmful to both the person suffering them and to those around them is easy enough. Most of us would think twice about inviting someone over for Thanksgiving dinner who spoke openly and often of his belief that space aliens were telepathically giving him or her instructions to discriminate against people from North Dakota. We don't normally associate with those who suffer from the kind of pathology that allows them to hear voices and alter reality. Unless, of course, these psychotic delusions pertain to religion.

It is even more the case when it is *our* religion.

> *I trust God speaks through me. Without that, I couldn't do my job.*

> —President George W. Bush[41], speaking with an Amish group, July 9, 2004, about a year after the invasion of Iraq

---

[41] Politicalwire.com, *George W Bush*, http://politicalwire.com/archives/2004/07/16/quote_of_the_day.html

He walked past me, and then a voice in my head said, "Do it, do it, do it," over and over again, saying "Do it, do it, do it, do it," like that.

—Born-again Christian Mark David Chapman[42], describing the voices in is head before he murdered John Lennon

The lack of any cognitive dissonance allowing otherwise rational people to dismiss fundamentalists who conflate fact and fiction is possible only because of the umbrella of religiosity. To some extent, even passive theists have undergone enough brainwashing to selectively ignore religious craziness for what it is. As such, simply by religious fundamentalism's unwillingness, if not inability, to accept factual information and rational determinations, it is the exact opposite of what it purports to be. It is darkness presented as enlightenment.

Imagine no religion.

—John Lennon[43]

Which is to say that religious fundamentalism is neither benevolent nor benign. It's dependent upon spreading fear and ignorance. And whether cultural Christians want to admit it or not, their silence abets the cruelty, bigotry, ignorance, and violence of Christian fundamentalists in America. So, before we undergo another thousand years of barbarism and blind adherence to mythology, before we allow ourselves to be duped again into ignoring the obvious truth about religious tenets, in favor of what less-than-rational zealots want reality to be ... allow me to offer some perspective:

---

[42]   Crimelibrary.com, *Mark David Chapman,* http://www.crimelibrary.com/terrorists_spies/assassins/chapman/8.html

[43]   Quotesplanet.com, *John Lennon,* http://www.quotesplanet.com/quote/10310/

A Story of Creation

In the beginning ... there was only chaos. There was only empty, silent, endless darkness. It was like waiting for your number to be called at the DMV.

Then, out of the void, appeared Erebus, an unknowable place where death and night dwell, which to be honest, was not much of an improvement. Somehow Love was born, bringing a start of order. From Love came Light and Day. Once there was Light and Day, Gaia (the earth) appeared, as did Uranus (the sky). As one might expect, a little celestial nookie occurred between Gaia and Uranus (as they were the only two cosmic beings in existence), and they gave birth to six pairs of adorable, bouncing baby Titan twins named Oceanus and Thethys, Coeos and Phoebe, Hyperion and Thea, Creos and Themis, Lapetos and Clymene, and finally, Kronos and Rhea.

Gaia and Uranus also managed to spawn a few multiarmed Cyclops children, which didn't make Uranus very happy. Unable to purchase sweaters off the rack, Uranus forced the little freaks back into their mother's womb. Now, as anyone who has every indulged in a late-night White Castle binge can attest, neither did this make Gaia very happy. So she channeled her inner Lorena Bobbitt and planned a little revenge.

Calling on her youngest (and probably cutest) child, Kronus (the god of time), to help her play an empyrean practical joke on her husband, Gaia made a supernatural sickle, which Kronus then used to cut off the nut sack from whence he came. Hell hath no fury like a woman with a few Cyclops's in her vag. So, as one might correctly assume, Uranus was no longer the man of the household, and thus, his cutlery-wielding offspring took over as the honcho of the heavens.

Seriously, who was going to mess with Kronus after he just cut off his father's 'nads? So, as only gods and southerners can do, he started screwing around with his sister, Rhea. In order to make their relationship legitimate, they married, conjured a house in the suburbs, and had six children, named Hestia, Demeter, Hera, Hades, Poseidon, and Zeus.

Fearing the prophecy that he would be overthrown by his own son in cosmic retribution for the whole "cutting off his Dad's junk" thing, Kronus swallowed each of his children as soon as they were born. Kind of like a giant astral goldfish. Tiger-mom Rhea wasn't wild about this. So after five of her children were lost to her brother/husband's carnivorous appetite, she came up with a brilliant scheme to save *her* youngest, Zeus. Rhea fed Kronus a giant stone wrapped in the clothes of an infant, and not being the sharpest knife in the celestial drawer, the ruler of the cosmos fell for it.

Despite a severe case of indigestion, Kronus thought that he was in the clear. But Zeus eventually grew up and forced his dad to disgorge the swallowed offspring. This was most probably accomplished by tricking him into watching *2 Girls 1 Cup*. Fortunately, Kronus hadn't yet gone to the transcendental men's room. Once the six siblings were free from their father's intestinal prison, they waged a ten-year war against the Titans, whom they eventually defeated.

Zeus then exiled Kronus and the other Titans who had fought against him and his siblings to the isle of Tartarus, which was the Mount Olympus version of Detroit. However, Zeus had different plans for Atlas, who was singled out for the special punishment of holding the world on his shoulders, so the Z-man could collect royalties from the future works of Ayn Rand.

To this day, Zeus remains the ruler of all the gods on Mount Olympus.

Transcendental Transgression

The pursuit of truth will set you free; even if you never catch up with it.

—Clarence Darrow[44]

---

[44]   BrainyQuote.com, *Clarence Darrow*, http://www.brainyquote.com/quotes/quotes/c/clarenceda154035.html

There was a time when the story of Zeus and the Titans was the prevailing wisdom about the origins of humanity and the world we live in. Most of a certain region of the world actually believed this explanation of how the world came to be and worshipped these gods. But as time has passed, so, too, did these beliefs. Virtually no one alive today takes these myths seriously, and I doubt that I'll get any flack for having taken some literary license or for poking a little fun at them. However, it would make me extremely happy if I were to receive hate-mail from people who still believed that Zeus rules the cosmos.

It is generally understood that these, and other mythological stories, were written by primitive men as a means to explain the world around them, of which they had little understanding. Myths exist because people were ignorant of science. Today, we make movies about these stories and categorize them in the fiction/fantasy genre. And I figure that if no one got their panties in a bunch at the casting of Harry Hamlin, there is little chance of *me* actually offending anyone.

The dice of Zeus always fall luckily.

—Sophocles[45]

But still, there was a time when temples were built in fear and reverence to these gods, and animal sacrifices were carried out in tribute. Had I lived in the fourth century BCE, my flippant attitude toward Zeus might have even earned me torture for having blasphemed. However, now just about everyone understands that these are just stories. They not to be taken literally.

Yet as I sit at my computer and write this book in the second decade of the twenty-first century, I am dismayed that some things have really not changed all that much. Maybe no one believes in Zeus anymore, but there are other, equally irrational, myths that people claim to believe. It seems

---

[45]   Ibid., *Sophocles*, http://www.brainyquote.com/quotes/quotes/c/clarenceda154035.html

that we have not evolved as much as we'd like to think over the last few millennia. Despite our great strides in science and what we've come to learn about the universe and the world around us, there are still widely held axioms that not only defy reason, but that are tantamount to insanity when objectively observed.

For instance, according to the Church of Scientology, millions of people worldwide—including many high-profile celebrities—derive their worldview and beliefs about the origins of our species from a science-fiction writer.

Another Story of Creation

I'd like to start a religion. That's where the money is.

—L. Ron Hubbard[46]

Once upon a time, approximately seventy-five million years ago (give or take), there was a galactic ruler named Xenu. He was kind of like a district manager overseeing a group of planets in an Intergalactic Federation. As fortune would have, our own planet Earth (then called Teegeeack), as well as many of the other planets in our galactic vicinity, were all under Xenu's purview.

Now, Xenu had a population problem in his galactic district. Each planet had an average of about 178 billion people. When one considers that present-day Earth only has around 7 billion people, and what a pain-in-the-ass rush hour traffic can be, then one can understand how this might be a concern. It was kind of like a galaxy modeled after downtown Beijing.

So Xenu developed a brilliant, albeit sinister, plan to correct all of this overpopulation, and thankfully he didn't have any special interest groups to deal with. The X-man was able to take over complete control of the

---

[46] Great-quotes.com, *L. Ron Hubbard*, http://www.great-quotes.com/quote/1190331

Intergalactic Federation with the help of sympathetic renegades, and together they defeated his superiors. Once he was in power and sitting behind his big ruler-of-the-universe desk in his awesome, comfy ruler-of-the-universe chair, he ordered billions of people to be called in for income tax inspections.

A Democrat. I *knew* it.

Xenu then retained psychiatrists—who were pretending to be accountants—who, rather than offering sound financial advice, instead administered alcohol and glycol injections so that folks would become paralyzed. Once they were helpless, the tax scofflaws whom Xenu wanted to get rid of were loaded into space ships, which looked extremely similar to the American-made Douglas DC-8 commercial aircraft, except that since they were traveling in outer-space, they had rocket motors instead of propellers. These DC-8 space planes were flown to Teegeeack (Earth), where hundreds of billions of incapacitated people from various worlds were stacked around volcanoes. It must have really sucked to be at the bottom.

But when the stacking was done, Xenu had his henchmen drop hydrogen bombs into the volcanoes, killing everyone. Overpopulation problem, solved. Oh, the horror.

No shit, folks. This is really how the story goes.

However, Xenu was as sinister as he was clever. He knew that since everyone has a "thetan"—or, as shoemakers, R&B singers, and theists like to refer to it—a soul—Xenu realized that he had to do something to prevent the thetans/souls of those he had just blown to bits from returning. So, with hundreds of billions of souls being blown around by nuclear wind, the new intergalactic overlord had special electronic traps built so that he could capture the wayward thetans on electronic beams. Apparently, thetans/souls stick to electronic beams like flies on flypaper.

Once all of the thetans were captured, Xenu had them packaged into boxes and taken to giant cinemas where they were forced to watch specialized, false propaganda 3-D motion pictures for days on end. The purpose of these was to confuse the disembodied thetan viewership into believing a false reality. Kind of like attending a Michael Moore film festival. In these films, the thetans/souls were implanted with false information about God and the devil, and were at an utter loss to be able to determine whether or not it was rabbit season or duck season.

When the films ended, the thetans left the cinema and started to wander around aimlessly, as that is apparently the net effect of receiving so much misinformation. Confused as they were, these noncorporeal entities began clustering together, since they all had the shared experience of being the victims of religious propaganda. In fact, many were even under the impression that they were the same thetan. John Jacob Jingle Thetan Smith.

So the wandering thetans assembled together in groups of a few thousand. And since there were not many actual people who were still alive, these apparitional thetan clusters inhabited the bodies of those who had escaped the H-bomb fate of the masses. This is why we humans remain so screwed up about religion and other stuff until this day. We are psychologically impaired by thetan disinformation.

Now I get it. When it is written in plain English like this, it all seems so obvious.

Eventually, as is the case with most dictators, Xenu was overthrown by Loyal Officers of the Intergalactic Federation. As a punishment for murdering hundreds of millions of people and being such a naughty boy, they locked Xenu away inside a forced-field encapsulated mountain on one of the planets of the Intergalactic Federation. The force field is powered by an eternal battery, so there is no chance of escape. Xenu remains imprisoned there until this very day. For the sake of humanity, I hope that he at least has a deck of cards or basic cable.

*It's well known I'm a Scientologist, and that has helped me
to find that inner peace in my life, and it's something that
has given me great stability and tools that I use.*

—Tom "I'm in Love with Katie Holmes, So
I'm Obviously Not Gay!" Cruise[47]

But fear not, dear readers. One need not release oneself to the effects of
thetan reincarnation. In order to escape the intellectually and emotionally
compromised fate of the propagandized masses, all one has to do is pay
shitloads of money to achieve different levels of mental clarity … although
the details remain sketchy, as the specific information is all super, super
secret, and only privy to an elite few.

But if you think that story is a little tough to swallow, wait until I tell you
the one about the apple-eating harlot and the talking snake …

The Story of Creation

Well, *God created the world in seven days. So, I mean, ten
days is not out of the reach for the Senate to act, surely.*

—Rep. Lynn "Slightly Off on Both His Biblical
Math and His Rocker" Westmoreland[48]

Today, the prevailing religious wisdom in America believes that an all-
powerful, omnipotent Yahweh created the universe and all that's in it in
six days, and then kicked back to enjoy a few brewskies on the seventh.
This belief is the driving force behind much of our political discourse.
"Creationism" is so prevalent that one would immediately be discounted
from seeking the Republican nomination for president if one did *not* either

---

[47] Ibid., *Tom Cruise*, http://www.great-quotes.com/quote/1402271

[48] Patheos.com, *Lynn Westmoreland*, http://www.patheos.com/blogs/
friendlyatheist/2013/09/24/rep-lynn-westmoreland-god-created-the-world-in-
7-days-so-surely-we-can-avoid-government-shutdown-in-10-days/

claim to believe it as scientific and historically accurate, or capitulate to those who do.

It is for this reason that I am compelled to explain to people who are as of yet unaware, that this is fucking crazy.

The story on which this belief is based can be found in the Old Testament of the Bible, in the book of Genesis. It's the tale of how the Judeo-Christian Yahweh created everything. And even though he's the all-knowing and all-powerful super-awesome infallible kick-ass one true God, meaning that he must have known how his space/time/matter experiment was going to turn out before he started doing any of his creating in the first place … it still took him a week to complete for some reason. But to be fair, it took me longer than that to paint the basement.

The story goes like this:

Day 1: God had this great idea. He thought to himself, "Hey, here I am out of space/time with nothing to do, and no one to worship me … so I think I'll make myself a universe to hang out in and rule over." So he began by creating light, so that he could see what he was doing. *"And God said, 'Let there be light,' and there was light" (Genesis 1:3)*[49]. Hey Lord, while you're at it, let there be doughnuts, too.

Then God separated light from darkness, most probably figuring that he'd work out the details of photons and energy sources later. It was then that he ingeniously coined the terms "Day" and "Night," so as not to confuse anyone. God then came to the conclusion that light was kind of groovy, and determined that "it was very good" (if he did say so himself).

Day 2: God created the skies, so he wouldn't hit his head while he was doing all this other creating stuff. He also needed to separate rain water from earth water, so he figured out a place to put them both, and divided

---

[49]   Holy Bible, *Genesis 1:3*, Holy Bible. New International Version ®, Copyright © 1973, 1978, 1984, 2011 by Biblica, Inc.®

them thusly. *"Then God commanded, 'Let there be a dome to divide the water and to keep it in two separate places'—and it was done. So God made a dome, and it separated the water under it from the water above it. He named the dome 'Sky'"* *(Genesis 1:6–8)*[50]. This begs the question, as sports stadium names go, isn't then, the Toronto Skydome just a tad redundant?

But in just two days, Yahweh had created light, and done this whole dome/water thing. So the grandest of all Poobahs was really starting to get the feeling that he was onto something, and determined that this too, "was very good."

Day 3: It was a busy day for the almighty. Lots to do, lots to do. Ignoring the rest of the universe, God turned his focus to our home planet, and created both dry land and the seas on this day. *"He named the land 'Earth,' and the water which had come together he named 'Sea'"* *(Genesis 1:10)*[51]. He also conjured all of the plants and trees, which includes hallucinogenic mushrooms and marijuana.

Mountains as throw pillows, meadows as area rugs. Yahweh's plan for his favorite celestial spheroid was really starting to come together, and he determined (as any pot grower will agree) that this was all "very good" too, dude.

Day 4: By this time, the Big Fella was really working his cosmic mojo, as he created the sun, the moon, and the billions upon billions of stars on the first Wednesday. *"So God made the two larger lights, the sun to rule over the day and the moon to rule over the night; he also made the stars"* *(Genesis 1:16)*[52]. Never mind that the moon doesn't actually give off light, but merely reflects it. That's not as important as understanding that, regardless, the great Task Master made us our own moon.

---

[50]   Ibid., *1:6-8.*

[51]   Ibid., *1:10.*

[52]   Ibid., *1:16.*

If one is remotely into astronomy, he or she would know that Yahweh got a shit-ton of work done this day. The cosmos is pretty friggin' big. Even though the majority of his focus would be on one tiny little planet in the corner of the universe, he decided to make it so vast and ever expanding that Earth amounted to a metaphoric grain of sand in an ever-expanding desert. Maybe he wanted to leave himself room for growth, in case he ever decided to franchise his idea.

But the day-four to-do list gave that whole day-and-night thing a little more focus as well as determined days, seasons, and years. Yahweh must've figured that since the previous day's accomplishments took approximately twenty-four hours (which only existed in his mind, since the creation of the universe is what determines space/time), that he'd make an earth day the same length of time. Because if we take the Bible literally, and we should, since it's God's own written word, a day is a day is a day.

I'm sure that there was a good reason for the almighty to make the earth's annual orbit around the sun not quite divisible by his twenty-four-hours-per-day planetary rotation, forcing us to have a leap year every four years. But Yahweh works in mysterious, and mathematically inconvenient, ways. Still, despite his orbital faux pas, modesty notwithstanding, he thought that this too was "very good."

Day 5: Since God made the seas and the sky, he got this great idea to make avian, and aquatic creatures, and place them in the correct spots (except for flying fish, which he probably couldn't make a decision on). *"Let the water be filled with many kinds of living beings, and let the air be filled with birds" (Genesis 1:20)*[53]. The Earth at this point was kind of like a giant fish tank/bird cage, only with sharks and pterodactyls.

Swim little fishies. Fly little birdies. Sorry for making most of you food for the bigger fishes and birds, but them's just the breaks. Yet, as any fish or bird owner will tell you, it's really easy to lose interest.

---

[53] Ibid., *1:20.*

Still, God being God and all, he determined that, despite being kind of boring, this was also "pretty friggin' good". After all, who was going to argue?

Day 6: This is where all the fun starts, unless you're a bird or a fish at the top of the food chain, in which case that was the day before. Yahweh created all of the land animals on this day, including—but not limited to—cows, cockroaches, and dinosaurs. *"Let the Earth produce all kinds of animal life: domestic and wild, large and small—and it was done" (Genesis 1:24)*[54]. This also includes every animal that ever existed, the vast majority of which are presently extinct. It is not clear whether God created penguins on this day or the prior one, since they are technically birds, even though they don't fly.

But then Yahweh got to thinkin' that all of this other stuff is really cool, but what good is it if there's no one but a bunch of dumb animals around to enjoy it? So since there were still some hours left in the day (it obviously takes less time to create land animals than it does birds and fishes), he came up with another brilliant scheme (he *is* God, after all) to make a smaller version of himself, with no godlike superpowers, to play and have loads of fun on this fabulous planet he had made. *"So God created human beings, making them to be like himself. He created them male and female" (Genesis 1:27)*[55]. Kind of like when someone gets a puppy, and they think it'll be all shits and giggles on a daily basis.

So Yahweh named his "mini me" Adam, and since there were no sports or X-Box around to occupy his time, he figured that eventually Adam would get bored out of his socks, that is, had socks been invented. As it was, Adam, was buck naked, and in all of his dangling penis, made-in-God's-image glory. However even though it was still the first day he was alive, Adam was already starting to realize that a social calendar that limited him to a Rubik's Cube and playing hide-and-seek by himself really sucks.

---

[54]   Ibid., *1:24.*

[55]   Ibid., *1:27.*

But since Yahweh is a totally awesome, all-powerful, super-smart God, he had the answer to Adam's dilemma. He decided that he was going to surprise young Adam with an unexpected celestial perk. God put Adam down for a nap, and, unbeknownst to the world's first person, while he was engaged in blissful slumber, the supreme ruler of the cosmos created the first woman from one of his ribs … which means that Adam must have been created with an odd number of ribs originally.

"So the LORD God caused the man to fall into a deep sleep; and while he was sleeping, he took one of the man's ribs and then closed up the place with flesh. Then the LORD God made a woman from the rib he had taken out of the man, and he brought her to the man" (Genesis 2:21–22)[56]. God named her Eve, and the chances are that, regardless of her boobs to ass ratio, Adam had most probably thought she was hot, having no dysmorphic, unreal Hollywood body-type issues to compare her against.

Yahweh so loved his creations, he blessed Adam and Eve and gave them every creature on Earth to rule over, and care for. *"I am putting you in charge of the fish, the birds, and all the wild animals" (Genesis 1:28)* [57]. Then, in a real piece of narcissistic egomania, he looked at the beings he created in his own image, and once again determined that "they were good." And he did all of this in under twenty four hours.

Day 7: Yahweh created hanging out. He sat back, admired his handiwork, and totally chillaxed. Then he figured, "What the hell; I am so friggin' amazing that once a week, these puny humans that I've created should totally pay homage to my awesomeness, and pray to me."

"By the seventh day, God had finished the work he had been doing; so on the seventh day he rested from all his work. Then God blessed the seventh day and made it holy, because on it he rested from all the work of creating that he had done" (Genesis 2:2–3)[58]. Yahweh loves us and all, but only insofar as we

---

[56]   Ibid., *2:21:22.*

[57]   Ibid., *1:28.*

[58]   Ibid., 2:2-3.

pacify his enormous ego. He *is* God, after all. If he doesn't have an ego, then who else should?

But here's where the story gets a little hard to believe. ...

Bimbo

In the Bible, it says, 'God made man in his own image.'
He made women after, from a rib—a cheaper cut.

—Archie Bunker[59]

God had planted this really terrific-looking garden that he called Eden, which was so beautiful that had there been a *Better Homes and Gardens* magazine at the time, it would have undoubtedly taken every award. This is where Adam resided, and where Eve was created from his rib. In the Bible, they refer to the Garden of Eden as paradise, and who am I to argue? I live in New Jersey.

God was a pretty hands-off landlord, and he asked only one thing of Adam. "Dude, do you see that tree with those really delicious-looking red fruits hanging from it? Stay the frig away from it. All the other trees are cool to eat from, but not that one. That tree contains knowledge, and just like people who will live six thousand years from now and actually believe this story, you don't want knowledge."

And the LORD *God commanded the man, "You are free to eat from any tree in the garden; but you must not eat from the tree of the knowledge of good and evil, for when you eat from it you will certainly die."*

—Genesis 2:16–17[60]

---

59 All in the Family (1971).*Archie Bunker*, Bud Yorkin Productions, Norman Lear/Tandem Productions

60 Holy Bible, *Genesis 2:16-17*, Holy Bible. New International Version ®, Copyright © 1973, 1978, 1984, 2011 by Biblica, Inc.®

Ignorance is bliss. Stay stupid. Trust me on this.

At the beginning, Adam seemed pretty cool with this idea. Stay away from the tree of knowledge? No apples? No problemo. To be fair, it's not like God told them that they couldn't eat from the Cinnabon tree. He had this covered.

But as is often the case when men are telling the story, Adam's troubles begin when a woman enters the picture. Yahweh realized that when he created Adam in his own image, he had also created the first heterosexual male, since God ain't no homo. Hence, he had to do that whole "make a helper with a vagina out of his rib" trick.

And as every hackneyed antifemale cliché has since suggested, Eve was not too bright, and she couldn't really be trusted to make any important decisions around the homestead. Like a teenager with her first credit card, she was gullible, naive, and susceptible to suggestion. I bet she would have been a bad driver too.

> *Now, the serpent was more crafty than any of the wild animals*
> *the* LORD *God had made. He said to the woman, "Did God*
> *really say, 'You must not eat from any tree in the garden?'"*

—Genesis 3:1[61]

Enter Satan, who—disguised as a serpent—decides to have a little fun with the world's first bimbo. He cunningly convinces Eve that, not only can she eat from the forbidden tree, but that doing so will make her like a god. I guess the fact that a snake was actually *talking* to Eve wasn't enough to tip her off that something might be amiss. But still, the world was young, and so was she. So she took the apple.

Then Eve goes to Adam and offers one to him, and like every guy does with a pair of tits in his face, he feebly goes along with whatever she

---

[61]   Ibid., *3:1.*

suggests. Disobey God? Sure. Just do a few more of those jumping jacks, you seductive little temptress, you.

> *When the woman saw that the fruit of the tree was good for food and pleasing to the eye, and also desirable for gaining wisdom, she took some and ate it. She also gave some to her husband, who was with her, and he ate it.*

—Genesis 3:6[62]

And with the hope of becoming wise—like the God who created them but who didn't have enough foresight to see that a talking snake in his garden paradise might be a potential problem—Adam and Eve ate the apples from the forbidden tree of knowledge of good and evil (which, let's face it, is an awfully long name for a tree). But their plan didn't work, and instead of becoming wise, they became self-conscious and realized they were naked, promptly covering themselves with fig leaves. I guess being naked became a big deal all of a sudden, as apples contain a lot of carbs. But on the bright side, it did eventually spawn an entire garment industry.

Tough Love

> *If you're going to do something wrong, do it big, because the punishment is the same either way.*

—Jayne Mansfield[63]

This really pissed Yahweh off, and who could blame him? He gave *one* order ... *one* freakin' order! ... and this is how they repay his kindness? How incompetent were they? I mean they were made in his image and all, but boy were they dumb. A talking snake? Really? They fell for that?

---

[62] Ibid., 3:6.

[63] BrainyQuote.com, *Jayne Mansfield*, http://www.brainyquote.com/quotes/quotes/j/jaynemansf315575.html

What was a supreme being to do? Well he did the only thing he could do. This situation required some stern discipline. Despite his love for Adam and Eve, God expelled them from paradise. My roof, my rules.

So the LORD God banished him from the Garden of Eden
to work the ground from which he had been taken.

—Genesis 3:23[64]

Adam, and all who came after him were sentenced to work and toil for their survival rather than get really cushy public sector jobs, and Eve, and all who came after her would be forced to be really cranky for three to seven days out of the month and endure agonizing pain during childbirth. The serpent was also punished, by having his legs taken away and being forced to slither around on his belly the next time he wanted to screw around with the almighty's playbook.

Junior, this is gonna hurt me more than it'll hurt you.

But God wasn't done. Not by a long shot. Because of Adam and Eve's "original screwup," God determined that they, and all of their future offspring—any human being who would ever be born—would be marked with this sin before they ever took their first dump. By heavenly decree, humans would henceforth be born guilty and unworthy. As such, they would be subjected to spend eternity in a fiery hell, where they would be tortured until the end of time.

Now *that's* love, baby.

So skip ahead to the New Testament—four thousand years or so, give or take—after people had been living brutal lives, suffering and dying from things like bad teeth, the harsh elements, and being eaten by animals (after the sky-boss had already repopulated the earth after killing everyone in a

---

[64] Holy Bible, *Genesis 3:23*, Holy Bible. New International Version ®, Copyright © 1973, 1978, 1984, 2011 by Biblica, Inc.®

giant flood, but that's another story). Yahweh gets another idea. Thinking that he may have overreacted a little, he comes up with yet another great and wonderful plan, one befitting only a supreme ruler of the universe.

This is how the birth of Jesus the Messiah came about: His mother, Mary, was pledged to be married to Joseph, but before they came together, she was found to be pregnant through the Holy Spirit.

—Matthew 1:18[65]

In order to allow some people into heaven, God decided that he needed to ghost-rape and impregnate a young virgin. Obviously, once Yahweh had a human son of his own, he could rationalize saving a few of those earthbound souls he was damning to hell. Luckily, there was just such a prude named Mary living in the most illiterate part of the world, who was the idyllic choice to birth to a savior. This was a great idea, since we couldn't have had a slut giving birth to the messiah. Bambi, Mother of Christ just doesn't quite have the same ring to it.

I am the Lord's servant, may your word to me be fulfilled.

—The Virgin Mary, Luke 1:38[66]

Men are so willing to respect anything that bores them.

—Marilyn Monroe[67]

But the plan doesn't end there. The true genius in God's plan lies in the details. You see this savior, Jesus, is not *only* God's son. He is *also* an incarnation of God himself. In sensationally nonsensical Christian

---

[65] Ibid., *Matthew 1:18.*

[66] Ibid., *Luke 1:38.*

[67] *BrainyQuote.com, Marilyn Monroe, http://www.brainyquote.com/quotes/quotes/m/marilynmon382334.html*

monotheistic terms, it's explained as the holy trinity of the Father, the Son, and the Holy Spirit.

I and the Father are one.

—Jesus Christ, Superstar, John 10:30[68]

This is where we get to see the majesty of Yahweh's cosmic scheme, and how he expresses his love for us pathetically flawed humans. You see, on the surface it appears that God sacrificed his only begotten son so that we might avoid eternal torture and be forgiven for what is considered— at worst—a misdemeanor. But in reality, Yahweh is actually sacrificing himself, *to* himself, so that he can forgive us all for something we never did and that only *he* determined that we needed to be forgiven for in the first place.

This all makes perfect sense, provided one's umbilical cord was wrapped around one's throat at birth.

Dealing with Idiots

Is it not a species of blasphemy to call the New Testament revealed religion, when we see in it such contradictions and absurdities?

—Thomas Paine[69]

I will acknowledge that there are those who will find fault with my biblical interpretations and point out how the above description of biblical creation is not an accurate representation. For instance, the book of Genesis does not actually refer to the serpent as being Satan, although that is how many interpret the role of the talking snake, due to a correlation made later, in

---

[68]   Holy Bible, *John 10:30*, Holy Bible. New International Version ®, Copyright © 1973, 1978, 1984, 2011 by Biblica, Inc.®

[69]   BrainyQuote.com, *Thomas* Paine, http://www.brainyquote.com/quotes/ quotes/t/thomaspain393407.html

the book of Revelation. Maybe the serpent went by the name Irving. Also, the forbidden fruit in the story of creation is not specifically named as an apple. But that is how it's represented in many of the church-sanctioned paintings. Maybe it was a pomegranate.

So work with me here, folks. Looking at the message of the story is more important than finding semantic discrepancies. The specifics are accurate. I didn't make any of this up.

Still, some will even take exception to a nonbeliever like me sarcastically blaspheming about the serpent or the forbidden fruit at all. There are those who will claim that I am taking things out of context. There are also those who are so deeply in denial that they'll use any excuse to not admit that their fundamentalism resembles the lunatic ravings of irrational zealots.

But they are. These stories—among many other absurdities—are what some elected members of our government actually believe.

> *The essence of Christianity is told to us in the Garden of Eden history. The fruit that was forbidden was on the Tree of Knowledge. The subtext is: All the suffering you have is because you wanted to find out what was going on. You could be in the Garden of Eden if you had just kept your fucking mouth shut and hadn't asked any questions.*
>
> —Frank Zappa[70], May 2, 1993

I am not going to even make an attempt to account for all of the physical and scientific impossibilities in the biblical story of creation. If you don't already understand *why* it is a myth—much like the account of Zeus and the Titans—and *not* an accurate historical account written by the hand of God—then nothing that I or anyone else can say will ever serve as sufficient proof to convince you. The chances are that Christian fundamentalists

---

[70] PlayboyMagazineStore.com, *Frank Zappa*, http://www.playboymagazinestore. com/playboy-magazine-may-1993-dian-parkinson/detail.php?p=440136

have already been exposed to the shitload of evidence against the biblical account of creation. They just choose to ignore it.

Nor will I try to explain why creationism—as a belief based upon the literal translation of the Bible—is patently insane. The truth is, that if you already believe in this drivel as a factual account of how the universe came into existence, then—as I said at the onset of this book—you're psychotically delusional, willfully ignorant, or incredibly stupid. In which case, I neither have the time, nor the inclination, to engage you in the hope of having a reasonable exchange of ideas.

Such a person would have had to already abandoned reason, and as such, their less-than-sane beliefs do not belong in any twenty-first-century political, or socioeconomic discussions. I hope you're not that type of Christian. For if you are, you're an asshole.

Better Dumb Than Sorry

Say what you will about the sweet miracle of unquestioning faith,
I consider a capacity for it terrifying and absolutely vile.

—Kurt Vonnegut[71]

A huge, however diminishing, majority of Americans say they are Christian. But are they really?

Coming to terms with one's own cultural hypocrisy can be difficult. Most Christians are lovely people. But yet they are so *despite* their religious beliefs, not because of them. Many cultural Christians even understand this.

Still, although cultural Christians fathom that the premise of their faith is not exactly rational, due to the mental abuse they've been inundated

71 Quotesplanet.com, *Kurt Vonnegut*, http://www.quotesplanet.com/quote/16874/

with since they were children, many can't bring themselves to admit that the belief they tether themselves to is simply is a myth like any other. So, many learn to rationalize, or make mental deals with themselves, so they won't have to concede to themselves that they are full of shit.

One such introspective check-off is something called "Pascal's Wager," and although most cultural Christians have never heard of it, they make this wager just the same. A seventeenth-century French philosopher named Blaise Pascal devised a clever way for theists to remain in denial about the doubts they have as they pertain to the more outlandish claims made by their orthodoxy, and it goes something like this:

> *Belief (in God) is a wise wager. Granted that faith cannot be proved, what harm will come to you if you gamble on its truth and it proves false? If you gain, you gain all; if you lose, you lose nothing. Wager, then, without hesitation, that He exists.*

—Blaise "Let It Ride" Pascal[72]

Ah … *now* I get it. Thanks a diaper load, Blaise. There is more to be gained from wagering on the existence of God than against it. So we should all—whether we believe in God or not, or if we are dubious because, deep down none of these stories make any sense—pretend that there is one. Because if the cantankerous, all-powerful egomaniac in the sky *does* exist, then we'll get invited to his postlife after-hours bash with all of the cool kids. If he doesn't, then no biggie. We'll just be the same worm food we would have been anyway.

Better safe than sorry, that's what good ole' Blaise Pascal always said.

Pascal actually formulated his introspective gambit within a Christian framework. Which is to say that he had Christianity in mind when he

---

[72]   BrainyQuote.com, *Blaise Pascal*, http://www.brainyquote.com/quotes/quotes/b/blaisepasc159845.html

articulated the most convenient way to rationalize a casual approach to faith.

The gospel to me is simply irresistible.

—Blaise Pascal[73]

How else could any rational person remain a "Christian" when confronted with the craziness of its orthodoxy?

But here's where the logic of Pascal's Wager fails.

Belief is not a choice. One cannot simply affirm that something is true if they know, or even suspect, that it might not be. That is more commonly known as bullshit. One cannot decide to believe in myths unless those myths were accompanied by facts and information that allowed one's sensibilities to make that determination. In which case they would cease to be myths; they would be redefined as history.

As it stands with cultural Christians who capitulate to Pascal's wager, it is religious fear that makes that determination, not faith. Hence, the denial. The facts and evidence simply do not support Christian tenets as science or history.

Faith is believing what you know ain't so.

—Mark Twain[74]

Which is to say that faith is not actually the "belief" in something in the absence of facts. Rather it is acquiescing to denial and surrendering reason and thought. Faith that magical, physics-defying impossibilities actually happened is little more than a capitulation to willful ignorance so that one might not feel so afraid in this great-big, scary universe.

---

73   Ibid., http://www.brainyquote.com/quotes/quotes/b/blaisepasc159848.html

74   Twainquotes.com, *Mark Twain*, http://www.twainquotes.com/Faith.html

In any other acceptance we hold dear, conclusions may only be drawn from the acumen of our life's experience, based upon evidence. For instance, we'd never "choose to believe" that werewolves or vampires really exist. Despite the myriad of stories about these creatures, we all understand that they are fiction. There is no proof, beyond Anne Rice's novels. So, however hard we may try, or whatever claims we might make inwardly or outwardly to the contrary, no adult without a mental impairment can truly believe that werewolves and vampires are real.

Believing in things one knows can't be true is not a choice that a sane person can make. Which suggests that Yahweh is more fear-inducing than vampires and werewolves. Moreover, if every atheist and non-Christian are entirely wrong, and if there is a wonderful Christian Yahweh up there looking down into our minds and he is willing to convict us for the thought crime of nonbelief—wouldn't he know that the fakers were full of shit? Wouldn't he understand why they are making this illimitable wager?

Hell, God would already know that you masturbate (don't deny that too). In case you hadn't noticed, the other thought crimes that virtually every Christian on earth is guilty of don't exactly conform to the Christian ideal, either. An all-seeing Muckety-Muck would know what's on your hard drive. So, wouldn't an omnipotent Yahweh also know that the only reason you claim to believe this madness is to avoid his potential cosmic retribution?

According to the stories in the Bible, this all-powerful space God is already very much aware of what we think and the depths of our faith. So if a cultural Christian were to make certain admissions based upon Pascal's wager, I'm sure that a deity as sharp as Yahweh could see through that little ruse. Considering that people cannot control what they truly believe, but rather only what they say they believe, the omnipotent interstellar kahuna would surely figure out when someone is stroking his almighty johnson.

He knows when you are sleeping. He knows when you're awake. He knows when you're in denial, so stop bullshitting yourself, for goodness' sake.

May the Farce Be With You

I believe with all my heart that the Bible is the infallible word of God.

—Rev. Jerry "Puts the Hippo in Hypocrite" Falwell[75]

The Bible is the truth. It's completely accurate both scientifically and historically because it is the perfect word of God. We know that it's the perfect word of God because it says so in the Bible. Therefore, the Bible is the truth.

This is what's known as "circular logic," and if you're having trouble wrapping your mind around it, I find it helpful to inhale some modeling glue when reading the above statement. Christian fundamentalism tends to come into clearer focus as one's brain cells are being killed off. So, in order to help cultural Christians out of denial, here are a few things that they don't teach you in Bible camp or parochial school:

The Christian faith is based on the writings in the New Testament of the Holy Bible. It tells the story of Jesus Christ, the son of Yahweh, who sacrificed himself so that all those who would eventually be born—and who believed that he was the one true savior—would be able to ascend into heaven. Having been absolved of original sin via crucifixion restitution, Christians could join the King of Kingpins in eternal bliss upon their earthly demise. Tough luck on the rest.

The New Testament is Jesus's book. He is the main character. He is like Luke Skywalker in Star Wars.

The Bible itself is actually sixty-six different books and has about forty different authors. There were probably around nine different people who wrote the New Testament alone. I say "probably" and "about" because the exact numbers are uncertain. Many of the origins of these stories are either

<hr>

[75] BrainyQuote.com, *Jerry Falwell*, http://www.brainyquote.com/quotes/quotes/j/jerryfalwe262058.html

anonymous or have assigned names that are questionable. From Genesis to Revelation, the Bible was written over approximately fifteen hundred years, and in several different languages. So it's safe to say that, if the Bible were Yahweh's means of expressing how we should act toward one another, he did a lousy job of maintaining continuity.

Read the Bible. Work hard and honestly. And don't complain.

—Rev. Billy "Easy for You to Say" Graham[76]

The general assumption that I've heard from Christians is that, through Yahweh's guiding hand, the New Testament came into existence via holy ghostwriting. The Bible itself is God's word, as authored by people who were having their hands guided by the Big Wheel himself. The thing is, most Christians have never considered the Bible's origins or how the books were put together. Even worse, many have never even read it.

In fact, there is an appreciable proportion of Christians who are unaware of how the book known as the New Testament actually came to be what it is today. Many are unaware that there is a significant history of censorship by the Roman Catholic Church. Various religious texts were discarded and destroyed in favor of those of which powerful clergy approved. The infallible word of God is actually plagiarized, rewritten, poorly translated, handpicked stories chosen by sadomasochistic lunatics who hoped to control the masses with an invisible overseer.

To those who understand its history, the construction of the Bible constitutes nothing short of fraud.

---

[76] Brainyquote.com, *Rev. Billy Graham*, http://www.brainyquote.com/quotes/quotes/b/billygraha403083.html

The Jedi Council

You must unlearn what you have learned.

—Yoda[77]

Many Christians I meet are under the impression that the gospels of Matthew, Mark, Luke, and John were written during the time of Jesus, by four of his apostles who followed him around and documented miracles, as his BFFs should. But that isn't the case. The New Testament gospels were not actually named after their authors. Rather, they were written many years after the supposed death of Jesus, by various sources. It would be like attributing the writing of *The Hound of the Baskervilles* to Sherlock Holmes.

For instance, the Gospel of Mark—the first gospel written—is estimated to have been composed between 65 and 80 CE. When you consider that the main character in the book supposedly died in 30 CE, that would be like nothing having been written about Winston Churchill until after the year 2000. The Gospel of Matthew is approximated to have been recorded in 80–100 CE, while the Gospels of Luke and John were calculated to have been written around 80–130 CE and 90–120 CE respectively. I guess the actual apostles weren't much for jotting things down.

If there actually was a Jesus—*and that is a big if*—the writers of these gospels never knew him. Moreover, the manuscript that we have come to know as *the New Testament of the Holy Bible* wasn't actually pieced together in its entirety until the fourth century AD. That is some 350 years after the time the Church claims that a man named Jesus Christ walked the earth.

But there is a reason why there was no such thing as the New Testament until the fourth century. Some of it was not written until then, and none of it was written until well after the time that the main character in the story

---

[77] Star Wars: Episode V - The Empire Strikes Back (1980), *Yoda,* http://www. imdb.com/character/ch0000015/quotes

allegedly existed. Unbeknownst to the vast majority of cultural Christians is the actual story of how the New Testament became this Frankenstein monster of sewn-together, edited, plagiarized works of fiction.

The suppression of the origins of the New Testament and how it fails to hold up to even the slightest scrutiny is the greatest hoax perpetrated on mankind of all time.

> *We believe in one God, the Father, the Almighty, maker*
> *of heaven and earth, of all that is, seen and unseen.*

—First line of the Nicaean Creed[78]

Many people are aware of something called "the Council of Nicaea," mainly because of the movie *The Da Vinci Code*. But as often happens when history is introduced via pop culture, the subject matter is treated cavalierly. That is actually understandable, since the movie's purpose was to entertain, not to educate. Hell, Tom Hanks and Sir Ian McKellan are awesome.

The reality is that, when you study the Council of Nicaea (as well as other early Christian congregations) and their effect on present-day American politics, it's kind of scary. Indeed, much of the Republican Party has come to adopt the watered-down tenets of a group of corrupt and ignorant fourth-century religious leaders. Many of the doctrinal decisions made sixteen hundred years ago are GOP mantra today.

However, there are many contradictory sources of information about what actually happened at Nicaea.

Certainly, there is an academic distinction—where it concerns credibility—between historians who make determinations based on evidence and Christian sources, who begin their research knowing the answers they want, and who disregard evidence that doesn't coincide with their

---

[78] Vatican.va @2014, *Nicean Creed*, http://www.vatican.va/archive/ccc_css/archive/catechism/credo.htm

predispositions. Not so coincidentally, the greatest consensus and the most reliable sources tend not to be from within the Christian community. But fundamentalists don't give a shit about credibility.

Flavius Constantinus, more famously known as the Roman Emperor Constantine (272–337 CE) was the man responsible for authorizing the compilation of writings that have come to be known as the New Testament. There was much civil unrest at the time, and rival "god factions" were violently vying for sociopolitical power. So Constantine gathered these groups together in what history calls "the First Council of Nicea, much as the "commission" convened to settle the bad blood among the heads of the five families after that unfortunate Virgil Sollozzo business.

Little did Constantine realize, until after this council was concluded, that it was Barzini all along.

Now to be fair, the history of the Council of Nicea is highly disputed. So I won't get into the non-Christian elements or the claims that, at this council, many different religious cults debated on a great number of divine and ritualistic preferences. There are even those who claim that Jesus Christ was actually an assemblage of other deities, and that the council settled on the Jesus myth as a great compromise. There is much evidence to support this.

However, to better frame the insanity, I think that perhaps we should keep the happenings at the Council of Nicaea within a Christian framework.

> *If the Father begat the Son, he that was begotten had*
> *a beginning of existence: and from this it is evident,*
> *that there was a time when the Son was not.*

—Fourth-century Alexandrian priest Arius[79], whose applied logic that a father and son are two different, unequal entities earned him the brand of "heretic" at the Council of Nicaea

---

[79] Izquotes.com, *Arius*, http://izquotes.com/author/arius

There are some Nicaean retrospectives that have—for the most part—garnered a historical consensus. Bishops disputed what to include and what to exclude in what was to be their new holy writ. They argued about the nature of Jesus Christ and whether he was to be portrayed as divine at all. It was at this council that the matter of monotheism was settled; it became an issue once they decided to make Jesus divine, and not merely a man.

Indeed, among the questions they deliberated over are: If Jesus were to be portrayed as the son of God, then would he be equal to God? What would be the hierarchal relationship? As it obviously turned out, the Nicaea Council eventually voted to make Jesus Christ a full deity, and it decided that the Holy Trinity of the Father, the Son, and Holy Spirit would become official church doctrine. So there you have it, One God, three heads ... kind of like a Targaryen dragon.

Faced with the daunting task of trying to define what Christianity would become, and having to choose from a variety of writs, the council members had many questions to settle before they could finalize what would eventually become the New Testament. What books should be included? What books should be excluded? Do any of these books contradict one another? Do any of them need a little editing so that they might conform better to what the Church feels they should say?

In addition, if any writing composed by Arius should be found, it should be handed over to the flames, so that not only will the wickedness of his teaching be obliterated, but nothing will be left even to remind anyone of him. And I hereby make a public order, that if someone should be discovered to have hidden a writing composed by Arius, and not to have immediately brought it forward and destroyed it by fire, his penalty shall be death. As soon as he is discovered in this offense, he shall be submitted for capital punishment.

—From an edict of the Emperor Constantine[80]

---

[80]   Fourthcentury.com, *Emperor Constantine*, http://www.fourthcentury.com/urkunde-33/

The suppression of knowledge by the Church is not limited to science. It comes at the expense of truth overall, even where it concerns its own history. Many documents that were written which either do not coincide, or which directly contradict the stories in the New Testament were presented at the Council of Nicaea, but those with the power of persuasion—and politics—omitted them.

Worse yet were historical works that were destroyed by the Church in the centuries following the First Council of Nicaea and the formation of the Roman Catholic Church. The omitted documents that have survived have cast serious doubt on the accuracy of the works that made it into the New Testament. We can only speculate on what was written about Jesus in the documents they chose to destroy.

Bunnies and Fatsos

And by the way, for all you kids watching at home, Santa just is white.

—Fox News's most prominent Christian blonde, Megyn
Kelly[81], debating the melanin content of a fictional
character in one of her least-bright moments

Even the holidays for Christianity were deliberated upon at the Council of Nicaea. Borrowing from preexisting pagan beliefs, and not wanting to upset the apple cart too much, they decided that Christmas and Easter should fall on pagan holidays of the winter solstice and spring harvest. Changing deities is one thing; ruining people's celebrations is quite another. So it's candy canes and chocolate bunnies for everyone!

But in my mind—as ridiculous as this all is—the most absurd component to American Christian fundamentalism is the editing of the Bible which has occurred *since* the Council of Nicaea. If one's faulty logic and disregard for evidence allows one to make the leap to believe that the hand of God

---

[81] Foxnews.com, *Megyn Kelly*, http://www.foxnews.com/us/2013/12/13/
megyn-kelly-responds-to-critics-over-santa-is-white-flap/

was involved in the original manuscript selection and editing process, then how can one reconcile the post-Council alterations? Is Yahweh, like George Lucas, in need of post-epic rewrites?

In the early 1600s, at the behest of King James I of England, somewhere in the neighborhood of fifty men were commissioned to *rewrite* the Bible according to His Grace's specifications. Since there was contention within the established Church, and His Highness was unable to read ancient Greek, Hebrew, or Aramaic, it became necessary to translate the Bible into English. And Jimbo was the King as chosen by God, so they better not screw this up.

> *The state of monarchy is the supremest thing upon earth: for kings are not only God's Lieutenants upon earth, and sit upon God's throne, but even by God himself they are called Gods.*

—King James I[82], displaying less humility than LeBron

King James—who believed that he had a *divine* right of monarchy—established a bunch of personal "rules" the translators were to follow, and since white-out hadn't yet been invented, they were obliged to do so. Then, upon its completion in 1609, The King James Bible was handed over to His Majesty for his final approval. However, good ole King James was really busy with the burden of divine awesomeness, so he passed the manuscripts onto the smartest cookie in the kingdom, Sir Francis Bacon, who was much more qualified to edit what the King's translators had done. And let's face it, one of the best Christian perks is that we love our bacon.

Moreover, since we Americans aren't very adept at reading Ye Olde English, the Bible been diluted further still. I know that whenever I suggest to a Christian that perhaps they should actually try *reading* the Bible, I always recommend the New International version. It's written in the plainest,

---

[82] Coursesa.matrix.msu.edu. *King James I*, http://coursesa.matrix.msu.edu/~hst201/SpeechParl.htm

most contemporary English, and, unlike the King James version, it's comprehensible to the average Joe.

Atheism leads a man to sense, to philosophy, to natural piety, to laws, to reputation: all of which may be guides to an outward moral virtue.

—Sir Francis "Respected by Jefferson" Bacon[83]

Needless to say, the infallible word of God was put together and edited over the centuries by men. The history of the New Testament, and how fundamentalist Christian Americans have come to regard it as a singular truth, is a total farce. To believe that the Bibles that they sell in Barnes & Noble are inconvertible proof of anything, let alone the life-coaching instructions of an omnipotent supreme being, requires an utter surrender of intellect and reason.

But even worse: the Bibles Americans have in their homes are not only severely edited, awkwardly translated, and altered over time—they are not even original stories. These books are, for the most part, plagiarized from preexisting works of Greek, Hebrew, Egyptian, and Aramaic fiction. And to add even a little more spice into the crazy Christian jambalaya, certain wording has been altered as the Bible has been translated so that Christian Americans can better succumb to brainwashing.

Sith Lords

Myth is what we call other people's religion.

—Joseph "Dude Knows His Myths" Campbell[84]

However, if the manner in which the New Testament was pieced together like a modern art mosaic wasn't enough to persuade a rational person to

---

[83] Quotesplanet.com, *Sir Francis Bacon*, http://www.quotesplanet.com/quote/2709/

[84] Quotingquotes.com, *Joseph Campbell*, http://quotingquotes.com/33130/

give his faith a little thought; if the omissions, misrepresentations and outright lies about the origins of the New Testament aren't enough to dissuade a person from his long-held dogma, here comes the good stuff:

As all good Christian folk know without a shadow of a doubt, any mockery of the one true savior is of no consequence to the true believers, because he existed well before his human birth, and he will endure until the end of time. He was born of a virgin, in a manger, and his birth is celebrated on December 25. His coming was announced by a star in the north. He was a child teacher and a fisherman, and he was baptized when he was thirty years old. He had twelve disciples who saw him perform miracles, like feeding the masses, healing the sick, and walking on water. He was crucified, buried in a tomb, and resurrected. He is known as "The Way," "The Truth," and The Light." They call him "The Messiah" and "The Lamb."

He lived approximately 3000 BCE. His name was Horus, the Egyptian sky god. And he had the head of a falcon. Wait ... what?!

Did you think I was referring to a disparate work of fiction about a different savior? Have you noticed any parallels in that story and the one you were taught was absolute truth growing up? Silly rabbit, Trix are for kids.

Three thousand years before the story of Jesus of Nazareth ambling around Judea performing magic tricks and pissing off Romans, there was a dude named Horus in Egypt, who apparently had the same gimmick. But the similarities—which is just a nice way to say plagiarizing—don't end there.

The infant Horus was carried out of Egypt to escape the wrath of Seth, who saw him as a threat to his power. The infant Jesus was carried *into* Egypt to escape the wrath of Herod, who saw him as a threat to his power. In through the out door.

Horus raised some guy named El-Azar-us, from the dead. But not to be outdone, Jesus raised a fella named Lazarus from the dead. And to one-up that hack Horus, he waited four days until Lazarus was good and ripe. I'm sure that the similarity in their names is a total coincidence.

It's too bad Horus wasn't a real sky god. He could have come back and sued Jesus's ass for stealing his act.

But to be fair, despite the similarities in these tales, there are also some striking differences. For instance, to the best of my knowledge, Jesus Christ did not have a bird's head. As we all know, Jesus was a six-foot-tall white guy with blue eyes, living in the Middle East during the Roman occupation.

Also, the manger that baby Jesus was born in was in a stable, whereas, Horus's manger was in a cave. Let's face it, how stupid would a cave scene look on anyone's lawn at Horus-mas time?

The Virgin Mary gave birth to Jesus after being divinely knocked up by the Holy Spirit. However the virgin goddess Isis conceived Horus posthumously with her deceased god/husband Osiris, after piecing him back together and substituting his missing wanker with a golden dildo. One can only assume that in ancient Egypt, the term "virginity" does not apply when the woman in question's gates are breached by an inanimate object.

And not to be confused with the guy who plays in the NHL, Jesus's nemesis was Satan, who tempted him with all sorts of libidinous indulgences on a mountain in a desert in Palestine. Whereas the Dr. Moriarty in the Horus story—who tempted ole' Falcon-head on a different mountain in someplace called Amenta—is named Set. You say tomato, I say Boris Badenov.

The Trinities in both stories are also different. The Egyptian holy trinity of Osiris, Isis, and Horus, is distinctly dissimilar to the Christian trinity of Father, the Son, and the Holy Spirit. Which is also a severe departure from Athos, Porthos, and Aramis let alone Kukla, Fran, and Ollie. See no evil, hear no evil, speak no evil.

Jesus's surname was Christ, while Horus was called "KRST." See? Totally different. Nothing to see here. Move along now, people.

And the guy who baptized Jesus was his cousin "John the Baptist," while Horus was baptized by "Anup the Baptizer." In an odd coincidence, they were both thirty years old when they took the literal plunge. It is not written whether either one of them took care of all "family business" as they were doing so.

Yet if the obvious plagiarism of the Horus story in the New Testament isn't enough to pique your skepticism, if you are still willing to remain in denial as to the historical validity of the Jesus story—or if you remain stubbornly steadfast about how the only way to gain admittance to "heaven" is to believe the Jesus story word for word, despite the overwhelming evidence against it ever having actually happened, worry not. Because the hits just keep on coming:

One-Hit Wonders

I reject your reality and substitute my own.

—*Mythbusters's* Adam Savage[85]

Yet another virgin-born savior of all mankind who managed to rise from the dead was the Phrygo (modern day Turkey)-Roman god Attis. Born of the virgin Nana, Attis also predated Jesus by several hundred years. He was both the divine son and the father, which is a pretty neat trick if you don't have a time machine, and his worshipers also ate his body as bread. His birthday was also celebrated on December 25. Attis was crucified during the spring season, having been nailed to a tree on a Friday, and then he rose from the dead on the third day, which, if you're not keeping score at home, is a Sunday—as in Easter.

---

[85] Goodreads.com, *Adam Savage*, http://www.goodreads.com/quotes/39019-i-reject-your-reality-and-substitute-my-own

Still, there are differences in the stories. For instance, Attis's blood soaked into the ground so as to resurrect the Earth, and rather than ascend into heaven, he instead ventured down into the underworld to rescue damned souls. So there is an obvious post-resurrection directional discrepancy.

Next up on the savior hit parade is a fella named Zoroaster, who has nothing to do with Mexican sword fighting. Also born of a virgin via an "immaculate conception of divine reason" several hundred years (at least, as the specifics of the timeline are in question) before the New Testament claim of the birth of Jesus Christ, Zoroaster was also a child prodigy, wowing holy men with his wisdom. Also beginning his ministry at thirty (which was apparently the chosen age for saviors to begin their savior-ing) and baptized in a river, he taught about heaven and hell and scared the crap out of people by teaching about the impending apocalypse.

It was taught that Zoroaster will have his second coming in the year 2341, which, let's face it, seems kind of arbitrary. But the good news is, he has promised to usher in a "Golden Age." So invest now.

Dionysus (around 800 BCE) was a divine, Greco-Roman badass. Yet another savior unsullied by paternal DNA, born of the virgin Semele and sired by none other than Zeus, this holy child was placed in a manger like all the other saviors. To be fair, mangers back then were like child-protective car seats today, so it really isn't that much of a coincidence. But the rest is.

This "savior" was also referred to as the "only begotten son," the "redeemer," the "sin bearer," the "anointed one," and the "Alpha and Omega." Dionysus also had his birthday celebrated on December 25. He was a traveling teacher whose primary mode of getting around was on the back of a donkey, and he performed miracles, most notably turning water into wine. Of course, he was killed for being such an awesome savior, and, more importantly, he came back from the dead, a la Bobby Ewing, in the shower. And like both Jesus Christ, and WWE champion Triple H, Dionysus was also known as "The King of Kings."

On his robe and on his thigh he has this name
written: king of kings and lord of lords.

—Revelation 19:16[86]

It is rumored that at the behest of his agent, after retiring from the savior business, Dionysus shortened his name and formed a singing group called the Belmonts.

Another hitherto savior of all mankind was Krishna, who was conceived a few thousand years before Christ via "mental transmission" from the pervy mind of Vasudeva directly into the womb of the virgin Devaki. However, if this were possible, then Kate Beckensale should be pregnant with my child right now. Sent from heaven to take the form of a man, Krishna was visited upon his arrival on earth by wise men who were guided to him by a star, and he had an adopted human father who was a carpenter and who was gullible enough to take his wife's word about how she got knocked up.

Angels warned of a plan to assassinate the baby Krishna by a local no-goodnick of a politician, much like angels would warn the parents of Horus, and Jesus, in their respective stories. Both Jesus and Krishna were hidden away from harm by their earthbound guardians: Mary and Joseph went to Muturea; whereas Krishna's parents stayed in Mathura. It was not known whether any of them did the Macarena.

Both Jesus and Krishna performed miracles, both had disciples, both cured disease before Obamacare. Both raised the dead. Both were meek and merciful. Both were criticized for hanging out with "sinners." And both Jesus and Krishna, along with every Italian mother in Brooklyn, were without sin.

---

[86] Usccb.org. *Revelation 19:16*, http://www.usccb.org/bible/revelation/19

He alone sees truly who sees the Lord the same in every creature, seeing the same Lord everywhere, he does not harm himself or others.

—Krishna[87]

Before either of them was crucified, Krishna and Jesus each held a last supper. Both were resurrected. They both forgave their enemies and were considered both human and divine. However, unlike the rest of these mythical deities—but just like Jesus—there are still people who are delusional enough to believe that Krishna was a historical figure and not just a myth. But at least followers of Krishna admit that he was brown.

And finishing up this segment of eerily similar saviors who predated Christianity is Mithra. Not to be confused with the giant flying arthropod and Godzilla nemesis who did the bidding of a couple of doll-sized Asian nightingales in a box, Mithra (approx. 600 BCE) was also a very Jesus-like savior. Or rather, Jesus was more of a Mithra-like savior. So much so that many of the rituals contained in a Christian mass are based on Mithraic worship.

As you might expect, all the usual similarities exist between Jesus and Mithra, although there are conflicting stories about Mithra's birth. One tale tells of him being born out of solid rock, while the other involves the Persian goddess Anahita—and, like all the other divine matriarchs, she was no slut. Saving her love button for supernatural procreation, Anahita's patience and diligence paid off, allowing her to give birth to her own omniscient Prince of Peace.

But regardless which Mithraic origin story has more validity, the lesson replete within all of these messiah stories is no less evident: Listen up young girls! Keep that aspirin between your legs, and who knows? Maybe you can birth a little savior yourself one day!

87   Entheos.com, *Krishna*, https://www.entheos.com/quotes/by_teacher/krishna

I am the way and the truth and the life. No one
comes to the Father except through me.

—Jesus "Mithra Is a Hack" Christ[88], John 14:6

Still, getting back on track, Mithra was also known as "the way, the truth, and the light." He was called the Redeemer, regardless of whether your coupons had expired. He was called the Lion and the Lamb. He was "the light brought into the world to fight darkness." He was the Good Shepherd and the Savior. They called him Messiah. But his friends called him "Mithy."

He had twelve companions while traveling around performing his one-man savior show. The Mithra posse, Yo. Like any messiah worth his salt, he performed miracles. Pick a card. Any card.

The followers of Mithra formed an organized church, which included a Eucharist and baptisms performed to purify oneself, and to cleanse one of sin. They taught of an immortal soul and a final judgment. Mithra redeemed damned souls and brought them to a better place. Perhaps a beach resort.

As the church's all-powerful honcho, Mithra was considered to be both human, and divine. It is not clear whether the head of the Mithraic church wore a giant pointy hat or not. Some early Christians believed Jesus to be an incarnation of Mithra. They were denounced as heretics. How dare they lie about the source of a plagiarized story.

Mithra's birthday was December 25. What a shock. Three wise men came to visit the baby/god and brought gifts of gold, frankincense, myrrh, and perhaps a Bundt cake.

---

[88]   Holy Bible, *John 14:6*, Holy Bible. New International Version ®, Copyright ©
1973, 1978, 1984, 2011 by Biblica, Inc.®

Mithra died on a cross, but before doing so, he had a "last supper" with his twelve disciples. He was buried in a tomb during the spring equinox and rose again after three days.

Faulty Premise

We must respect the other fellow's religion, but only in the sense and to the extent that we respect his theory that his wife is beautiful and his children smart.

—Great American satirist H.L. Mencken[89]

So here's the thing: there are many other deities who predate the New Testament and who have valid comparisons that I haven't even mentioned. I simply picked out a few of my favorites, and to be honest, the ones whom I felt I could write the best jokes for. But these myths all steal from each other so much that the satire just writes itself. Frankly, I don't know how anyone can write about any of this stuff *without* making fun of it.

Savior stories back then were like spy novels are today. There were tons of them, and some were written better than others. But what they all had in common is that they were fiction. Bond. Jesus Bond.

Which makes the premise from which cultural Christians might argue with their hate filled, violent fundamentalist brethren is extremely weak. There were a lot of so-called virgins popping little saviors out of their love tunnels when the world was young, and people were really ignorant. Thankfully, now we have the Maury Povich show to illustrate the futility of paternal deniability.

The individual savior stories I've mentioned above, as well as the illustration of the Council of Nicaea and the Roman Emperor Constantine each warrant their own book. I mention them, but in the interest of avoiding

---

[89] BrainyQuote.com, *H.L.Mencken*, http://www.brainyquote.com/quotes/quotes/h/hlmencke101720.html

tedium and keeping this book under four thousand pages, I mention them thusly.

People can research these topics to death and find varying discrepancies, as well they would for the New Testament scriptures themselves. Even a quick trip to Wikipedia will yield enough information for most Christians to realize that their understanding of their own faith is pedestrian at best. Many things are hidden from the average Christian; if most Christians were to be exposed to a true religious education and have their tenets juxtaposed with ideologies of various cultures over several centuries and they would scrutinize their beliefs with the same sense of reason that won't allow them to believe in Zeus, then they'd have little choice but to categorize Christianity together with every other myth.

> *I know that (America) is a Christian country, and I stand up*
> *for your right to be religious, but please know that you're wrong.*
> *Please know that you're living in a fantasy land, and that after*
> *you die, nothing happens; stop being a fucking child.*

—Australian comic, *creator of Legit*, and my
kind of asshole, Jim Jefferies[90]

But here's the thing about Christian Dominionism as it applies to your vote. It requires willful lunacy. The very premise of Christianity is based on the obvious fiction of Adam and Eve. Without the literal translation of the biblical story of the forbidden fruit and "original sin," the whole Jesus story makes even less sense than it already does. This is why Christian fundamentalists have to deny evolutionary science and claim that the biblical story of creation is true history.

—And they're hoping that you're crazy and stupid enough to believe it, too.

Because without the talking snake and the apple-eating bimbo, Yahweh would have had no reason to absentee bang an under-aged virgin in the

---

[90]   Jim Jefferies © 2014, *Jim Jeffries*, http://jimjefferies.ning.com/

first place. According to Christianity, the tenets clearly state that Jesus "died on the cross for our sins."

He himself bore our sins in his body on the cross, so that we might die to sins and live for righteousness; by his wounds you have been healed.

—1 Peter 2:24[91]

So if the Adam and Eve story is a work of fiction or a metaphor (and it obviously is, unless you're a complete idiot), then why would the all-knowing all-powerful Yahweh have to create an earthbound incarnation of himself? It only works if he has to undo Eve's fruit blunder.

No apple, no original sin. And with no original sin, there is nothing for Jesus to be "savior-ing" us from. According to the story, Jesus died so that his father/self could find it in his black heart to forgive us faulty humans after that no-good floozy ate from the wrong tree. All it would take is a human sacrifice as recompense to not compel the good lord to banish us all to an eternity of suffering. So then, unless one believes that Adam and Eve were created on the sixth day and were susceptible to reptilian propaganda, then the concept of Yahweh feeling the need to sacrifice his son/himself, *to* himself as a means to acquire the capacity to forgive us all for something that we never did (but we were born guilty of) falls to pieces.

As if it made any sense in the first place.

---

91   Holy Bible, *1 Peter 2:24*, Holy Bible. New International Version ®, Copyright © 1973, 1978, 1984, 2011 by Biblica, Inc.®

CHAPTER 3
The Handbook
(How to Be a Sociopath, in Sixty-Six Easy Lessons)

Have faith, hope, and charity. That's the way to live successfully. How do I know? The Bible tells me so

—Christian Hymn[92]

92   Ibid., *Christian Hymn*.

With circular logic comes a myriad of other intellective concessions. Beyond a Christian fundamentalist's assertion that the Bible is infallible word of God—which is a determination arrived at because it says so in the Bible—which is true because it the Bible says it is—and therefore, the Bible is the infallible word of God—exist many other obtuse and irrational presumptions.

Twenty-first-century biblical affirmations are made despite all the translations, alterations, and creative edits performed on the Bible throughout history. So, decades after we landed a man on the moon, we can go to Barnes & Noble to buy life-coaching instructions from the Supreme Being, as given to us via the writings of Bronze-Age goat-herders who had their hands guided by the Cosmic Czar himself. It's like a dictated autobiography. *God's Greatest Hits.*

And Christians claim that this book proves their moral compass.

Even low-pressure Christians like to speak of their loving God, because priests, ministers, reverends, and/or parents have told them so. In fact, God *is* love. That's what they've been taught growing up. It's not like the lord makes us eat vegetables or anything. Yahweh is a swell guy. There is no denying. Here is an example:

> *Dear friends, let us love one another, for love comes from God. Everyone who loves has been born of God and knows God. Whoever does not love does not know God, because God is love. This is how God showed his love among us: He sent his one and only Son into the world that we might live through him. This is love: not that we loved God, but that he loved us and sent his Son as an atoning sacrifice for our sins.*

> —John 4:7–10[93]

Thus, we are given many illustrations of God's love for us throughout the Bible. The thing is, some of the examples of God's love are a little sketchy.

---

[93] Ibid., *John 4:7-10.*

They say "love," but it kind of looks like the kind of "love" a battered wife receives from her drunk husband after serving dinner cold. The biblical, Judeo-Christian Yahweh shows love much in the same manner as any sadomasochistic sociopath who gets his jollies from tormenting others. Only he doesn't allow those whom he tortures for his own amusement a "safe word."

A Really, Really Honest Abe

We can start near the beginning, in the book of Genesis and the story of Abraham, who was chosen by God for a very special task.

> Then God said, "Take your son, your only son, whom you love—Isaac—and go to the region of Moriah. Sacrifice him there as a burnt offering on a mountain I will show you."

—Genesis 22:2[94]

"Hey, Dad, wanna toss the ball around? What's with the rope and duct tape?"

But Abraham was undaunted, despite loving his boy. Yahweh wanted the lil' fella dead, so knife to the chest it would be. So Abe suckered his not-too-bright progeny, Isaac, to his own human sacrifice by claiming that he was going to offer a lamb, despite their being no actual lamb present: "God himself will provide the lamb for the burnt offering, my son." (Genesis 22:8) [95]Nice boy, about as sharp as a sack of wet mice.

However, right before Abe was going to murder his own son—who was tied up and could not run away—because voices in Abraham's head told him to do so, Ike got a last-minute reprieve from God's secretary. "Miss Johnson, drop everything and stop that idiot from killing his son, and deliver this memo with your wings on, so he'll know it's from me ..." "Do

---

94 Ibid., *Genesis 22:2*.

95 Ibid., *Genesis 22:8*.

not lay a hand on the boy," the angel of the Lord said. "Do not do anything to him. Now I know that you fear God, because you have not withheld from me your son, your only son." (Genesis 22:12)[96]

"Abraham, dude … I can't believe you were really going to go through with that. Holy me, you're crazy, yo. Thanks for acknowledging the voice I put in your head as really being me, and not some neural hallucination brought about by eating bad mushrooms. You don't really have to brutally murder your son. I was only joshing. Sorry for the mix-up. You're my main man, Abe."

So God gave Abraham a ram to sacrifice in Isaac's stead, because everyone knows that a loving supreme being requires an occasional blood sacrifice, even if it's not a human. Then to show his appreciation for Abe being such a good sport about almost being punked into murdering his kid, God gave Abraham a major eternal genetic perk. The would-be kid killer's devotion was to be passed down to an innumerable amount of offspring who would be blessed and anointed with the ability to murder, rape, and pillage entire cities.

> *The angel of the LORD called to Abraham from heaven a second time and said, "I swear by myself, declares the LORD, that because you have done this and have not withheld your son, your only son, I will surely bless you and make your descendants as numerous as the stars in the sky and as the sand on the seashore. Your descendants will take possession of the cities of their enemies, and through your offspring all nations on earth will be blessed, because you have obeyed me."*

—Genesis 22:15–18[97]

Two things: One, does anyone else find it hilarious that Yahweh swears by himself? And two, how's that for some potent sperm?

---

[96]   Ibid., *Genesis 22:12.*

[97]   Ibid., *22:15-18.*

Then Abraham eventually settled in a place called "Beersheba," which, to be honest, sounds awesome. I would probably be casual about where my DNA wound up if I lived there too. Margaritaville was probably too far away.

So in retrospect, who's to say? Maybe Andrea Yates and Susan Smith heard the voice of God telling them to kill their children, too. The alibi has biblical precedence, and Dominionist Christian politicians claim that God speaks to them all the time. "Rick Santorum, my son, it's me again, God. You shall continue to wear awful sweater-vests, and you shall run for President of the United States."

But for the record, if you ever hear voices telling you to kill your child—or to do anything, for that matter—I highly recommend seeking psychiatric help.

We're Gonna Need a Bigger Boat

A little over a thousand years after God's perfect creations—Adam and Eve—disobeyed him, the lord decided he needed to hit the cosmic reset button and murder every person on earth, with the exception of a centuries-old fella named Noah and his family. You see, Yahweh was kind of pissed off that humans were not living up to his standards. So, rather than euthanizing tens of millions of people by having them die in their sleep, God had to make sure that everyone knew how naughty they'd been by drowning them.

> *In the six hundredth year of Noah's life, on the seventeenth day*
> *of the second month—on that day all the springs of the great*
> *deep burst forth, and the floodgates of the heavens were opened.*
> *And rain fell on the earth forty days and forty nights.*

—Genesis 7:11–12[98]

---

[98]   Ibid., *7:11-12.*

Take *that*, Al Gore. Noah must have been a spry six hundred years old, and that was before Medicare. I guess Yahweh warning people with his big booming voice in the sky was inappropriate. Using his God powers to convey dissatisfaction and allowing people to alter their behavior is unbecoming of a supreme being. So genocide via drowning it was. Lead by example:

> *So the LORD said, "I will wipe from the face of the earth the human race I have created—and with them the animals, the birds and the creatures that move along the ground—for I regret that I have made them." But Noah found favor in the eyes of the LORD.*

—Genesis 6:7–8[99]

To be fair, I once spent an entire morning trying to make pancakes, resulting in a garbage pail full of burnt batter. Maybe God had the flame too high when he made the first batch of humans. Regardless, into the cosmological dumpster they went.

But forcing people to struggle to breathe—gasping in abject horror until water filled their lungs—wasn't quite enough of a punishment for Yahweh's burnt pancakes. Although the all-knowing Nabob loved his burnt pancakes, he had to teach them a lesson. So God—as any loving parent would do when their children disappoint them—sent every person on earth other than Noah and his kin to their room without supper. And by room, I mean Hell, and without supper, I mean for an eternity of torture.

God is love.

Never mind that the story of Noah makes the concept of God needing to sacrifice his only begotten son in order to atone for Adam and Eve's original sin even more implausible than it already is. When one considers that, since Noah and his family were Yahweh's chosen humans to repopulate

---

[99] Ibid., 6:7-8.

the earth, it's a logical conclusion that an all-powerful, omnipotent space deity might have chosen *this* moment to lift his "you're all going to spend eternity being tortured in hell" restriction before he allowed Noah to litter the planet with more original sin-stained humans.

If nothing else, it shows bad planning. But then again, God works in illogical ways.

However, murdering millions of people via drowning also presented another problem for the big enchilada in the sky. When Yahweh took the better part of a week to actualize the universe, he spent almost an entire day creating millions of species of land animals. Damn if he was going to go through that again. Do you know what a pain in the ass it is to make an armadillo or a proboscis monkey from scratch? What if he didn't still have all of the ingredients? Or if he lost the instructions?

So Noah was going to need a bigger boat. But being an awesome, loving space deity, Yahweh thought of everything.

So make yourself an ark of cypress wood; make rooms in it and coat it with pitch inside and out. This is how you are to build it: The ark is to be three hundred cubits long, fifty cubits wide, and thirty cubits high. Make a roof for it, leaving below the roof an opening one cubit high all around.
Put a door in the side of the ark and make lower, middle, and upper decks. I am going to bring floodwaters on the earth to destroy all life under the heavens, every creature that has the breath of life in it. Everything on earth will perish. But I will establish my covenant with you, and you will enter the ark—you and your sons and your wife and your sons' wives with you. You are to bring into the ark two of all living creatures, male and female, to keep them alive with you. Two of every kind of bird, of every kind of animal, and of every kind of creature that moves along the ground will come to you to be kept alive. You are to take every kind of food that is to be eaten and store it away as food for you and for them.

Noah did everything just as God commanded him.

—Genesis 6:14–22[100]

Blueprints down to the last detail. Heck, a three-hundred-cubit by fifty-cubit ark must've been pretty big. After all, that's a lot of animals, not to mention a lot of poop. A brachiosaurus alone can drop a deuce the size of a Volvo. The Bronx Zoo is gigantic, and they don't even have dinosaurs.

However, a search on the Christian website "Answers in Genesis" reveals that a biblical "cubit" is the distance between one's elbow and one's fingertip. Granted, it is an inexact measurement. A Shaquille O'Neal cubit would be much larger than a Danny Devito cubit. So let's be generous and say that Noah must've had an abnormally large, Popeye-esque forearm, and an elbow-to-fingertip span of about two feet. That would mean that Noah crammed his family, and two of every animal on earth, into a six-hundred-by-one-hundred-foot ark.

I know how difficult it is to seat feuding relatives apart from one another at a wedding. Can you imagine what a pain in the ass it must've been to keep a pair of tyrannosauruses from devouring every other living thing on that ship? But hey, I'm sure that, although it didn't actually say it in the scriptures, God must've shrunk everything down to a manageable size and suppressed their natural inclinations for the duration of the cruise. "Now Rex, I know that cow looks really yummy, but you'll just have to wait until we disembark and she has the opportunity to make more cows before you eat her."

Regardless, Yahweh so loved his creations that he killed all of them, with the exception of a six-hundred-year-old man, his family, and two of every animal on earth. Now if that's not love, I don't know what is.

---

[100]   Ibid., *6:14-22.*

The Wizard of Uz

God and Satan were having a chat. Sure, one of them was all-loving and the other pure evil, but that should never get in the way of compelling conversation. So, after some preliminary small talk about sports and the weather, they eventually started chatting it up about a fella named Job. God said to Satan, *"Have you considered my servant Job? There is no one on earth like him; he is blameless and upright, a man who fears God and shuns evil" (Job 1:8)[101]*. This must have been as annoying to Satan as when your neighbor brags about his awesome lawn while you're trying to pull out weeds.

Good guy/bad guy conversations like this happen all the time in movies, where they meet to talk like gentlemen before the big showdown. As it is written, it's a lot like when Sheriff Rick and the Governor were discussing the fate of Michone in *The Walking Dead*. If you don't get the reference, I'm sure you can figure it out.

Now Job (rhymes with lobe, not lob) lived in the land of Uz, and he really loved the all-powerful space magician who treated him so well. Job would offer burnt sacrifices to God as a token of his esteem, because he knew that supreme beings like their ritual blood sacrifices risk-free from salmonella. And Yahweh, being awesome, rewarded Job's devotion by lovingly bestowing good fortune upon him. Job had a beautiful family (seven sons and three daughters), a great collection of livestock, fertile lands, a terrific home, good health, and a smokin' hot wife. Life is good when you suck up to Yahweh.

Then the Lord of Darkness retorted to God's boast with something to the effect of: "Sure Job loves you, look at all the cool stuff he has, and check out the tits on Mrs. Job. I'd love you too if you gave me wealth and let me tap that. Let's see what would happen if we Murphy's Law'ed Job's ass." And Yahweh, never one to back down from a challenge, took Satan up on his bet and laid down a few ground rules: *"The LORD SAID TO SATAN, 'VERY*

---

[101]   Ibid., *Job 1:8*.

WELL, THEN, EVERYTHING HE HAS IS IN YOUR POWER, BUT ON THE MAN HIMSELF DO NOT LAY A FINGER'" (JOB 1:12)[102].

So the bet was on. Challenge accepted. Peer pressure succumbed to. Satan could fuck with Job all he wanted to, as long as he didn't harm him personally. Gotcha. That makes everything all right then. Now we'd get to see how faithful to the sky wizard Job really was. Winner gets dinner at Chili's.

So the devil—with God's okay—went to work to prove that Job's reciprocal love was conditional: *"One day when Job's sons and daughters were feasting and drinking wine at the oldest brother's house, a messenger came to Job and said, 'The oxen were plowing and the donkeys were grazing nearby, and the Sabeans attacked and made off with them. They put the servants to the sword, and I am the only one who has escaped to tell you!'" (Job 1:13–15)[103].* Damn Sabeans, they really know how to ruin a party. But donkeys, oxen, and servants? A tough break for sure, but in the big picture it's not too big of a deal. Job can just put up a help wanted sign and head to the Ass and Ox Emporium later in the week.

But little did Job know, this is when the fun was really about to start.

"While he was still speaking, another messenger came and said, 'The fire of God fell from the heavens and burned up the sheep and the servants, and I am the only one who has escaped to tell you!'" (Job 1:16)[104]. Geez. Fireballs from the sky landing in Job's fields? What are the odds? Well at least Job didn't have to pay any severance to his murdered former employees. I hope the Ass and Ox Emporium sells sheep.

"While he was still speaking, another messenger came and said, 'The Chaldeans formed three raiding parties and swept down on your camels and made off with them. They put the servants to the sword, and I am the only one who has

[102] Ibid., *1:12.*
[103] Ibid., *1:13-15.*
[104] Ibid., *1:16.*

escaped to tell you!'" (Job 1:17)[105]. Jiminy Cricket! The ACLU better not find out about this. Job's servants are dropping like flies. The paperwork is going to be unbearable.

"While he was still speaking, yet another messenger came and said, 'Your sons and daughters were feasting and drinking wine at the oldest brother's house, when suddenly a mighty wind swept in from the desert and struck the four corners of the house. It collapsed on them and they are dead, and I am the only one who has escaped to tell you!'" (Job 1:18–19)[106]. Okay ... shit just got real. Livestock and servants were one thing, but now the Job family legacy just got snuffed. That was some of his best DNA, right there.

I'm thinking that this would have been a bad day for Job to be in Vegas. But still, ever the optimist, he still had at least four servants. That had to count for something. Sure he'd miss his kids. Family picnics were going to suck from now on. But hey, God is the boss, and if he deems it fit to murder innocent people and wreck Job's life for whatever reason, that's cool with good ole' easy goin' Job.

"In all this, Job did not sin by charging God with wrongdoing" (Job 1:22)[107]. Heck, the all-powerful, loving space God probably had a good reason for murdering my kids, servants, and livestock. I'm sure it wasn't something stupid like a bet or anything. Maybe God hadn't had his coffee yet.

So Yahweh was winning the bet, and this was pissing off Satan because he really liked Chili's cheese fries. In your face, Satan! This moron still loves me. I told you! Predictably, the Lord of Darkness dared his ex-landlord to double down:

"'Skin for skin!' Satan replied. 'A man will give all he has for his own life. But now stretch out your hand and strike his flesh and bones, and he will surely curse you to your face.' The LORD said to Satan, 'Very well, then, he is in your

---

[105] Ibid., *1:17.*

[106] Ibid., *1:18-19.*

[107] Ibid., *1:22.*

hands; but you must spare his life'" (JOB 2:4–6)[108]. Once again, God caved into peer pressure and went back on his original condition for the bet. All right, you can mess with Job, but just don't kill him. That would be cheating. *"So Satan went out from the presence of the LORD and afflicted Job with painful sores from the soles of his feet to the crown of his head" (Job 2:7)[109]*.

Naturally, oozing puss on the sofa was a little much for Job's wife. She and his three pals urged him to call God out for his excessive douchiness. But Job was a glass-half-full kind of guy, and remained faithful to the almighty sadist. *"He replied, 'You are talking like a foolish woman. Shall we accept good from God, and not trouble?'" (Job 2:10)[110]*.

That kind of sealed the bet. Satan knew he was going to have to pony up for dinner. God was probably going to order appetizers, too, the asshole. And this Job dude was hardcore. I mean, if painful, open sores weren't enough to knock the Jobster off his game, he didn't know what would. Okay, God, you win—*again*. Darn your omnipotence.

But don't fret, dear Christian readers. Because in the epilogue of this story, Yahweh sets everything right as rain again. He uses his awesome magical God power to not only cure Job of his skin disease, he also offered Job a stimulus package. Yahweh doubled Job's livestock losses, replaced his laborers, and gifted him with a new family, since the old family members were all burning in hell because this story took place before original sin was forgiven. All's well that ends well.

Job, you were fabulous. Sorry for killing those kids you loved so much, but trust me, you're gonna love this new batch of moppets even more. And sorry I allowed you to be tortured so I could prove a point to my arch nemesis. Satan is a dick, and any time I can one-up him, I feel obligated to do so. So I'll toss in a few more perks that you didn't even have before to make it even. No hard feelings, right?

---

[108]   Ibid., *2:4-6.*

[109]   Ibid., *2:7.*

[110]   Ibid., *2:10.*

Ah … God's love.

Ares Too

An eye for an eye only ends up making the whole world blind.

—Mahatma Gandhi[111]

Throughout the good book, Yahweh seems to have trouble getting his core message out. He's the one true God and all, but why can't some of these dopes get that through their thick skulls? People in various geographic locations—many of whom had never even heard of Yahweh—worshipped other gods? Why must they be so petulant?

Well, perhaps it's because the deranged schizoids who wrote the Old Testament were made in Yahweh's petulant image … and by that, I mean that Yahweh was written in their image. If the Yah-meister had permitted the invention of the printing press a few millennia earlier, maybe he'd have been able to avoid some needless carnage of the human creations he so loved. As it was, he chose the most illiterate part of the world to make his appearance during a time of incomprehension. He gave the death sentence to a whole lot of people before they had the technological benefit of mass communication and the tools to make informed decisions.

But ignorance is no excuse for breaking the rules. Yahweh is a stern, no-nonsense kind of loving God. As any BDSM submissive will tell you, sometimes love is expressed via torture. So Yahweh did what any loving father would do when his children disobey his wishes. He has them slaughtered, raped, gutted, enslaved, and forced to sit in a corner for a time-out.

His planet, his rules. Yahweh or the highway.

---

[111] Goodreads.com, *Mahtama Ghandi*, http://www.goodreads.com/quotes/750816-an-eye-for-an-eye-only-ends-up-making-the

Of course, despite God being all-powerful and surely able to accomplish mass capital punishment all by himself—with a simple series of well-placed lightning strikes or an impromptu tsunami—he would instead send armies of his followers to kill those born into geographically dissident locations. Yahweh loves him some combat. It was his favorite way to teach heretic no-good-nicks a much-deserved lesson.

When it comes to invading, conquering, bloodshed, and killing, Ares, the Greek god of war, has nothing on the biblical Judeo-Christian God of love.

I hate war as only a soldier who has lived it can, only as one who has seen its brutality, its futility, its stupidity

—Dwight D. Eisenhower[112]

In fact, the God of the Bible not only directs his minions to invade and conquer the cities and lands occupied by those who had the audacity to pray to a different god, but he also offered rewards of rape and slaves to the faithful. And if you attack before midnight tonight, God will throw in a second virgin free of charge. Kill now, our operators are standing by.

So go figure. Some people were heretic enough to think that their religious needs could be met by worshipping gods who would not be so-fiendish as to invade anyone's lands and slaughter them for such petty transgressions. Silly them. Yahweh—the slumlord zillionaire—loves his loyal tenants so much that he gives them the gift of righteous mass murder, whatever lands and possessions an enemy had, and however many unbreached hymens might be ambling about their heathen abodes.

For instance, Midian was a biblical place where people prayed to gods other than the one true murderous psychopath in the sky. Descended from Abraham and his second wife Keturah, they should have known better. So those assholes had to go.

---

[112] BrainyQuote.com, *Dwight Eisenhower,* http://www.brainyquote.com/quotes/quotes/d/dwightdei136897.html

Enter Yahweh's favorite earth-bound conqueror, Moses. Fresh off an Egyptian ass-kicking and subsequent sea parting, "Mo the Merciless" was on a mission to do the Lord's bidding. "So Wuddaya want me to do, boss?"

The LORD said to Moses, "Take vengeance on the Midianites for the Israelites. After that, you will be gathered to your people." So Moses said to the people, "Arm some of your men to go to war against the Midianites so that they may carry out the LORD's vengeance on them. Send into battle a thousand men from each of the tribes of Israel." So twelve thousand men armed for battle, a thousand from each tribe, were supplied from the clans of Israel. Moses sent them into battle, a thousand from each tribe, along with Phineas son of Eleazar, the priest, who took with him articles from the sanctuary and the trumpets for signaling.

—Numbers 31:1–6[113]

Wow, twelve thousand soldiers is larger than the army Saruman sent from Isengard to attack Helm's Deep. That's a whole lot of angry Jews. And to make matters worse, they couldn't even get a group discount on their swords. Yahweh spoke directly to Moses, who in turn instructed his army. That's how the chain of command works. So the Israelites were pissed off, and motivated to kill them some no-good Midianites.

They fought against Midian, as the LORD commanded Moses, and killed every man. Among their victims were Evi, Rekem, Zur, Hur, and Reba—the five kings of Midian. They also killed Balaam son of Beor with the sword. The Israelites captured the Midianite women and children and took all the Midianite herds, flocks and goods as plunder. They burned all the towns where the Midianites had settled, as well as all their camps. They took all the plunder and spoils, including the people and animals, and brought the captives, spoils and plunder

---

[113] Holy Bible, *Numbers 31:1-6*, Holy Bible. New International Version ®, Copyright © 1973, 1978, 1984, 2011 by Biblica, Inc.®

to Moses and Eleazar the priest and the Israelite assembly at their
camp on the plains of Moab, by the Jordan across from Jericho.

—Numbers 31:7–12[114]

Not a bad haul. Herds, flocks, and lots of cool stuff. Hey, it's not really stealing when you take someone else's shit during a holy conquest, right? Some burning, some pillaging ... boy this was fun. Yahweh is the bestest God ever.

Oh, by the way ... what do you want us to do with all of these hostages?

Moses, Eleazar the priest and all the leaders of the community
went to meet them outside the camp. Moses was angry with
the officers of the army—the commanders of thousands and
commanders of hundreds—who returned from the battle.

"Have you allowed all the women to live?" he asked them. "They
were the ones who followed Balaam's advice and enticed the
Israelites to be unfaithful to the Lord *in the Peor incident, so*
that a plague struck the Lord's *people. Now kill all the boys.*
And kill every woman who has slept with a man, but save for
yourselves every girl who has never slept with a man.

—Numbers 31:13–18[115]

What part of God's order didn't you morons understand? Massacre all the women and boys. Rape all the virgins. It's really not that complicated, you dummies.

But Moses had a good point. It was probably the women's fault that the Medians became such blasphemous assholes to begin with. Biblically speaking, it was *usually* the woman's fault. Evil temptresses they were, with

---

[114]   Ibid., *31:7-12.*
[115]   Ibid., *31:13-18.*

their diabolical vaginas, shapely, hairless heinies, and irresistible powers of female seduction. Median men would do anything for a little pussy. Had the Israelites done their jobs right the first time, we'd have probably been spared all of those Tyler Perry movies.

In turn, the boys had to be murdered too, because raping *them* was against God's rules. Yahweh did not allow same-sex compulsory molestation. The only type of forcible fornication he permitted when it involved a grown man deflowering a young girl. The biblical Top Banana is a loving god, with morals … not some depraved nutcase. Boy rape is bad, girl rape is fine and dandy. Duh.

But to put God's love into proper context:

> *The plunder remaining from the spoils that the soldiers took was 675,000 sheep, 72,000 cattle, 61,000 donkeys and 32,000 women who had never slept with a man.*

—Exodus 31:32–35[116]

Four calling birds, three French hens, two turtle doves, and a virgin in a pear tree. Then they sacrificed a bunch of animals to the Judeo/Christian Yahweh, just in case killing an entire population wasn't enough.

Brotherly Love

Sure, it's easy to love a god who rewards you with rape and plunder, but only an omnipotent supreme being like Yahweh would think to put his earthbound servants to a true test of faith.

Sometimes the biblical God even required that a person murder his or her own friends and family. Absolute obedience to Yahweh was required, and if your loved ones were being disrespectful to his clear-cut third-party

---

[116] Ibid., *Exodus 31:32-35.*

instructions, then they had to be stabbed or hacked to death. That much should be obvious. After all, rules is rules.

And speaking of rules, this is where this tale begins:

> *When the LORD finished speaking to Moses on Mount Sinai, he gave him the two tablets of the covenant law, the tablets of stone inscribed by the finger of God.*

—Exodus 31:18[117]

Shortly after Moses returned from his "alone time" with Yahweh, carrying the ten commandments, he ran into a few problems. You see, he left an incompetent dolt named Aaron in charge, and things got out of hand in a hurry. There was festive jubilation going on, with a big fire, whimsy, song, and frolic. It was like a friggin' *Burning Man* down there.

> *He said to Aaron, "What did these people do to you, that you led them into such great sin?"*

—Exodus 32:21[118]

I can't leave these morons alone for one damn minute! What's with all this singing and dancing? And a golden calf? You gotta be shittin' me!

Some of those ingrates he led from Egypt were dirty dancing and worshiping a false-calf-idol. Moses couldn't let this unsanctioned party go on. It must've been like when parents go away for the weekend and their teenagers throw a major kegger. I know that my parents wanted to kill me when they came home and found the house a wreck and my buddy's puke on the carpet. John Lithgow was way too lenient in *Footloose*.

---

[117] Ibid., *31:18*.

[118] Ibid., *32:31*.

So Mo' was in a tough spot. He couldn't be seen as being too lenient. But like any good lieutenant, he knew what the Grand Custodian wanted without even needing to ask. Good leadership requires proper discipline. And by discipline, I mean murder. Yahweh's chosen lackey had little choice but to order compatriot and sibling executions.

> So he (Moses) stood at the entrance to the camp and said, "Whoever is for the LORD, come to me." And all the Levites rallied to him. Then he said to them, "This is what the LORD, the God of Israel, says: Each man strap a sword to his side. Go back and forth through the camp from one end to the other, each killing his brother and friend and neighbor." The Levites did as Moses commanded, and that day about three thousand of the people died. Then Moses said, "You have been set apart to the LORD today, for you were against your own sons and brothers, and he has blessed you this day."

—Exodus 32:26–29[119]

But to be fair to Moses, perhaps he hadn't yet read what was engraved on those two giant stone tablets he lugged down from Mount Sinai. And even if he had, apparently one can be exempt from that "don't kill" rule when one is answering to Yahweh directly. God is allowed to break his own rules, because they are rules written for us, not him. Like when a CEO takes home a stapler.

And let's not forget that this was the same Moses who—on a sheep-tending junket—had received ethical edification from a combusted hedge. *"God called to him from within the bush, 'Moses! Moses!'" (Exodus 3:4).* So obviously Holy Mo was Yahweh's chosen mouthpiece. Even though Moses was alone when this bush started yapping at him, there was no reason to not take him at his word. It's not like Moses was prone to irrationalities, like asking people to commit murder because of voices in his head or anything. So orating shrubbery? Sure, why not?

---

[119]   Ibid., *32:26-29.*

It is kind of ironic though, that God's response to people breaking the "thou shalt not worship false idols" commandment, is to break the "thou shalt not kill" commandment. Levites wear their war wounds like a crown.

Collateral Damage

God's mercy is fresh and new every morning.

—Christian author, speaker, and emotional predator,
Joyce Meyer[120], explaining how the celestial sociopath
from the Bible is just a swell friggin' fella

To anyone with the correct amount of chromosomes, intellectually reconciling this whole "God is Love" thing—when juxtaposed with God's actions as described in the Bible—requires mental gymnastics. Hilariously, the Bible also states—in more than one verse—that Yahweh is jealous *"For the Lord your God is a consuming fire, a jealous God" (Deuteronomy 4:24)[121]*. So, by extension of this logic, God is love, God is jealous, so love is jealous. Right.

God is like a box of chocolates.

The reality is that the Bible is replete with appalling examples of God-sanctioned rape, torture, murder, and other forms of benevolent violence that Yahweh commands us to so lovingly perpetrate on one another. It is dizzying that anyone with enough cognitive capability to read the Bible can rationalize its main character as something noble or loving. Yet Christians do just that on a daily basis.

Sure, Uncle Fred molested us as kids. But he also bought us ice cream.

---

[120] BrainyQuote.com., *Joyce Meyer*, http://www.brainyquote.com/quotes/quotes/j/joycemeyer567540.html

[121] Holy Bible, *Deuteronomy 4:24*, Holy Bible. New International Version ®, Copyright © 1973, 1978, 1984, 2011 by Biblica, Inc.®

Perhaps the single most effective way for a normal person who refers to himself or herself as a Christian to become an atheist is to actually sit down and read the Bible. The stories are horrifying. But there is a willful denial—even on a subconscious level—on the part of many Christians who have been raised be afraid of Hell. So they'll just go with "God is love, Jesus loves me, All you need is love, love is what makes the world go 'round" approach to Christianity, and not dig any deeper into the actual tenets of their own faith—for fear of raising doubts.

In their minds, it's better to not know.

However Christian fundamentalists—unlike the general Christian population—usually *are* familiar with all of these stories. But like any enabler for violent, abhorrent behavior, they have internal mechanisms to justify the psychopathic nature of the Judeo-Christian biblical God: "Sure, Yahweh drowned the entire population of the Earth, and he sent the Israelites to slaughter people, and he allowed his followers to rape virgins and own slaves—but he did so lovingly. He's God. It's not for us to question. God was trying to teach us lessons. We need to put all of this murder, rape, slavery, and whatnot into its proper context."

Hilarious. It's like when NAMBLA tries to rationalize institutionalized child molestation as something "natural". *Uncle Fred let me get sprinkles.*

Since Christians are monotheists—and only believe in the "One True God"—and therefore conclude that Jesus and God are one in the same, as explained through the miracle of the Holy Trinity of the Father, Son, and Holy Spirit—creating one isosceles triangle supreme being— they must then acknowledge that the Jesus in the New Testament and the Yahweh of the Old Testament are the same super-duper space God in different incarnations. Bruce Wayne is Batman.

The conflation of sociopathic commands given by Yahweh, and the concept of "Jesus love" is all most Christians feel they need to understand about the intentions of the supernatural creator of the cosmos. This overly simplistic approach to reconciling the moral contradictions from different parts of the Bible accompanies an ambiguous understanding of monotheism. Moreover, it's dependent upon accepting lunacy.

Christians surely don't believe in many gods like some heathen Pagans, nor do they believe that Jesus is less than his father. Christians pray to Jesus when they get cancer or they need their air conditioner to hang on for one more summer. Hence, the father and son are one and the same.

Savvy? Me neither. But still, the Holy Trinity is the premise of the Christian faith in monotheistic terms. Jesus answered, *"I am the way and the truth and the life. No one comes to the Father except through me" (John 14:6)[122]*. No secondary god could make that claim. This is one of the quotes that Christians hang their hats on. It's not like the divine offspring said "Hey, let me ask Dad, and I'll get back to you."

So Christians have to mitigate the morality of the New Testament Jesus—*"A new command I give you: Love one another. As I have loved you, so you must love one another. By this everyone will know that you are my disciples, if you love one another" (John 13:34–35)[123]*. With that of his father/self from the Old Testament whose actions defied the son's precepts. *"Kill them all—old and young, girls and women and little children. But do not touch anyone with the mark. Begin your task right here at the Temple. So they began by killing the seventy leaders" (Ezekiel 9:6)[124]*.

It's staggering, I know. And if you're thinking to yourself, *what the fuck?!* It's only because you're not crazy. None of this makes the slightest bit of sense to anyone who's not a complete idiot.

The reality is—in the twenty-first century—anyone with even a modest sense of morality understands why it's wrong to kill people who have different religious beliefs. It's wrong to take their possessions, hold people in captivity, and rape young women. Yet if it is Yahweh who provides our

---

[122] Ibid., *John 14:6.*

[123] Ibid., *13:34-35.*

[124] Ibid., *Ezekiel 9:6.*

moral compass, then why don't Christian Dominionist politicians call for us to kill our fellow Americans who *do not* believe in the Judeo-Christian God, like they did in the Old Testament? For that matter, why not call for the death penalty for gays and adulterers? Why don't Christian politicians try to repeal the Thirteenth Amendment of the Constitution and restore slavery to its original, biblical correspondence?

> *But I believe it's a lot easier to change the Constitution than it would be to change the word of the living God. And that's what we need to do is amend the Constitution so it's in God's standards.*

—Former Arkansas governor and Republican presidential candidate, Mike "Christian Sharia in America" Huckabee[125]

In America, we don't follow biblical law because our sense of morality has evolved enough that we know better. That's why the morality of Bronze-Age theologians—to whom savagery was a part of life—is inferior. The "morality" of the Judeo-Christian God of the Bible sucks, and everyone understands why. Casual Christians would turn away from their evangelical cousins in a nanosecond if the biblical law of stoning children to death who freak out in Chuck E. Cheese were part of their platform.

So evangelical Dominionists have to temper their hate speech in accordance with what they think they can get away with in a modern world.

Yet despite this, the bullshit from the Christian fundamentalist, Dominionist right continues. Despite the God of the Bible being a murderous sociopath, they'll continue to tell you that "God is Love." Despite what the Bible actually says, they lie to you and hope that the brainwashing from your childhood still holds enough sway that you will ignore facts and believe what they want you to.

---

[125] Thinkpress.org, *Mike Huckabee*, http:// thinkprogress.org/politics/2008/01/15/18870/ huckabee-amend-the-constitution-to-gods-standards/

They need your votes. So they hope that you're in enough of a fearful religious stupor to not question God's or, more importantly, *their* authority. Jesus loves me, this I know, for the Bible tells me so.

The Gift That Keeps On Giving

A dog barks when his master is attacked. I would be a coward if I saw that God's truth is attacked and yet would remain silent.

—Sixteenth-century French Theologian John Calvin[126], unintentionally helping me make my point by comparing a Christian's relationship with Yahweh to that of a dog and its master

I've highlighted a few of the more infamous stories from the Bible in the hopes of jarring loose some repressed memories. Hopefully, casual Christians might recall some of the reasons why they've never considered these stories to be crazy. What is it that allows an otherwise decent person to hear a story about a supreme being who drowns all of the people on our planet and sentences them to an eternity of pain and torture, and still equate that very same magical overseer to their concept of love? Where is the cognitive dissonance between love and cruelty? Are humans so inherently masochistic?

Perhaps we are rather afraid. A dog loves its master, but only after learning to fear him. And perhaps Christian Americans don't realize how fear manifests as faith. Then again, perhaps there are just a whole lot of pseudo-Christians who'll claim to believe the unbelievable, just so that they can justify being assholes.

So let's take one more stroll down biblical lane and showcase some of the more awful, albeit hilarious, excerpts from the handbook of hate. Just in case some folks were under the mistaken impression that I was taking biblical child sacrifice, genocide, slavery, or rape out of context. Or perhaps

---

[126] BrainyQuote.com, *John* Calvin, http://www.brainyquote.com/quotes/quotes/j/johncalvin144215.html

some might think that in the broader sense, these acts can somehow be justified as righteousness. Let's see what other representations of the benevolent God's love are contained within the pages of the not-so-good book. Here are but a few, of the many examples:

"The people of Samaria must bear their guilt, because they have rebelled against their God. They will fall by the sword; their little ones will be dashed to the ground, their pregnant women ripped open" (Hosea 13:16)[127]. Little ones dashed. Pregnant women ripped open. Loving God. Gotcha.

"If a man is caught in the act of raping a young woman who is not engaged, he must pay fifty pieces of silver to her father. Then he must marry the young woman because he violated her, and he will never be allowed to divorce her" (Deuteronomy 22:28–29[128]*).* This is why any decent rapist should carry silver with him. But it does kind of get you out of that whole awkward, old-fashioned "asking Dad for permission for his daughter's hand" thing. "Damn, I only have forty-three pieces of silver. Dude, can you lend me seven? Look at the ass on that twelve-year-old."

When a man sells his daughter as a slave, she will not be freed at the end of six years as the men are. If she does not please the man who bought her, he may allow her to be bought back again. But he is not allowed to sell her to foreigners, since he is the one who broke the contract with her. And if the slave girl's owner arranges for her to marry his son, he may no longer treat her as a slave girl, but he must treat her as his daughter. If he himself marries her and then takes another wife, he may not reduce her food or clothing or fail to sleep with her as his wife. If he fails in any of these three ways, she may leave as a free woman without making any payment.—Exodus 21:7–11[129]. Wow, all these criteria for proper slave ownership. It almost make a potential master say "fuck it, it ain't worth it if you're gonna hit me with all of these dumb

---

[127] Holy Bible, *Hosea 13:16*, Holy Bible. New International Version ®, Copyright © 1973, 1978, 1984, 2011 by Biblica, Inc.®

[128] Ibid., *Deuteronomy 22:28-29.*

[129] Ibid., *Exodus 21:7-11.*

rules." Where was the tea party when you needed them? But you do have to love the buyer's remorse clause.

"If a man lies with a male as with a women, both of them shall be put to death for their abominable deed; they have forfeited their lives" (Leviticus 20:13)[130]. God hates fags. Everyone knows that. And it's our earthly duty to snuff these sissy-Marys. "Thou shall not kill" obviously doesn't apply to homos.

"Whoever strikes his father or mother shall be put to death" (Exodus 21:15)[131]. On the bright side, the punishment for not cleaning your room is only getting beaten into a coma. Then again, this rule would make eating out much more bearable.

"If a man commits adultery with another man's wife, both the man and the woman must be put to death" (Leviticus 20:10)[132]. Well there goes half of Congress. Come to think of it, there goes most of the country. Sorry, Newt.

"See, I will stir up against them the Medes, who do not care for silver and have no delight in gold. Their bows will strike down the young men; they will have no mercy on infants, nor will they look with compassion on children" (Isaiah 13:15–18)[133]. Kid killing 101. The infants are surely the acorns from which the mighty blasphemers will grow. So the brats of your enemy must die.

"Anyone arrogant enough to reject the verdict of the judge or of the priest who represents the LORD your God must be put to death. Such evil must be purged from Israel" (Deuteronomy 17:12)[134]. Do what your priest commands. His word is law, no matter how big of a child-molesting scumbag he is. "Hey Timmy, meet me in the rectory after the service, and wear something

---

130 Ibid., *Leviticus 20:13.*
131 Ibid., *Exodus 21:15.*
132 Ibid., *Leviticus 20:10.*
133 Ibid., *Isaiah 13:15-18.*
134 Ibid., *Deuteronomy 17:12.*

without a lot of buttons." And remember Timmy, Father Murphy commanded that you not tell a soul.

"When a man strikes his male or female slave with a rod so hard that the slave dies under his hand, he shall be punished. If, however, the slave survives for a day or two, he is not to be punished, since the slave is his own property" (Exodus 21:20–21)[135]. So remember, all you good-intentioned slave owners out there, be careful when beating your slaves, because you don't want them dying on you and getting the Lord all pissed off. Nor do you want to spare the rod and spoil them either. The trick is to give them a sound enough beating that they survive a couple of days—and learn their lesson.

"Happy is the one who seizes your infants and dashes them against the rocks" (Psalm 137:9)[136]. Maybe by "dashes them against the rocks" they meant "gives them a cookie." Sometimes these things don't translate very well.

"If you buy a Hebrew slave, he is to serve for only six years" (Exodus 21:2)[137]. Kosher slaves have different rules. Okay, your six years are up, see ya, Shlomo. Well at least they won't have to pay off student loans.

"The one who has stolen what was set apart for destruction will himself be burned with fire, along with everything he has, for he has broken the covenant of the Lord and has done a horrible thing in Israel" (Joshua 7:15)[138]. There's nothing like a little ritual human sacrifice to set everyone straight. So there is no stealing from the bounty collected from slaughtering God's enemies which has been set aside to be burnt as an offering, lest you shall become part of the sacrifice yourself. And while you're at it, keep your mitts out of the cookie jar.

"Put the entire town to the torch as a burnt offering to the Lord your God. That town must remain a ruin forever; it may never be rebuilt. Keep none of the

---

[135] Ibid., *Exodus 21:20-21.*
[136] Ibid., *Psalm 137:9.*
[137] Ibid., *Exodus 21:2.*
[138] Ibid., *Joshua 7:15.*

plunder that has been set apart for destruction. Then the Lord will turn from his fierce anger and be merciful to you. He will have compassion on you and make you a great nation, just as he solemnly promised your ancestors. The Lord your God will be merciful only if you obey him and keep all the commands I am giving you today, doing what is pleasing to him" (Deuteronomy 13:15–19)[139]. Yeah, burning and plundering an entire town is pleasing to the Lord. Maybe his ex-wife lived there. But all that ill-gotten booty was his. Boss God has to get his vig. Running the cosmos can be an expensive endeavor. But if you're a good earner and you keep your nose clean, the Godfather won't have you whacked.

"They entered into a covenant to seek the Lord, the God of their fathers, with all their heart and soul; and everyone who would not seek the Lord, the God of Israel, was to be put to death, whether small or great, whether man or woman" (2 Chronicles 15:12–13)[140]. This sounds a lot like "kill all the infidels." Gee, when you put it this way, it kind of makes flying planes into buildings seem like a just another way of carrying out Yahweh's orders.

"Now go, attack the Amalekites and totally destroy all that belongs to them. Do not spare them; put to death men and women, children and infants, cattle and sheep, camels and donkeys" (1 Samuel 15:3)[141]. What the hell did the sheep and donkeys do wrong? If you are a Christian and belong to PETA, you have a serious conflict of interest.

"Meanwhile, the Lord instructed one of the group of prophets to say to another man, 'Strike me!' But the man refused to strike the prophet. Then the prophet told him, 'Because you have not obeyed the voice of the Lord, a lion will kill you as soon as you leave me.' And sure enough, when he had gone, a lion attacked and killed him" (1 Kings 20:35–36)[142]. Well you have to hand it to Grand Master G for his creativity. Death by random lion attack is a pretty

---

[139] Ibid., *Deuteronomy 13:15-19.*

[140] Ibid., *2 Chronicles 15:12-13.*

[141] Ibid., *1 Samuel 15:3.*

[142] Ibid., *1 Kings 20:35-36.*

neat trick. I bet the next prophet was willing to sucker punch whomever Yahweh needed to straighten out.

"But the territory of the Danites was too small for them; so the Danites marched up and attacked Leshem, which they captured and put to the sword. Once they had taken possession of Lesham, they renamed the settlement after their ancestor Dan" (Joshua 19:47)[143]. Anyone who knows anything about real estate will tell you that back then, it was a killers' market. But I'm sure that property taxes were reduced, as they could share schools and services. This also opened up the downtown area for commerce and a Walmart shopping plaza.

"Unto the woman he said, I will greatly multiply thy sorrow and thy conception; in sorrow thou shalt bring forth children; and thy desire shall be to thy husband, and he shall rule over thee" (Genesis 3:16)[144]. Lemme tell ya something Alice, I'm the king, and you're nuthin'."

Here's the thing. This could go on and on. I could easily fill a hundred pages with examples of biblical immorality directly from the pages of the Bible itself. But if people don't get the point by now, I doubt they're able. If they are inclined to dismiss God's biblical commands for murder, rape, torture, pillaging, slavery, and copyright infringement as something other than psychotic and immoral, then they would have to be so utterly fucked in the head that the thought of them being part of a civilized society—let alone elected to public office—is counter-intuitive to anyone with the slightest sense of true morality.

Is it any wonder why so many religious fundamentalists are complete assholes?

---

[143]   Ibid., *Joshua 19:47.*
[144]   Ibid., *Genesis 3:16.*

Bread and Salt

Yet another hilarious example of biblical rape culture takes place in the book of Genesis, with a righteous fella named Lot, who lived in a town called Sodom. You see, Lot was not just a holy man, but he was also a gracious host, and thus he allowed a couple of strangers to stay in his home. Soon thereafter, an angry mob appeared at Lot's door, demanding that he hand over the two strangers for the town's customary welcome, which in Sodom involved a friendly ass-raping. Howdy strangers!

Because Lot did not want to offend Yahweh, as recompense to the mob, he offered his virgin daughters for sexual violation instead.

Look, I have two daughters who have never slept with a man. Let me bring them out to you, and you can do what you like with them. But don't do anything to these men, for they have come under the protection of my roof.

—Genesis 19:8[145]

As it turns out, the two dudes Lot invited into his home were not just any couple of fellas sportin' exit-only assholes. They were angels of the Lord. It's a good thing that he was hospitable enough to try to protect them from the raucous crowd of heinie enthusiasts.

As a reward for protecting the integrity of these angels' back gates, Lot and his family were given the suggestion by Yahweh to flee Sodom, as the almighty arsonist planned to burn the city to the ground: *"Then the LORD rained down burning sulfur on Sodom and Gomorrah—from the LORD out of the heavens"* (Genesis 19:24)[146]. After Lot's stupid wife gets turned into a pillar of salt for the misdemeanor crime of looking over her shoulder to see the mass murder occurring behind her, the family unit was reduced to Lot, and his two virgin daughters.

---

[145]   Ibid., *19:8.*
[146]   Ibid., *19:24.*

But Lot was old, and since he only had daughters, his family lineage was about to end. But ever the loyal, grateful kids, these very same virgin daughters come up with a terrific scheme to extend the family name. They get their dad drunk and screw his brains out.

> *Thus both the daughters of Lot became pregnant by their father. The firstborn bore a son and called his name Moab. He is the father of the Moabites to this day. The younger also bore a son and called his name Ben-ammi. He is the father of the Ammonites to this day.*

—Genesis 19:36–38[147]

You gotta hand it to ole' Lot. Maintaining wood while being wasted enough to bang your own slutty daughters is a tough task to accomplish. Obviously, Lot would have never done this sober. Women: you can't live with 'em and you can't stop them from making dumb, God-defying decisions or seducing you when you're drunk.

Meet the New Boss

> *As the Father has loved me, so have I loved you.*

—Jesus "I Hope Not" Christ[148]

Christian apologists like to point out that the Old Testament God had to be a cruel, crotchety curmudgeon because times were different back then. If one has any biblical knowledge, they might have noticed that the previous few pages all contained passages from the Old Testament. Sure God was a murderous psychopath in the *old* book, but Christians are more concerned with the loving Jesus version of God in the New Testament. The Old Testament stuff was just a few thousand years of Yahweh getting his bearings and figuring out how to rule the world. Cut the incorporeal overseer some slack.

---

[147] Ibid., *19:36-38.*

[148] Ibid., *Matthew 10:34-37.*

Once Yahweh got the brilliant idea to inseminate a virgin with an earthbound incarnation of himself, he really started to mellow out. The Big Fish was New Testament chillin'. He was handing the family business over to his boy, Jesus. No need to kill, rape, enslave, or torture anymore. From Christ's birth on, God was turning over a new fig leaf.

Well, not really.

You see, Jesus could be a jerk too. Most casual Christians like to think of Jesus as a sandal-wearing hippie who tried to teach us to not be such assholes to one another. And for the most part, they're right, he was. But there was certainly a moral duplicity that carried over mixed messages from the Old Testament. And although Yahweh definitely had some better ideas about peace love and understanding once he sired himself, he still often missed the mark.

A quote from Jesus in the Gospel of Matthew: *"Think not that I am come to send peace on earth: I came not to send peace, but a sword. For I am come to set a man at variance against his father, and the daughter against her mother, and the daughter-in-law against her mother-in-law. And a man's foes shall be they of his own household"* (*Matthew 10:34–37*)[149]. This does kind of support the NRA's claim of a bad-ass, gun-toting Jesus. Prince of peace, my ass. Get me a damned sword. Apparently, Eve Arden and Kaye Ballard owed much of their careers to the Gospel of Matthew.

Now, I understand that the New Testament—as morally reprehensible holy writs go—is miles ahead of the Old Testament and the Koran. But that's kind of like saying that Moe was smarter than Larry and Curly. Less crazy is still crazy.

To illustrate a point, slavery is the fundamental moral blight on human history. Among the myriad of morally demeritorious acts humans have perpetrated on one another, slavery is at the top. As subject matter, slavery was the New Testament Jesus's chance to reestablish morality as it pertained

---

[149] Ibid.

to ownership of another human being. Here was his chance to define the rudimentary concept of right and wrong. It's a morality no-brainer.

And yet what did ole' son of himself do? He doubled down on the douche-baggery.

> *Slaves, obey your earthly masters with deep respect and*
> *fear. Serve them sincerely as you would serve Christ.*

> —Ephesians 6:5[150]

Is it me, or are the words "slavery is wrong" too difficult to comprehend? Christian apologists will claim that in the larger context, these are instructions to treat your slaves benevolently if they behave. Be nice to your slaves. Well, isn't that special? Go fuck yourself.

In the New Testament Epistle to the Ephesians, the author writing as St. Paul makes it very clear. Slavery is just fine and dandy in the eyes of God. No wonder the tea party wants to do away with the minimum wage. Would you like fries with that?

As you might suspect, St. Paul—whose hand was guided by the Great Sky Daddy—and his take on slavery is not an isolated incident within the New Testament:

> *Christians who are slaves should give their masters full respect so that*
> *the name of God and his teaching will not be shamed. If your master is*
> *a Christian, that is no excuse for being disrespectful. You should work*
> *all the harder because you are helping another believer by your efforts.*
> *Teach these truths, Timothy, and encourage everyone to obey them.*

> —1 Timothy 6:1–2[151]

---

[150]   Ibid., *Ephesians 6:5.*
[151]   Ibid., *Timothy 6:1-2.*

or:

The servant will be severely punished, for though he knew his duty, he refused to do it. But people who are not aware that they are doing wrong will be punished only lightly. Much is required from those to whom much is given, and much more is required from those to whom much more is given.

—Luke 12:47–48[152]

Listening to Christian fundamentalists do a theological tap-dance around the words in their own book is hilarious. It's like listening to a stutterers spelling bee. These are the words in the *New* Testament. In what other context can we take them?

But at least the good book sees fit to explain a slave's place and to not just put restrictions on the job creators. It isn't like Jesus was okay with beating a slave who didn't deserve it, or anything. So make sure those new summer interns can take a punch.

Same as the Old Boss

The authors of the gospels were unlettered and ignorant men, and the teachings of Jesus have come to us mutilated, misstated and unintelligible.

—Thomas Jefferson[153]

Now, as ancient plagiarized holy heroes go, I won't deny that Jesus did do some really cool things. Certainly he wasn't a total dick. Feeding the hungry, helping the poor, and healing sick were awesome, moral things to do. Bravo, liberal Jesus.

---

152   Ibid., *Luke 12:47-48.*

153   Thinkexist.com, *Thomas Jefferson,* http://thinkexist.com/quotation/ the_authors_of_the_gospels_were_unlettered_and/163976.html

However, in early twenty-first century America, being a Christian Republican involves an utter departure from all of the actual morality that Jesus Christ espoused, and instead concentrates on Old Testament precepts. Dominionist, American Christians will mix and match Old and New Testament scripture so as to coincide with a world view that appeals to morons. Love thy neighbor only insofar as he shares your same bigoted, perverse sense of morality. Otherwise, it's hate thy neighbor, as the Old Testament Yahweh directed, and the New Testament Jesus reaffirmed:

> *Do not suppose that I have come to bring peace to the*
> *earth. I did not come to bring peace, but a sword.*

> —Jesus Christ, from Matthew 10:34[154]

Surely the Prince of Peace was kidding, right? How was he to know that one day a bunch of assholes who call themselves the NRA would take him seriously? Maybe the word "sword" translated awkwardly from the Gospel's original Greek, and Christ actually said "party."

> *Do not think that I have come to abolish the Law or the Prophets;*
> *I have not come to abolish them but to fulfill them.*

> —Jesus Christ, from Matthew 5:17[155]

Listen folks, Jesus didn't come to Earth, perform all of those impressive magic tricks, and then spend a really horrible weekend getting crucified just so we can stop obeying Old Testament law. Oh, no, no, no. He did all of that to redeclare for Dad.

So, sure, JC was cooler than Yonder Poppy. But blood is thicker than sacramental wine. Sometimes he needed to turn the other cheek, and other times he needed to kick the other ass-cheek.

---

[154] Holy Bible, *Matthew 10:34*, Holy Bible. New International Version ®, Copyright © 1973, 1978, 1984, 2011 by Biblica, Inc.®

[155] Ibid., *5:17*.

The rule "spare the death, spoil the child" was still very much intact in the New Testament *"Whoever curses father or mother shall die" (Mark 7:10)[156]*. But junior, before Mommy and Daddy kill you for insubordination, make sure that your room is tidied up and to finish your homework. Or else we might have to kill you twice.

Nor did the estrogenic internment end with the birth of Tot-God: *"Let the women learn in silence with all subjection. But I suffer not a woman to teach, nor to usurp authority over the man, but to be in silence. For Adam was first formed, then Eve. And Adam was not deceived, but the woman being deceived was in the transgression" (1 Timothy 2:11–14)[157]*. Shaddup, ya dumb broads. The Lord commands it so. Now why don't you bring me my slippers and give me a blow job while I watch the game.

However none of this is meant to demean the greater body of Jesus's work. Most of what New Testament Jesus did was just wonderful. I only point out a few moral contradictions in the New Testament to illustrate moral perspective. Dwight Eisenhower is a hero of mine. I think he could have done a better job handling the communists after the war, but that doesn't mean that I am willing to denounce his entire career. The same is true with Jesus Christ. A few fuckups unbecoming of a savior, but overall not a bad guy.

Rock me, sexy Jesus.

So sure, New Testament God 2.0 is less imperfect and less immoral than the first version. But nevertheless, by any reasonable standard, Christ is morally inferior to most twenty-first century Americans. I, for one, despite my own questionable sense of morality, would never dream of owning a slave, killing my child, or torturing anyone for eternity. Not even Roger Ailes.

All right. Maybe Roger Ailes.

---

[156]   Ibid., *Mark 7:10.*
[157]   Ibid., *Timothy 2:11-14.*

And of course, speaking of New Testament Jesus in the context of being an historical figure whose life eerily—not to mention, impossibly—paralleled a myriad of other mythical saviors who came before him is kind of crazy to begin with. But that's kind of the point. Any literal interpretation of the Bible, or for that matter, even a metaphoric comprehension that cherry-picks the passages that abide morality—while dismissing those that make Jeffery Dahmer seem like Gandhi—requires a leaving of one's senses. Christianity begins with a premise of crazy, and it gets worse from there.

So never mind the total lack of morality it takes to believe that the almighty intergalactic sky God required a blood sacrifice of the earthbound progenical incarnation of himself in order to make it okay for him to open the doors of his ethereal country club so that a select few could spend eternity worshipping him while the rest of humanity—whom he loves—spends forever getting tortured. Never mind the utter stupidity of going through all of this when God is the one making the rules in the first place.

The bottom line is, rape, slavery, plundering, and murder are morally wrong. You know that. The Judeo-Christian Yahweh of the Bible doesn't.

CHAPTER 4
Alternate Anterior
(How the Founding Fathers Battled the Forces of Mordor, and Other Nonevents)

We learn from history that we do not learn from history.

—Georg Wilhelm Friedrich Hegel[158]

---
[158] Goodreads.com, *Georg Wilhelm Friedrich Hegel*, http://www.goodreads.com/author/quotes/6188.Georg_Wilhelm_Friedrich_Hegel

When metaphoric, biblical fiction is promoted as science and history, it accompanies an adulteration of *actual* science and history.

Indeed, if Christian Dominionists are to coerce voters away from reason and have them base their sociopolitical predispositions upon mythology, then they are faced with an additional conundrum concerning researched and recorded discoveries and events. Historians and scientists have actual data. It's one thing to bullshit people about invisible sky gods but another thing entirely to deny the material world in which we live.

However, those prone to crazy and stupid affirmations are undeterred by reality.

Now, denying science is easy to do when one is not very bright. Since said not-too-bright person doesn't possess the ability to understand how science works to begin with, science denial doesn't require mental gymnastics from a synaptic spastic. In order for a neutered intellect to enter into a state of denial, all that is needed is an adolescent reaction to the fear of inadequacy (due to not being very bright) and projecting one's own deficiencies back at whatever exposes them as intellectually inferior. It's like when a twelve-year-old lacks the skills to properly articulate her emotions and reacts with something like, "I didn't want to go to that dumb party anyway."

No one wants to be the person not invited to the party, and no one wants to be labeled dumb. So those incapable of comprehension have the need to insulate themselves from the pain of social exclusion by making rationalizations about their own intellectual limitations. Hence, Christian fundamentalists react to science with skepticism, rather than having the emotional maturity to admit they just don't get it. Crazy, stupid people have thrown their own science-denying and history-revising (tea) party. So there.

We were certainly safe between 2000 and 2008 (under George W. Bush). I don't remember any terrorist attacks on American soil during that period of time.

—Fox News Host Eric Bolling[159], overlooking that easy-to-forget September 11, 2001, national security hiccup.

But revising history is a whole other ballgame. Especially American history. It's not like Dominionists are translating ancient hieroglyphics and interpreting them for would-be voters. American history was written in English, and, historically speaking, it was not that long ago. So when evangelical Christian politicians and their sympathetic media affiliates propagandize about how our country's founders intended for this to be a "Christian nation," it requires a want on the part of those being deceived.

Republican and tea party voters who buy into revisionist history truly have a desire for past events to have occurred other than the way that they did, so that Dominionist lies can be justified, even when the facts don't fit. Where a corrupted acceptance of American history is concerned, it's not the same lack of comprehensive ability that accords science denial, but rather a willful capitulation to bullshit.

… And the farther one goes back in history, the deeper the Dominionist bullshit gets. So to offer a little historical perspective:

I Would Have Words

There have to be people who are vocal about the advancement of knowledge over faith.

—Seth "Rarely Misses" Macfarlane[160]

There was a time, in our more-distant past, when Christianity ruled over what we now designate as Western Civilization. The fall of the Roman Empire (roughly 500 CE) brought about the rise of the Roman Catholic

---

159   Huffingtonpost.com, *Eric Bolling*, http://www.huffingtonpost.com/2011/07/14/eric-bolling-terrorist-attacks-bush_n_898135.html

160   BrainyQuote.com, *Seth MacFarLane*, http://www.brainyquote.com/quotes/quotes/s/sethmacfar519516.html

Church as the ruling authority. They remained the pointy-hat-wearing honchos for a thousand years. Life was wonderful, and much simpler then ... and by wonderful, I mean full of pain and despair, and by simpler, I mean shorter.

Today, we refer to that period of history as the Dark Ages.

Now, regardless of what religious propagandists tell us about what it was like to live under Roman rule, history actually notes that the Romans did manage to offer a few things to the civilized world in the way of science, art, literature, architecture, and invention. Now, I won't pretend that the Romans weren't barbaric conquerors or deny that they had many societal flaws. Spartacus was one of my favorite TV shows. The Romans were total dicks. I get it.

I understand that, by our standards, the Romans were primitive, cruel, and often ruthless. But what I am saying is that when one considers what occurred throughout Europe over the thousand years *after* the fall of Rome, that in comparison, the Roman Empire were the good old days.

For instance, plumbing was a Roman innovation. Sewers and public baths really came in handy over those hot summer months when a centurion's armpits could chase a bear away from a dumpster. It doesn't take a historian to understand that not having to eat where you had just defecated is a nice little contribution to civilization.

The advances in engineering and construction were miraculous for the time. Bridges, mining, dams, aqueducts, machinery, metallurgy, and sanitation—to name just a few—were all also part of Roman civilization. As such, there were accompanying trades and an economy. For the most part, it was kind of like today ... if you had tools and ambition, you could probably eat.

Education was also part of Roman culture. Many Roman citizens could read and write. The Romans based much of their society on Greek culture and philosophy. As it was with the Greeks before them, there was a desire to better understand the world around them. The Greek philosopher Aristotle—long deceased—was very much an influence in Rome, and it was evident.

Education is an ornament in prosperity and a refuge in adversity.

—Aristotle[161]

Enter the Christians, who replaced efforts to understand the world via scientific advancement with an attempt to know God. Observation-based study of nature was accordingly subordinated to faith-based study of scripture. A decline in learning consequently afflicted every cognitive dynamic ... among them, literacy.

Under Christian rule, science was denounced as heresy. Truths that defied Christian dogma—or as we call it today, common sense—were forbidden to be spoken, under penalty of torture and death. Technology actually regressed. Famine recurred so insistently for centuries that it became a part of everyday life. Millions suffered and died needlessly. It was a wonderful time to be alive if you liked having open sores.

For almost one thousand years under Christian rule, there was virtually no economic growth or rise in per capita income. People lived in the same squalor—with primitive, temporary shelters and barely any food or clothing—for a millennium. Think about that. Today, if our economy stagnates for consecutive fiscal cycles, the talking meat puppets on cable news want the president's head on a spike.

For almost one thousand years under Christian rule—with the exception of torture devices used by clergy—there was virtually no significant scientific advancement. In fact, whatever advances that might have occurred during the period before the Renaissance had virtually no socioeconomic impact, and moreover, when compared to the periods in history that both preceded

---

[161] Ibid., *Aristotle,* http://www.brainyquote.com/quotes/quotes/a/aristotle104903. html

it and came afterward ... it is an embarrassing retrospective. Praise be the Lord.

For almost one thousand years under Christian rule, in the areas of sewage and sanitation, there was an actual regression from the technology of the Roman Empire, which resulted in the diseases that occur when feces are dumped into the streets or into the local rivers from which a population gets its drinking water. Vermin and germs permeated the garbage strewn streets. Hallelujah.

For almost one thousand years under Christian rule, medical advancement all but ground to a halt. Whatever medical advances had occurred under the Greeks and Romans gave way to mysticism. Advances in anatomy and biology faded into oblivion. There was no need to find the cause of disease when it was explained as "demonic" possession by the church. Take two leeches and call me in the morning.

For almost one thousand years under Christian rule, the average life expectancy was less than thirty years of age. About one third of all babies born died within their first year. In the 1300s, the bubonic plague—the infamous "Black Death"—ravaged Western Europe, obliterating roughly twenty million people. That was about one-third of the human population. Must've been God's will.

It is during our darkest moments that we must focus to see the light.

—Aristotle Onassis[162]

For almost one thousand years under Christian rule, heretics and other freethinkers were continually suppressed, tortured, and murdered for the crimes of heresy and blasphemy. Poets, artists, and philosophers were accused of satanic worship and tortured in various creative and sadistic ways until they either confessed their imaginary sins or died. Women

---

[162]   Ibid., *Aristotle Onasis,* http://www.brainyquote.com/quotes/quotes/a/aristotleo119068.html

who dared defy biblical gender subjugation were accused of witchcraft or demonic possession and were summarily tortured or burned to death by church decree. The church's authority could not be questioned under the penalty of long, painful, maddening, agonizing—but eventually welcomed—death. Testify, brothers and sisters!

For almost one thousand years under Christian rule, the accomplishments of ancient Greek scholars were lost to the general population. Ignored were the achievements of intellects like Aristotle—who instructed Alexander the Great, and whose teachings ranged from physics to poetry, from music to linguistics, and from government to biology; Plato—the founder of the Academy in Athens, Greece, which was the first institute of higher learning for science and mathematics in Western civilization; and Hippocrates—considered the father of Westernized medicine. Can I get an amen?

For almost one thousand years under Christian rule, those who were either not in the clergy or part of the ruling class lived in utter destitution. They lived in misery and died young. If they questioned authority, they were made to suffer further. For almost one thousand years, ignorance reigned.

Praised be the lord, Jesus Christ.

Renaissance and Stimpy

There are three classes of people: Those who see; those who see when they are shown; those who do not see.

—Leonardo da Vinci[163]

Well, needless to say, eventually people had enough of dying prematurely and crapping in the same room where they slept and ate, while a scant, crucifix-wearing few were rewarded with privilege by an almighty absentee landlord. So, toward the end of the fourteenth century, there began a social

---

163   Ibid., *Leonardo Da Vinci*, http://www.brainyquote.com/quotes/quotes/l/
leonardoda387197.html

push toward human expression beyond needless suffering at the hands of the clergy. Kind of like the death of disco.

Among the many casualties of medieval church rule were art, music and science. But as Dr. Ian Malcolm so douche-chillingly stated in the movie *Jurassic Park,* "Life uh, finds a way." Indeed, although it took almost a thousand years, the human spirit eventually—to some degree—broke free.

The European Renaissance was a cultural movement that spanned the fourteenth to the seventeenth centuries. Essentially, it was inspired by a desire to not suffer and die prematurely, and to not live in constant fear of the church. Go figure. Beginning in Italy and spreading to the rest of Europe by the sixteenth century, its influence was felt in literature, philosophy, art, music, politics, science, and other aspects of phrenic inquiry. Things started to not suck as much.

So, regarding this period of history, think of intellectual and artistic giants like Leonardo Da Vinci, Michelangelo, and Galileo. Understand that if they were born two hundred years earlier, they'd have never had the opportunity to create or discover. In fact, many of the scientific observations during this time (such as the earth revolving around the sun) were still considered blasphemy by the church, and much of the art created was only allowed under church administrations. Like when the mob takes protection money.

And as much as I would like to drone on about how awesome the geniuses were during this period of history (and they were), and how they persevered despite Church totalitarianism, the sad part about this creative and intellectual surge in human history is that it was impeded upon in the name of Christianity. The European Renaissance is only germane to the subject matter of this book because of how it affected what was to ensue.

These wonderful contributions to civilization occurred despite the church, not because of it. If the authoritative clergy of the time had had their way, little or none of the advancements in art, literature, science or medicine would have ever been allowed to see the light of day. The period of history that immediately followed the Renaissance proved a violent backlash by the Roman Catholic Church against the discoveries during that era.

The church didn't like not being in control.

The Reformation(s)

Reason is a whore, the greatest enemy that faith has; it never comes to the aid of spiritual things, but more frequently than not struggles against the divine Word, treating with contempt all that emanates from God.

—Martin Luther[164], inadvertently explaining why religion is for idiots

Even though there was a cultural and scientific renaissance occurring throughout Europe, it's not like the entire population of the continent suddenly was awoken from the Matrix overnight. After all, a thousand years of brainwashing via mental and emotional abuse is a difficult thing to undo. I mean, paintings of women's dirty parts are awesome and all, but what if God noticed that you got a chubby?

The answer for some who embraced the human spirit—but who did not wish to abandon their faith—lay in the concept of symbolism.

Enter Martin Luther (not the civil rights leader who was assassinated in 1968, but the guy he was actually named after) who loved him some Jesus, but who also recognized the Roman Catholic Church authorities for the sadomasochistic bullshit peddlers that they were. So good ole' ML no K decided to do something about it, and protested the church via his "Ninety-Five Theses." Among them were challenges to certain Catholic standards, such as the infallibility of the Pope and the silliness of wearing headgear that resembles a large order of McDonald's French fries.

Hence, the Protestant religion was born.

---

[164] Goodreads.com, *Martin Luther*, http://www.goodreads.com/quotes/38024-reason-is-a-whore-the-greatest-enemy-that-faith-has

But the Roman Catholic Church still wasn't done ruling, nor did they like not being in absolute control. So they began a counter-reformation, initiated at the Council of Trent. It was one thing to blaspheme by carving naked people statues and saying that the Earth is not the center of the universe, but suggesting Church fallibility and a different way to follow Jesus? Well, them's fightin' words.

So the Roman Catholic Church needed to act, and act it did. Back to the ole' drawing board, and a little more of what made the Catholic dynasty great. Illiteracy, with a heaping spoonful of female subjugation, a dash of sexual control, and a jigger of fear at the hands of clergy should one defy the Church's rule, and everything will be right as rain again. I mean, what the hell was going on? People were actually thinking? And what's all this bullshit about wanting to live past thirty?

If only they'd thought of the tea party.

In order to regain the political power it had held until recently, the Catholic Church had to make the population stupid, afraid, and unhealthy again. That was the plan. And it would have been a terrific plan, too, if it were not for those pesky Protestants exposing the Catholic hierarchy for what they were.

As such, Europe became a bloody mess. For the most part, with the exception of most of Ireland, Northern Europe became Protestant, whereas most of Southern Europe remained under Roman Catholic purview. Central Europe was a contentious disaster, with Catholicism and Protestantism vying for influence.

Christians killing Christians ... all in the name of the Lord Jesus Christ.

Blind Spots

Don't get saucy with me, Béarnaise!

—Count de Monet[165], *History of the World Part 1*

I realize that from the perspective of a true historian, the retrospective of the last few pages is far too generalized. The reality is that two thousand years of history cannot be discussed responsibly in such a limited space. The formation of Christianity, the Renaissance, and the Protestant Reformation have all had volumes written about them. I get that.

So are there exceptions to what I've written here? Of course there are. But is the overall depiction accurate? Damn straight it is.

The thing is, the quick reflection in the last few pages is not intended to be a history lesson. It is meant to provide some perspective for those moments when one hears a twenty-first-century Dominionist blather utter bullshit about the past. As such, the historical generalization that I've made are—in themselves—merely dotted points on a timeline designated to make a greater point, which is that Christian theocrats in twenty-first-century America are deceptive and mentally unstable.

An analysis of past events is why the Dominionist GOP feels the necessity to rewrite history at their own convenience. It's almost like they want us all to ignore the horrible things that their own religion has brought upon the world and assign them an undeserved nobility. So as the twenty-first-century tea party/GOP bastardizes history in order to accommodate present-day psychosis, they likewise feign altruism and claim ethical uprightness and the moral high ground as authorized by a higher power.

The reality is that history contradicts all of that. An audit of the past shows that Christianity—or for that matter, any religion—as the core of a society

---

[165] History of the World Part 1(1981), *Count de Monet,* http://www.imdb.com/character/ch0070483/quotes

brings about poverty on a grand scale, a ceasing of progress, impedes civil rights in general and women's rights in particular, and cause an attenuation of a populations' thought processes. Dominionists in our legislature—of course—know this. But they just don't want you to know it.

Study the past if you would define the future.

—Confucius[166]

Moreover, the formation of the United States of America did not occur out of space and time or in a bubble. Like everything else, who we are is very much dependent upon who we were. This brief look back is germane to contemporary politics insofar as our nation's founding was predicated on the periods of history that came before.

I did not mention events between the fall of Rome and the rise of Protestantism because of the lies told by the tea party/GOP about those time periods. If the worst historical lie Dominionists told was about Christianity's effect on Galileo, I would have skipped this entire chapter. But Dominionist pontiffs and politicians make stuff up about more recent history all the time, too. Because of the way both lies and history work, if one distorts the more distant past, these distortions beget more contemporary perversions of the truth.

The closer we get to the present day, the greater the humbuggery.

---

[166] Goodreads.com, *Confucius*, https://www.goodreads.com/ quotes/129296-study-the-past-if-you-would-define-the-future

The Enlightened Few

No kingdom has shed more blood than the kingdom of Christ.

—French sociologist, political architect, and scholar
Charles de Montesquieu[167] (1689–1755)

As Western civilization struggled during the post-Renaissance era with the choice between art, science, and discovery and the Church's attempts to re-impose its authority in the form of the Christian Reformation, a few lesser-known historical figures helped shape Western culture for the next few centuries. Faced with the prospect of having their imagination stymied, their curiosity arrested, and their expression proscribed, the choice of sociopolitical direction was clear for a generation who defined themselves by their intellect.

Christian rule? Hell no.

The Church had its chance to govern, and for a thousand years, humanity suffered needlessly, died young, and lived in fear, poverty, and squalor. Although the Dark Ages sounds like it must have been a whole lot of fun, we'd been there and done that. Choosing to revert to ignorance after Western civilization had the chance to experience Da Vinci would have been somewhat equivalent to returning to prison for a crime one never committed once one had already watched midget porn. Thanks, but no thanks.

In what's known today as the Age of Enlightenment—or the Age of Reason—there was a cultural movement of intellectuals whose purpose was to reform society using reason, and advance knowledge through the *scientific method*. Brilliant dudes, such as Isaac Newton, Voltaire, and John Locke, built upon the genius-level contributions to humanity of the Renaissance and challenged ideas grounded in tradition, mythology, and

---

[167] BrainyQuote.com, *Charles de Montesquieu*, http://www.brainyquote.com/
quotes/quotes/c/charlesdem382678.html

faith. They determined that societal precepts should be able to survive the test of scrutiny.

To put it simply, truth should supersede superstition.

During the seventeenth and eighteenth centuries, the Enlightenment was a movement that hoped to undo the abuses of power by Church-run states via promoting factualism as arrived at through peer-reviewed evidence. Folklore and unfounded beliefs promoted by the Church were assaulted with skepticism, and as such were exposed as blatant falsehoods. It wasn't enough to believe that demons caused illnesses when there were cures that needed to be found.

> *The Christian theory is little else than the idolatry of the ancient mythologists, accommodated to the purposes of power and revenue; and it yet remains to reason and philosophy to abolish the amphibious fraud.*

—Thomas Paine[168], *The Age of Reason*

It was in the eighteenth century that the Enlightenment reached the American colonies, which eventually led to the founding of the United States of America. Such men as Thomas Jefferson, John Adams, Benjamin Franklin, Thomas Paine, and James Madison—intellectuals all—recognized that, when church and state become one, the people suffer. The beliefs of the founders were based upon facts and the scientific method, not baseless superstition. Hence, they wrote the single greatest document in the history of civilization specifically disassociated from church authority: the United States Constitution.

The founders of our nation were men of the Enlightenment.

Which leads us to today, and the rules of socioeconomics, which mirror those of the Reformation, leading to the equal and opposite reaction to the force of enlightened reason. A contemporary Christian reformation

---

[168] The Theological Works of Thomas Paine, *Thomas Paine, Page 15.*

is underway. There is a concerted political effort at a reimposition of Church authority, and it goes by the name of Christian Dominionism. It is as rooted in ignorance, greed, and lust for power at the expense of the populace as its Medieval predecessors.

For the twenty-first-century Dominionist Christian hopes to transform our nation back to a time when fear, intolerance, and superstition governed our choices and science was viewed as heresy. We see it today, with Dominionist politicians denying genetic biology (evolution), the origin of our species, the age of our planet, and even climate change. Dominionist Christians are replete within the legislative branch of our government—they help write our laws, for cryin' out loud—and in the 2012 presidential election, several Dominionist candidates ran.

One almost got the Republican nomination.

Apocalypse Then

No man shall be compelled to frequent or support any religious worship, place, or ministry whatsoever.

—Thomas Jefferson[169], the Virginia Act for Religious Freedom

It really takes a malevolent, psychotic derangement—at this point in history—to deny peer-reviewed, scientific facts and evidence in favor of promoting superstition and fairy tales. However, political Dominionists need to do this in order to create a fearful, ignorant—albeit fervent—voting base. It's a daunting task, but one should never underestimate the national capacity to embrace the absurd. Yet the main difference between twelfth- and twenty-first-century Christian fundamentalists is that the former had the luxury of scientific incomprehension, whereas the latter are burdened with contradictory, scientific peer-reviewed facts. Which means that the contemporary Dominionist has to outright lie to his or

---

[169] Vahistorical.org, *Thomas Jefferson*, http://www.vahistorical.org/ collections-and-resources/virginia-history-explorer/thomas-jefferson

her constituency, and voters must capitulate to crazy and stupid scientific and historical affirmations.

For example, the Dominionist conceptions that our nation needs to "return to" mosaic (biblical) law are based on the fundamental lie that is that our nation was founded on "Christian principles." As if political conservatives—in the name of Christianity—can claim ownership of patriotism while simultaneously ignoring the founders' departure from the Church when forming the precepts of our nation. The truth is that, upon the founding of our nation, the United States citizenry were never subject to biblical law or Church authority in the first place.

The most glaring example of the founders' intentions regarding Christianity's place within our legislative process is that there is no mention of God, Jesus, or Christianity anywhere in our constitution. In fact, the First Amendment is specific in this regard:

> *Congress shall make no law respecting an establishment of religion,*
> *or prohibiting the free exercise thereof; or abridging the freedom of*
> *speech, or of the press; or the right of the people peaceably to assemble,*
> *and to petition the Government for a redress of grievances.*

So either our founders simply forgot to mention Yahweh while they were allegedly basing the entire document on his precepts—which is a preposterous assumption—or they did not define their moral or legal principles in Christian terms. This might also explain why seven of the ten commandments are unconstitutional to enforce. Amazing for a group of men who purportedly intended to found a nation based on Christianity.

And God spoke all these words in Exodus 20:1–17[170]:

---

[170] Holy Bible, *Exodus 20:1-17*, Holy Bible. New International Version ®, Copyright © 1973, 1978, 1984, 2011 by Biblica, Inc.®

I am the LORD your God, who brought you out of Egypt, out of the land of slavery. You shall have no other gods before me.[171]

Right off the bat, this commandment is contradicted in the first amendment to the "Jesus-inspired" Constitution. If you're an American, you can worship any damn god you want, from a multiarmed Hindu elephant deity to a sentient flying plate of spaghetti. The government can't tell you whom to pray to.

You shall not make for yourself an image in the form of anything in heaven above or on the earth beneath or in the waters below. You shall not bow down to them or worship them; for I, the LORD your God, am a jealous God, punishing the children for the sin of the parents to the third and fourth generation of those who hate me, but showing love to a thousand generations of those who love me and keep my commandments.[172]

I'm not sure if most Christians understand this when they hang a crucifix around their necks or when they put the Virgin Mary on a half-shell on their lawns. Not to mention that the other gods protected by the First Amendment also have the right to have their images viewed. And although the Muslims are much bigger assholes about this rule, nevertheless it's important to point out what a petty, jealous douche Yahweh is. He even admits as much.

You shall not misuse the name of the LORD your God, for the LORD will not hold anyone guiltless who misuses his name.[173]

Jesus Fucking Christ on roller skates, are you kidding me? I do this all the time, and I am not breaking the law when I do. Jesus, Moses, and Mohammed walked into a bar with a monkey ... Again, that pesky First Amendment getting in the way. If you are reading this book, understand

---

[171] Ibid.

[172] Ibid.

[173] Ibid.

that I am breaking this commandment just by having written it. I will freely admit that I enjoyed doing so, because as rules go, it's really stupid.

Remember the Sabbath day by keeping it holy. Six days you shall labor and do all your work, but the seventh day is a Sabbath to the LORD your God. On it you shall not do any work, neither you, nor your son or daughter, nor your male or female servant, nor your animals, nor any foreigner residing in your towns. For in six days the Lord made the heavens and the earth, the sea, and all that is in them, but he rested on the seventh day. Therefore the LORD blessed the Sabbath day and made it holy.[174]

If by "keeping the Sabbath holy" you mean getting woken up with a blowjob, making a pot of Italian sauce, and watching football, then I'm totally with you. However I am under no legal obligation to do so. Everyone who does little more than lie around like a beached Manatee on Sunday breaks this commandment.

Honor your father and your mother, so that you may live long in the land the LORD your God is giving you.[175]

Now I'm not saying that we shouldn't all be nice to our parents or that the Menendez brothers aren't assholes. I'm just saying that there is no constitutional mandate to be nice to Mom and Dad. What if you got molested by your dad? Do you still have to "honor" him?

You shall not kill.[176]

Duh. A no-brainer. Although Yahweh—his omnipotent, rule-making self—has a lot of trouble with this one, including once destroying the entire population of the Earth in a great flood, not to mention all of those other orders God gives to kill people who piss him off, like gays, pregnant spouses of the enemy, and adulterers. So I guess this is more about we

---

[174]   Ibid.

[175]   Ibid.

[176]   Ibid.

humans not taking the initiative to kill unless we receive explicit orders from the great space honcho himself. Like George Bush did. So gotcha. Killing is not only a bad idea, it's also against the law.

You shall not commit adultery.[177]

If this were unconstitutional, half of Congress would have committed treason. AshleyMadison.com would also be illegal (which it's not) and a whole lot of so-called Christian politicians would be up for the death penalty. While cheating on one's spouse might be a bad idea, it's not in the nation's founding document.

You shall not steal.[178]

Another no-brainer, however most of Congress is guilty of this too. It's a good thing we had Yahweh to tell us all to not steal from one another. We'd have never figured this out on our own. Ugh.

You shall not give false testimony against your neighbor.[179]

This one actually makes sense. We call it perjury, but regardless, making shit up in court in order to frame someone for a crime they did not commit is uncool and illegal.

You shall not covet your neighbor's house. You shall not covet your neighbor's wife, or his male or female servant, his ox or donkey, or anything that belongs to your neighbor.[180]

For some reason, it is biblically common to differentiate between wanting to bogart your neighbor's wife and his new sports car. But coveting stuff is the fundamental principle of capitalism. That's the basis for our entire

---

[177] Ibid.

[178] Ibid.

[179] Ibid.

[180] Ibid.

economy. Not only is none of this in the Constitution, our entire economic system operates from the opposite premise. And as far as coveting your neighbor's wife, well, that all depends on her level of MILFiness. *Mrs. Robinson, you're trying to seduce me.*

> *It's in the Ten Commandments to not take the Lord's name in vain.*
> *Rape is not up there, by the way. Rape is not a Ten Commandment.*
> *But don't say the dude's name with a shitty attitude.*

—Sociological genius Louis C.K.[181]

As things turn out, the three "commandments" that happen to work within our constitutional framework are not Christian-only principles. In fact, virtually every civilized culture in history has had these very same laws. Still, Dominionist politicians blur the concept of "morality," as they do science and history, to coincide with their socioeconomic agenda. So, for the tea party Republican voters, it is known that Jesus himself helped guide the hands of our founders as they wrote the Constitution.

This might come as a shock to good Christian folks, but Jesus wasn't the first character in literature to have determined that we should try not to be complete dicks to one another.

Hands Off

> *Deism is the belief that reason and observation of the natural world are*
> *sufficient to determine the existence of a God, accompanied with the*
> *rejection of revelation and authority as a source of religious knowledge*

—Wikipedia

---

[181] ThoughtCatalog.com, *Louis C.K.*, http://thoughtcatalog.com/nico-lang/2013/10/55-brilliant-louis-c-k-quotes-that-will-make-you-laugh-and-think/

The truth is, many of the founders were not Christians, but rather they were Deists. Meaning that they—to whatever extent—believed there to be a god, however, they did not adhere to Christian dogma. A Deist believes that God does not intervene with the functioning of the natural world, allowing it to run according to the laws of nature. It is certainly not a belief that a Christian God is "watching over" us, or that said deity has a specific interest in America. Nor is it a belief that a mystical overseer knocked up an unwed teen to bear his son.

Some books against Deism fell into my hands ... It happened that they wrought an effect on me quite contrary to what was intended by them; for the arguments of the Deists, which were quoted to be refuted, appeared to me much stronger than the refutations; in short, I soon became a thorough Deist.

—Benjamin Franklin[182]

I have generally been denominated a Deist, the reality of which I never disputed, being conscious I am no Christian, except mere infant baptism makes me one; and as to being a Deist, I know not strictly speaking, whether I am one or not.

—Ethan Allen[183], *Reason: The Only Oracle of Man*

Now, despite whatever doubts some of the founders may, or may not have had, they were also politicians. As such, some said contradictory things regarding faith, and Christianity in particular. But would a true follower of Jesus who intended for the United States of America to be founded as a "Christian nation" ever say this:

The detail of the formation of the American governments may hereafter become an object of curiosity. It will never be pretended that any persons

---

182   Goodreads.com, *Benjamin Franklin*, https://www.goodreads.com/work/quotes/598905-autobiography-of-benjamin-franklin

183   "Ethan Allen the Robin Hood of Vermont" By Henry Hall, *Ethan Allen*, Page 20. D. Appleton & Company

employed in that service had any interviews with the gods, or were in any degree under the inspiration of heaven. It will forever be acknowledged that these governments were contrived merely by the use of reason and the senses.

—John Adams[184]

or this:

I have recently been examining all the known superstitions of the world, and do not find in our particular superstition (Christianity) one redeeming feature. They are all alike founded on fables and mythology.

—Thomas Jefferson[185]

or this:

What is it the New Testament teaches us? To believe that the Almighty committed debauchery with a woman engaged to be married; and the belief of this debauchery is called faith.

—Thomas Paine[186]

or this:

During almost fifteen centuries, has the legal establishment of Christianity been on trial. What has been its fruits? More or less, in

---

[184] Goodreads.com, *John Adams*, http://www.goodreads.com/work/quotes/94827-the-political-writings-of-john-adams-representative-selections

[185] Thinkexist.com, *Thomas Jefferson*, http://thinkexist.com/quotation/i_have_recently_been_examining_all_the_known/226006.html

[186] Goodreads.com, *Thomas Paine*, https://www.goodreads.com/author/quotes/57639.Thomas_Paine?page=5

all places, pride and indolence in the clergy; ignorance and servility in the laity; in both, superstition, bigotry and persecution.

—James Madison[187]

Yet tea party Christians and their GOP representatives gather at rallies all over the country and quote the founders as if they had never said such things. They purposefully misrepresent men they claim to admire and bastardize their words so as to accord fundamentalist predispositions. Just as Holocaust deniers attempt to revise history in order to accommodate those with anti-Semitic predispositions, so, too, do Dominionists politicians misrepresent American history so as to acquiesce to a Christian voting base.

Sadly, when seeking political power via votes, truth matters less than what you can get people to believe. Pay no attention to the founders behind the curtain.

Another Brick in the Wall

We also know that the very founders that wrote those documents worked tirelessly until slavery was no more in the United States.

—Rep. Michele "Hey Marcus, Where's My Strap-On?" Bachman[188], providing a unique historical retrospective

However, the founders of the United States of America were not limited to mere quotes regarding their lack of Christian fundamentalism. They performed historically recorded deeds which no devout Christian anywhere would do.

---

[187] Searchquotes.com, *James Madison*, http://www.searchquotes.com/quotation/ During_almost_fifteen_centuries_has_the_legal_establishment_of_ Christianity_been_on_trial._What_has_/289430/

[188] Nymag.com, *Michele Bachmann*, http://nymag.com/daily/ intelligencer/2011/06/michele_bachmann_stands_by_rid.html

For instance, Thomas Jefferson—third president of the United States, the author of the Declaration of Independence, and one of the main overseers of the writing of our Constitution—also took the time to rewrite the New Testament of the Bible. But rather than leave in the mythology and physical impossibilities—rather than tell stories of Jesus performing magic tricks as evidence to supernatural "miracles"—Jefferson created a naturalistic narrative of the life of a man named Jesus of Nazareth. In other words, he removed all of the bullshit from the book. Hardly a "fundamentalist Christian" approach to theology, let alone governance.

You can go to Amazon.com right now and order yourself a copy.

It was Thomas Jefferson who is credited for having coined the term "Separation of Church and State" in the first place. In a letter to the newly elected president, a group who called themselves "the Danbury Baptists"—a Christian minority in the state of Connecticut who were concerned that larger, more powerful religious groups would be able to exert disproportionate influence in government—appealed to Jefferson with the following:

> *It is not to be wondered at therefore, if those who seek after power and gain, under the pretense of government and Religion, should reproach their fellow men, [or] should reproach their Chief Magistrate, as an enemy of religion, law, and good order, because he will not, dares not, assume the prerogative of Jehovah and make laws to govern the Kingdom of Christ.*

—Danbury Baptists[189]

In other words, "We're worried that other, more wealthy Christian churches will take over the nation in the name of their particular ministry, and that those of us who do not knuckle under to them will suffer at the hands of an oppressive, fundamentalist regime." If I do say so myself, it's a valid concern. It had happened many times before, and in fact, two different Christian denominations are still shedding blood in Ireland today.

---

[189] Marta E. Greenman Leaders, Nations, and God, *Danbury Baptists*, Page 141.

To which President Jefferson[190] responded, *"I contemplate with sovereign reverence that act of the whole American people which declared that their legislature would 'make no law respecting an establishment of religion, or prohibiting the free exercise thereof,' thus building a wall of separation between Church and State."*

In other words, "Don't worry dudes. We got this. It ain't never gonna happen while we're in charge. We have a wall of separation between church and state, and I should know, because I helped write the Constitution. This ain't no theocracy, yo."

Yet there are revisionist historians who—in the name of Christian Dominionism—claim that is not what Jefferson meant, despite his words. As if he was misinterpreting the meaning of the First Amendment to the Constitution which he helped write in the first place. The balls it takes to suggest that Thomas Jefferson—flawed genius that he was—was either mistaken or perfidious in declaring his intent of his own words regarding the separation of church and state is staggering.

While it was Jefferson who first defined the separation of church and state, it was his successor, James Madison[191], who articulated it for generations thereafter: *"The purpose of separation of church and state is to keep forever from these shores the ceaseless strife that has soaked the soil of Europe in blood for centuries"* in an 1803 letter objecting use of government land for churches.

Remember earlier in this chapter, the part about the Dark Ages and the Christian Reformation? This is what James Madison is referring to with this quote. The separation of church and state must be maintained here in America, so as to not repeat the nightmarish millennia of Christian rule that occurred in the lands from whence they came.

---

[190] Goodreads.com, *Thomas Jefferson*, http://www.goodreads.com/author/quotes/1673.Thomas_Jefferson

[191] Ibid., *James Madison*, https://www.goodreads.com/author/quotes/63859.James_Madison

(I have) always regarded the practical distinction between Religion and Civil Government as essential to the purity of both and as guaranteed by the Constitution of the United States.

—James Madison[192]

Is it me, or did Founding Father James Madison just plainly state that *the Constitution* guarantees the separation of church and state? Yet Dominionist Christians claim the founders intended for meaning of the document that defines our entire political system of government to mean the exact opposite of what James Madison plainly stated here.

Thus we get this blatant bullshit like this from a guy who claims to be a constitutional absolutist:

The notion of a rigid separation between church and state has no basis in either the text of the Constitution or the writings of our Founding Fathers.

—Rep. Ron "It Takes a Tough Man to Make a Tender Chicken" Paul[193]

Really Dr. Paul, you pedantic putz? No basis in their writings? Since Ron Paul is not an idiot, one can only assume that statements like this are born of ignominiousness. There are volumes written by the founders that contradict Dr. Paul's perfidy-laden statement.

However, this is the tactic of Dominionists in our legislature. This is how they coerce Christians to vote against their own self-interest. This is how they get crazy, stupid people to do the bidding of those who would benefit financially from an American theocracy.

They lie. They keep lying until those predisposed to believe the Dominionist lie will repeat the lie. Eventually the lie will become tea party mantra. The

---

192 Ibid., https://www.goodreads.com/author/quotes/63859. James_Madison?page=2

193 Ibid., *Ron Paul,* http://www.goodreads.com/author/quotes/395622.Ron_Paul

Founding Fathers of our nation, despite all they have written and recorded for historical posterity, were not who their writings say they were. They were who Dominionists want you to believe them to be. After two hundred and fifty years of church-state separation, tearing down that wall in the name of Christianity is being repackaged as patriotism.

God created this nation and God created the
Constitution; it is written on biblical principles.

—Former House Majority Leader, born-again Christian, and sack of shit whose political connections managed to have his criminal conviction for influencing Texas state elections with corporate money overturned - Tom "the Hammer" DeLay[194]. Brilliant, in that extra chromosome kind of way.

However if one is inclined to research, both Jefferson's and Madison's quotes are many in this matter, their intentions plainly stated, and their convictions unwavering. A wall of separation between church and state must be maintained. And they were not the only founders who felt this way.

Preceding both Jefferson and Madison was the second president of the United states, John Adams who in the Treaty of Tripoli stated the following:

As the Government of the United States of America is not,
in any sense, founded on the Christian religion.

—John Adams[195]

Gee, I wonder what John Adams meant by that? For a guy who was an essential part of building a "Christian nation," that seems a curious thing

194   Huffingtonpost.com, *Tom Delay*, http://www.huffingtonpost. com/2014/02/20/tom-delay-god-constitution_n_4826503.html

195   Goodreads.com, *John Adams*, http://www.goodreads.com/author/quotes/1480. John_Adams?page=4

to write into an agreement with another nation. President Adams must've known that it was to be recorded for history. So why say it?

Yet according to Dominionist Christians, John Adams meant the exact opposite. As did Jefferson, Madison, Franklin, and Paine when they wrote similar musings. Thus we have Dominionists trying to coerce frightened voters to tear down the wall between church and state, based on an insane premise that the founders often lied about their religious inclinations (or lack thereof) for no reason. If the founders intent was to give rise to a "Christian nation" then they sucked at it. But rational people know better.

How can you have any pudding if you don't eat your meat?

Signatories

In the affairs of the world, men are saved not by faith, but by the lack of it.

—Ben Franklin[196]

Since we do not have the benefit of being able to invite any of the founders who contributed to the writing of our Constitution to a televised inquiry, we must look at the greater body of their work and their writings. I won't (nor will anyone committed to telling the truth) deny that most of the founders did also say things that could be interpreted as "Christian-friendly." But they were not just Deists, they were also politicians.

So one must ask oneself, "Is it more likely that Christian fundamentalists—who intended for the United States to be a Christian nation—wrote so many disparaging things about their faith and called for a wall of separation between church and state? Or is it more likely that a group of Deist politicians occasionally acquiesced to religious platitudes so as to do what politicians do?"

---

[196] Ibid., *Benjamin Franklin*, http://www.goodreads.com/work/quotes/1957101-poor-richards-almanack

For it was Thomas Paine[197]—arguably the most vocal opponent of religion among the founders—who stated it most simply, and eloquently *"Of all the tyrannies that affect mankind, tyranny in religion is the worst."* And yet, self-proclaimed tea party patriots seem to long for that very tyranny, having had the meaning of freedom confounded by Christian theocrats. Even the founders who did identify themselves as Christians—among them, George Washington[198]—understood the need for a separation of church and state: *"Religious controversies are always productive of more acrimony and irreconcilable hatreds than those which spring from any other cause. I had hoped that liberal and enlightened thought would have reconciled the Christians so that their religious fights would not endanger the peace of Society."*

It was the oppression of the Church and its relationship with the King of England that caused many of these intellectual giants to brave the Atlantic Ocean and start life anew in the Colonies in the first place. However, despite these very researchable historical reveries, there are many who modify history to coincide with their astigmatic, Dominionist Christian predispositions. Despite the founding of the United States of America being just about two hundred and fifty years ago, and having books written by and about our nation's founders—some specifically about their religious inclinations—there are still right-wing religious propagandists who revise, if not openly lie about, the affiliations and intentions of many of those who were intimately involved in forming this country. So we get cognitive incompetents blathering nonsense like this:

---

197 BrainyQuote.com, *Thomas Paine,* http://www.brainyquote.com/quotes/quotes/t/thomaspain384482.html

198 Goodreads.com, *George Washington,* http://www.goodreads.com/quotes/70318-religious-controversies-are-always-productive-of-more-acrimony-and-irreconcilable

*Go back to what our founders and our founding documents meant—
they're quite clear—that we would create law based on the God
of the Bible and the Ten Commandments, it's quite simple.*

—Sarah "I Think She Makes This Crap Up As She Goes Along" Palin[199]

It's kind of funny that Sarah Palin said this, considering that she'd have to
stone her own daughter to death for having had a child out of wedlock. But
these historical revisionists *need* the founders to be retrospectively viewed
as fundamentalist Christians so that they can push their Dominionist
agenda in the founders' name. So they attempt to rewrite history for their
easily led and gullible followers. Lying about the founders' religiosity is
easy enough to do, provided no one with credibility is there to contradict
their blatant and purposeful deceptions. Hell, listening to Sarah Palin
and Sean Hannity blather Dominionist propaganda to one another
about our "Christian founders" is not only devoid of any sense of reality,
it's objectively as funny as watching a couple of chimpanzees hurl feces
through their cage bars.

Sadly, all that's required for Dominionist pontiffs and their supporters
to pull the wool over the eyes of those willing to be blinded is to remove
quotes from context, state suppositions as fact, or simply make things up.
Or as it's known in the New York City neighborhood where I grew up,
have a good line of bullshit.

However, rather than simply take the word of people whose self-interest
would be served by having people buy into Dominionist propaganda, I'll
check in with someone who might have had an idea what he, and his fellow
constitutional signatories true intentions were:

[199] Mediate.com, *Sarah Palin*, http://www.mediaite.com/uncategorized/
sarah-palins-coming-back-to-fox-so-why-not-relive-9-of-her-greatest-hits/#1

Christianity neither is, nor ever was, a part of the Common Law.

—Thomas Jefferson[200], in a letter to Dr. Thomas Cooper, 1814

For some reason, "conservative Republican Christian" news people and politicians never seem to remember quotes like this. It must be an oversight. Yet those with any sense of history or commitment to truth understand that our great nation was founded by men of the enlightenment who defied Church authority and embraced the scientific method.

Not by idiots who believed in a literal interpretation of fairy tales.

The Looking Glass

This would be the best of all possible worlds, if there were no religion in it.

—John Adams[201]

But as easy as it is to convolute American history with Christian Dominionist nonsense, as we go back in history toward the alleged time of Jesus, even more historical revamping takes place. According to the Dominionist Christian version of history, not only were the writers of our Constitution devout Christians, but that Jesus Christ fella in the New Testament is a two-thousand-year-old Republican. Among other things,— if Christ lived today—he would go to war, cut aid for schools and the poor so that the wealthy can get subsidized, and demand that every American citizen be armed.

What would Jesus do? He'd say, "Fuck em' if they can't afford health insurance."

---

200   Goodreads.com, *Thomas Jefferson*, https://www.goodreads.com/quotes/509929-if-therefore-from-the-settlement-of-the-saxons-to-the

201   Ibid., *John Adams*, http://www.goodreads.com/quotes/120264-twenty-times-in-the-course-of-my-late-reading-have

*Religious bondage shackles and debilitates the mind
and unfits it for every noble enterprise.*

—James Madison[202], in a letter to Wm. Bradford, April 1, 1774

Although to the degree that the adage "the winners of the wars get to write the history" is true, there remains a lot of recorded history that contemporary Christian Dominionists would like to amend. There is certainly a reason why we refer to the millennium of Church rule as the Dark Ages and the period of discovery from which this nation was born as the "Enlightenment." One need only to read a few history or science books.

The struggle between Christian Dominionism and secularism literally pits the willful ignorance and intellectual subjugation of Christian fundamentalism against the sociological advancements in science, medicine, economics, and technology. It is an ongoing struggle between crazy and rational. And between stupidity and education.

The Dark Ages vs. the Enlightenment.

*The study of theology, as it stands in the Christian churches,
is the study of nothing; it is founded on nothing; it rests on no
principles; it proceeds by no authority; it has no data; it can
demonstrate nothing; and it admits of no conclusion.*

—Thomas Paine[203]

Darwin's *On the Origin of Species* was written in the mid-nineteenth century, roughly eighty years after the signing of our Declaration of Independence. What would be the reasonable assumption—based on what we know of our nation's founders—as to how they would react to the

---

202 Ibid., *James Madison*, http://www.goodreads.com/work/
quotes/28116730-letters-and-other-writings-of-james-madison-volume-3

203 Ibid., *Thomas Paine*, http://www.goodreads.com/work/quotes/1018077-the-age-of-reason-being-an-investigation-of-true-and-fabulous-theology

science of evolution? Is it that the signatories of that document believed in a six-thousand-year-old earth as described in the Bible? Or that they would more likely lend credence to the peer-reviewed evidence of evolution as arrived at via the scientific method?

Moreover, how would such men, many of whom loathed dogma and embraced the scientific method, react to the millions of pieces of genetic, astronomical, geological, and fossil evidence that have been discovered since Darwin's original theory? Does any rational person truly believe that Benjamin Franklin, Thomas Jefferson, John Adams, John Jay, John Hancock, James Madison, or George Washington—all of whom were men of the Enlightened Age of Reason—would look at this myriad of scientific fact and shrug their shoulders in favor of a story about a talking snake and an apple-eating whore?

Here's the thing about Dominionist Christianity. It is a totalitarian worldview applied to a Christian theocracy here in America. Totalitarians never announce themselves as such, and you won't realize that you are subjugated until it's too late. In the fourth century, the Church never told people that it was about to usher in a thousand years of ignorance and economic destitution. The same holds true for Dominionists in American politics.

Dominionist Republicans won't come right out and say what their intentions are. They can't. So they dance around their own crazy and stupid premise, recite Jesus-addled platitudes, and present their vile, egregious intentions as Christian morality. Judeo-Christian biblical law is no less oppressive than its Islamic counterpart, Sharia. They just can't let you comprehend that.

But, as it has been throughout history when theocrats offer themselves as messengers for a deity, it is never truly about their god. It is invariably about greed and lust for power. Christian Dominionism in America is no different.

The founders knew what would happen if there were no wall of separation between church and state—that's why they built one.

CHAPTER 5
Non Compos Civics

(The Twenty-First-Century GOP, from Dupe to Nuts)

You can only protect your liberties in this world by protecting the other man's freedom. You can only be free if I am free.

—Clarence Darrow[204]

204 Ibid., *Clarence Darrow,* http://www.goodreads.com/
search?q=clarence+darrow&search[source]=goodreads&search_type=
quotes&tab=quotes

The biblical and historical retrospective provided in the previous chapters brings us back to today's twisted right-wing socioeconomic affirmations and how evangelical Dominionist Christians in our political realm have come to dominate the Republican Party.

There was a time in America when news was reported rather than editorialized, and the political affiliation of a reporter was secondary to the story itself. While Walter Cronkite and Edward R. Murrow undoubtedly had strong feelings about the stories they were conveying, and while viewers might have known what those feelings were, their integrity as journalists usually prohibited them from interjecting their bias at the expense of the story. Even on those few occasions where that did happen, their credibility was established enough to offer them certain allowances. Today, however, there is a concerted effort on the part of those reporting news to steer their audience toward a particular sociopolitical inclination.

With the advent of ratings-driven cable news, reporting has become partisan and selective. The sad truth is, there are organizations that identify themselves as "news" but that in reality are little more than public relations extensions of whichever political party they cater to. Thus, there is a disturbing trend occurring in the United States regarding how many Americans fail to recognize the difference between sociopolitical illumination and propaganda.

It does not require extraordinary acumen to see that twenty-first-century America is infested with polarizing political partisanship. Yet it's staggering how impressionable "We The People" have become concerning the nature in which we form our political perspectives. We Americans (or at least, far too many of us) have come to view our political landscape through a black-and-white paradigm, never having learned that the color of reason is gray. Like rubes watching pro wrestling, we jeer whomever our enfeebled sensibilities have led us to believe is the political "bad guy."

News-ertainers have become celebrities in their own right, and it comes at the expense of not only journalism but our entire political process.

Dog Wag

Objective journalism and an opinion column are about
as similar as the Bible and Playboy magazine.

—Walter Cronkite[205], the most trusted man in America

When twenty-first-century Americans choose their news sources, they tend to gravitate toward their own political predispositions, meaning that someone who identifies as a Democrat will most likely watch MSNBC, Bill Maher, or—if he suffers from acute self-loathing—whatever vapid network Keith Olbermann is broadcasting for. Conversely, those with Republican leanings will probably watch Fox News and listen to conservative talk radio or other like-minded media.

We call it news, but in reality it is editorializing delivered as very specific public relations infomercials. After midnight, cable TV sells vacuum cleaners and fitness equipment. During prime time, they sell sociopolitical propaganda.

The "I'm on team X" method of formulating sociopolitical perspectives does little more than pacify one's own sense of self-indulgence. The reality is, most people who tune into cable news aren't seeking knowledge of current events. They are more likely hoping to have their predispositions verified by a like-minded third party.

Nowhere is this more true than with conservative news-ertainment.

There are a lot of socioeconomic reasons to identify oneself with a political party. But if you do so because your favorite TV and radio hosts have suggested that Republicans are closer to Jesus than Democrats, then frankly you're just too big of a moron to vote. Yet this is just what has

---

[205] BrainyQuote.com, *Walter Cronkite*, http://www.brainyquote.com/quotes/ quotes/w/waltercron169113.html

happened to Republican tea partiers across America, and it translates into some very suspect, un-Jesus-like social and economic policies.

Conservative Christian TV and radio profiteers have convinced the GOP and tea party electorate that if Jesus were alive today, he'd most certainly be a Republican. Biblical and constitutional illiteracy among the Christian rank and file has enabled conservative news-ertainers to capitalize on the average American Christian's lack of knowledge of their own faith and recast Jesus in their own right-wing image. The twenty-first-century Messiah is no pussy. He'd go to war, champion the wealthy, and fight for your right to have as many high-capacity magazine semi-automatic weapons as you want.

A sandal-wearing Rambo.

> *Where did the Second Amendment come from? ... From the founding fathers; it's in the Constitution. Well, yeah, I know that. But where did the whole concept come from? It came from Jesus, when he said to his disciples 'now, if you don't have a sword, sell your cloak and buy one.' I know, everybody says that was a metaphor.* It was not a metaphor! *... And the sword today is an AR-15, so if you don't have one, go get one. You're supposed to have one. It's biblical.*

> —Retired Lt. Gen. William G "Jerry" Boykin[206], exemplifying
> the need for periodic PTSD psychiatric evaluations

> *I'm a Christian first, and a mean-spirited, bigoted conservative second, and don't you ever forget it. You know who else was kind of "divisive" in terms of challenging the status quo and the powers-that-be of his day? Jesus Christ.*

> —Author and high-metabolism poster child, Ann Coulter[207],
> speaking with an unmelted pat of butter in her mouth

---

[206] Huffingtonpost.com, *Lt.Gen. William G. Boykin*, http://www.huffingtonpost.com/2014/02/20/general-boykin-gun-jesus_n_4826089.html
[207] Goodreads.com, *Ann Colter*, http://www.goodreads.com/quotes/63457-i-m-a-christian-first-and-a-mean-spirited-bigoted-conservative-second

To make matters worse, conservative radio and TV hosts have gained so much influence over the GOP electorate that they don't simply influence policy, *they make it*. The most powerful people in the GOP are not in public office. They are in the media. The worst thing for any Republican politician's career is to piss off Rush Limbaugh, Roger Ailes, or Glenn Beck.

Should any Republican not be "Christian conservative" enough or fail to acquiesce to the astigmatic, less-than-rational Dominionist vision quest, they'll be labeled a RINO (Republican in name only). And no Republican wants that. In the GOP Jesus-sphere, having been dismissed as a RINO is worse than being an HIV-positive, homosexual, Satan-worshiping communist with a black spouse.

> *All you CPS workers, all you corrupt bureaucrats, all of you that've had your way with innocent children over and over again, who think your evil is invincible, you're not invincible and God is gonna deal with you! And you are cursed to hell!*

—Radio host and certifiable lunatic, Alex "Get the Net" Jones[208]

Once a politician gets labeled a RINO, there is a distinct possibility that he or she will never make it out of the primaries, meaning that conservative media will get behind whichever candidate capitulates to crazy the most, regardless of that candidate's qualifications, sanity, or lack thereof. Psychos in; rational Republicans out. If the results of Republican politicians cowering in fear to media personalities weren't so frightening, it would kind of laughable. But as it stands now, they try to out-crazy one another so that they can keep their jobs.

But tragically, regardless of how dedicated any given Republican's service to the country has been, and regardless of whether his or her legislative voting record has harmonized with traditional Republican positions, if a

---

208 Prisonplanet.com, *Alex Jones,* http://www.prisonplanet.com/the-alex-jones-show-l-i-v-e-jan-9-with-russell-means.html

GOP politician doesn't abide the conservative TV and radio extremism, that politician is toast.

American scientific companies are cross-breeding humans and animals and coming up with mice with fully functioning human brains.

—Tea party candidate, deep thinker, and fundamentalist Christian Christine O'Donnell[209], who defeated fellow Republican incumbent Delaware Senator Mike Castle in a 2010 primary

The relationship between the Republican Party and the representative media has truly come off the rails. Conservative radio and TV hosts—in a quest to be the top dog in the crazy/stupid marketplace—continue to push the discourse farther and farther to the right—and away from traditional Republican politics. In order to both gain favor and avoid being labeled a RINO, Republicans both in and out of office keep saying crazier and more stupid things, just to keep up. It is truly the tail wagging the dog.

Moreover, conservative TV and radio hosts have not only abandoned the premise of journalism in favor of becoming news-ertainers, they've transcended their own fecklessness and morphed their brands into "political evangelism." As such, a big part of the twenty-first-century Republican crazy is based on biblical interpretations of TV and radio personalities. They've become more like a conservative media mafia than news. No one wants a political hit put out on them in the name of Jesus.

Thou shall not kill, unless the motherfucker is a liberal, a commie, a RINO, or wears a turban.

---

[209] ©2014 FOX News Network, LLC, *Christine O'Donnell*, O'Reilly Factor- Nov 15, 2007.

Dumb Like a Fox

I hired Sarah Palin because she was hot and got ratings.

—Roger "You'll Get Nothing and Like It" Ailes[210], CEO of Fox News

Of course, one could not speak of conservative media without mentioning Rupert Murdoch, who is to journalism what osteoporosis is to high-jumping; Roger Ailes, who is to patriotism what chemotherapy is to hairstyle; and their info-spawn, Fox News—which is to integrity what a hand grenade is to chocolate soufflé. They've created a lucrative industry around coercing their audience toward a Dominionist perspective. If nothing else, you gotta hand it to the gang over at Fox News, they are entertaining as hell.

If my mom had mixed alcohol with narcotics in the months prior to my birth, I would be addicted to Fox News today.

However Ailes and company are hugely popular among the geriatric, over-250 lb./under 100 I.Q. tea party crowd. But their votes count just the same as any Columbia graduate's. Fox News editorializes for an audience specifically predisposed toward baseless socioeconomic stereotypes and Christian propaganda. Thus, the cast of on-air Christian Fox News characters has a remarkable record of both promoting Christian Dominionism and saying really, really dumb things.

> *One night, I just woke up and went: Killing Jesus. And I believe, because I'm a Catholic, that comes from the Holy Spirit.*

—Fox News host Bill O'Reilly[211], claiming that he was visited by a member of the holy trinity, who conveniently suggested that he write a book and make lots of money

---

[210] Huffingtonpost.com, *Roger Ailes*, http://www.huffingtonpost.com/2011/10/05/roger-ailes-sarah-palin-fox-news_n_995691.html

[211] Nymag.com, *Bill O'Reilly*, http://nymag.com/daily/intelligencer/2013/09/bill-oreilly-killing-jesus-came-from-holy-spirit.html

Of course that was the holy spirit speaking to you alone in bed in the middle of the night, Billy O. Who else could it be? It's not like you suffer from psychotic delusions of self-importance or anything.

It doesn't say anywhere in the Constitution this idea
of the separation of church and state.

—Fox News host Sean "Facts Optional" Hannity[212]

Of course, Fox News poster-douche Sean Hannity would be correct, except that both Thomas Jefferson and James Madison clearly spelled out the intent of the First Amendment on numerous occasions. And one might think that, since they wrote it, their opinions on the matter might have a little relevance. The Supreme Court fortunately understood that. Hannity, not so much.

Not to mention that "Boy Scout Sean" ignores literalist interpretations when it doesn't suit him. His perspective is dependent upon whom he's making a case for—or against. So the duplicitous Hannity also remains inconsistent in his wing-nut interpretation of the Fourth Amendment:

Our techniques are working. We've got the NSA program, the
Patriot Act program … it's staggering to me that we're even
debating the use of these techniques in this country at this time.

—Sean Hannity[213], defending President George W. Bush for
spying on American citizens in the name of homeland security

But:

---

212   BrainyQuote.com, *Sean Hannity*, http://www.brainyquote.com/quotes/quotes/s/seanhannit183985.html

213   Dailykos.com, *Sean Hannity,* http://www.dailykos.com/story/2013/06/13/1215906/-He-Was-For-NSA-Surveillance-Before-He-Wasn-t-VIDEO

These actions by the Obama Administration are a clear, very clear, violation of the Fourth Amendment, which prohibits unreasonable search and seizure.

—Sean Hannity[214], denouncing President Barack Obama for spying on American citizens in the name of constitutional literalism

However, as Fox News' reporting of sociology and politics morphs according to the moment's conservative needs, so too does Roger Ailes's gaggle of shills modify the New Testament to coincide with a Dominionist perspective. Whether it's passive-aggressive blond-isms blathered by Gretchen Carlson, the viper-like vitriol of Michelle Malkin, or the vapid platitudes spoken by the innumerable talking meat puppets that Fox News employs, there are consistent underpinnings of Christian theocracy on the Fox roster.

We ask why there's violence in our schools, but we have systematically removed God from our schools. Should we be so surprised that schools would become a place of carnage?

—Former Arkansas governor, presidential candidate, and Fox News loon Mike Huckabee[215], suggesting that the Judeo-Christian God allowed children to be massacred at the Sandy Hook Elementary School because the all-powerful creator of the universe was butt hurt over not being praised enough

This is the Fox News/Roger Ailes business model. Extreme, right-wing conservative politics as rationalized through a historically revised Christ. Conservative Jesus hated handouts to the poor and sick. He would have never approved food stamps or public education. If only the son of God had a Glock, he might have been able to shoot his way out of the crucifixion. One could fill a book with all of the inane, fact-deficient pseudo-Christian utterances blathered on Fox News.

[214] Ibid.

[215] Businessinsider.com, *Mike Huckabee,* http://www.businessinsider.com/huckabee-fox-news-shooting-god-2012-12

What makes the round-the-clock Ailes-a thon particularly reprehensible—beyond its abysmal fact-check record—is the network's undermining of the Republican Party and its concession to Christian Dominionism. Indeed, Fox News' journalistic crime isn't simply having a conservative bias. It's the nefarious means by which that bias is presented and how, through a Dominionist perspective, Roger Ailes and company take advantage of fearful, crazy, stupid people for ratings-driven profit.

But to be fair, the Fox News brand of fact-deficient conservative newsertainment television has turned out to be a sound political and business strategy.

Don't Hate the Playaz

No one can terrorize a whole nation, unless we are all his accomplices.

—Edward "Good Night and Good Luck" R. Murrow[216]

Still, Fox News is not alone, and some conservative media personalities are more powerful than others.

For instance a tea party proponent, and the man who was too nutty for Fox News, Glenn Beck is a frequent speaker at tea party rallies and a favorite among those who require their ignorance to be validated. Never one to shy away from connecting imaginary Nazi dots to even the most socially benign organizations (he actually did so with the Peace Corps), he actually compared President Obama's "civilian national security force" to the Third Reich:

---

[216] Goodreads.com, *Edward Murrow*, http://www.goodreads.com/author/quotes/178884.Edward_R_Murrow

*This is what Hitler did with the SS. He had his own
people. He had the brown-shirts and then the SS.*

—Glenn "Nazis Everywhere" Beck[217], August 27, 2009

The self-proclaimed "rodeo clown" is ever fervent in his invocation of "God" as spoken through Beck himself. A political evangelist, Beck is masterful at garnering attention by saying proactive Yahweh-isms.

Crazy, stupid people love him.

I haven't seen a half-monkey, half-person yet.

—Glenn "Not Big on Science Comprehension"
Beck[218], calling evolution ridiculous

Perhaps Mr. Beck never noticed the Cro-Magnon sloped brows or the protruding jawbones of the typical tea party crowds that he gets huge sums of money to address—and who may have no socially redeeming features other than possessing the scientific value of serving as irrefutable Darwinian proof.

And rounding out (literally) the trifecta of journalistic abominations (yes, that was a fat joke) is none other than Rush Limbaugh. Truly one of the most politically powerful people in the country, Limbaugh has positioned himself—and his approval—as the singular litmus test that any Republican politician must pass. For if one finds himself in the Limbaugh crosshairs, the rest of Conservative news-ertainment invariably follows suit. And there is no more prolific RINO hunter than the great white Rush.

---

[217] Mediamatters.org, *Glenn Beck,* http://mediamatters.org/research/2009/10/13/
beck-continues-long-history-of-invoking-nazis-b/155673

[218] Huffingtonpost.com, *Glenn Beck,* http://www.huffingtonpost.
com/2010/10/20/glenn-beck-joins-the-rank_n_770331.html

Although no Republican politician will admit it, they all fear Rush Limbaugh. They are terrified that "Godzilla Strangiato" will label them RINOs. Because once he does, it's game, set, primary.

This is why there are so few rational people left in the GOP and why there is no longer such a thing as a "pro-choice" Republican. This is why virtually every member of the Republican Party—to whatever extent—bows to the evangelical lobby. For it is their willingness to engage in Jesus bromides that determines loyalty to the twenty-first-century tea/GOP voters, their Dominionist overseers, and Rush.

As such, Rush Limbaugh is the conservative standard-bearer. No one brings the irrational rationalizations quite like him. He is the Howard Stern for crazy and stupid people.

I pray to Jesus Christ often. I have read and studied the Gospels. I know Jesus Christ.

—Rush "Me and Jesus Are Pals" Limbaugh[219], on his radio show, September 12, 2008

The only way to reduce the number of nuclear weapons is to use them.

—Rush "What Does This Button Do?" Limbaugh[220], because if Jesus had a nuke, he'd have used it.

But to be fair, I was prescribed Oxycodone after back surgery. And I can attest to how terrific it is. I don't blame ole' Rushbo one bit.

---

[219] Rushlimbaugh.com, *Rush Limbaugh*, http://www.rushlimbaugh.com/daily/2008/09/12/millions_insulted_by_liberals_use_of_jesus_christ_pontius_pilate_line

[220] Liberalamerica.org, *Rush Limbaugh*, http://www.liberalamerica.org/2013/10/13/rush-limbaugh-idiot-ten-cigar-puffing-lunatics-worst-quotes/

To Infinity and Beyond

All you need is ignorance and confidence and the success is sure.

—Mark Twain[221]

Few people like to think of themselves as rubes.

Everyone who has a strong opinion about anything likes to believe that he or she arrived at that opinion via intellect and acumen. This is particularly true regarding conclusions drawn about politics, because it is embarrassing when one's affirmations are exposed as the result having been gullible, biased, and misinformed. Let's face it, no one wants to look like an idiot by voicing stupid opinions. Eddie Van Halen is the greatest guitar player ever.

However, in this age of potentially misleading information, the Dominionist influence in American politics has given rise to an interesting phenomenon known as "doubling down" on crazy and/or stupid statements. It's awe-inspiring to watch the double-down paradigm at work. Christian conservatives say really wacky things, that, if fact-checked, are easily debunked. Yet despite the debunkability of their statements, they not only stand by their crazy and stupid comments, they proudly—if not defiantly—reaffirm them.

(Paul Revere) warned the British that they weren't going to be taking away our arms, by ringing those bells and making sure as he was riding his horse through town to send those warning shots and bells that we were going to be secure and we were going to be free.

—Sarah "Tragical History Tour" Palin[222], explaining how Paul Revere's midnight ride was about the Second Amendment, which was yet to be written.

---

[221] BrainyQuote.com, *Mark Twain*, http://www.brainyquote.com/quotes/quotes/m/marktwain109620.html

[222] ABCnews.go.com., *Sarah Palin*, http://abcnews.go.com/blogs/politics/2011/06/sarah-palin-i-didnt-mess-up-paul-reveres-story/

... And the doubled-down crazy/stupid:

> *Part of his ride was to warn the British that were already there that, "Hey. You're not going to succeed. You're not going to take American arms. You are not gonna beat our own well-armed, uh, persons, uh, individual private militia that we have.' He did warn the British."*

—Sarah Palin[223], explaining to Fox News's Chris Wallace that she was correct about Paul Revere's ride, and how yelling, "The British are coming!" was actually a warning to the British, who apparently didn't know that they were on their way to defeat ... because we had guns

I realize that quoting Sarah Palin is like picking low-hanging fruit. But this is less about her than it is about the sociopolitical concept of doubling down. Admitting that one made a mistake is out of the question for the media-driven GOP. Emphatically and confidently reaffirming verbal blunders—bereft of any sense of reality—with a cavalier disregard for journalism or truth is conservative policy.

Thus, the tea party proletariat, who are susceptible to crazy/stupid statements, will not only believe them but defend them as if defending their nation. It's as if cognitive dissonance collides with counter-intuitiveness, creating a synaptic short circuit that tears the fabric of the space-time continuum. A Rod Serling–like altering of reality, erudition be damned.

> *There are many well-documented stories about God's intervention on behalf of our country during the War of Independence.*

—Dr. Ben Carson[224], who is a really smart guy
who says crazy things to stupid people

---

[223] Ibid.

[224] Newsmax.com, *Dr. Ben Carson*, http://www.newsmax.com/BenCarson/Religion-God-Jesus-Russia/2014/02/12/id/552357/

One would have to search far and wide to find something crazier or more stupid than Dr. Carson's statement above. In reality—despite Dr. Carson's decree—there are no such "documented stories" because—as he is well aware—any eighteenth-century tale regarding wartime divine intervention is subjective, anecdotal, and devoid of evidence. Therefore, no respected historian would be "documenting" such folly into history. Truth is, there's nothing in any Revolutionary War chronicles that warrants a claim of godly intervention, because nothing magical ever occurred.

But Dr. Carson states nonsense like this as fact because he knows that those to whom he is speaking are predisposed to accept such doubled-down nonsense. Affirmations made about magic, fairy tales, and the whims of Yahweh are amenable to those who find comfort in willful ignorance. There are no rules to the double-down game. It's like someone with a pair of threes telling someone with a straight flush that the pot is theirs: "I call your evidence and raise you insanity. Pair of threes; I win!"

This is the same phenomenon that existed when a con man named Joseph Smith convinced people *(less than 200 years ago)* that an angel had directed him to the location of golden plates containing the sacred texts of Yahweh—which Smith alone was allowed to see and translate from their original "Reformed Egyptian" via a magical "seer stone." Why did Americans in upstate New York believe such obvious horseshit? Because it was about God, stated emphatically, and reaffirmed even more emphatically. When called out on his fraud, Smith doubled down, and the Mormon religion was born. It would seem that's all idiots require to jump onboard the crazy train.

And excessively wealthy Dominionists are extremely cognizant of this.

However, with the erosion of the wall separating church and state, coercing people to believe silly things is no longer restricted to religion. The doubling down of crazy and stupid is as effective with bogus sociopolitical declarations as it is when applied to Christian perspectives on history and science. The tea party and the conservative entertainment complex have made sure of that by merging Christianity and politics.

*This president (Obama) I think has exposed himself over and
over again as a guy who has a deep-seated hatred for white people
or the white culture. I'm not saying he doesn't like white people,
I'm saying he has a problem. This guy is, I believe, a racist.*

—Glenn Beck[225], on July 28, 2009, making it clear that he
has no idea what a racist is and preying upon the fears of a
nation that is dependent upon its first black president leading
the recovery from a devastating financial collapse

Deranged, doubled-down affirmations made by conservative entertainers
have emboldened the susceptible. It has germinated fear among a Christian
conservative audience. This has resulted in a lot of people deciding to
engage politically—many for the first time in their lives—with the advent
of a black president.

Putney Swope is upon us. Guide us with your wisdom, oh Rush!

Suddenly, having never really given a shit before, there is a huge
demographic of novice political experts who—despite having no idea
what they are actually talking about—believe themselves adept at solving
complex socioeconomic problems. All one has to do now is either attend
a Koch-brothers-funded tea party rally or watch Rupert Murdoch-owned
Fox News to know all there is to know about "God and Country."

Little did those of us who actually went to school for this kind of stuff
realize that the nation's woes—as brought about by the election of President
Satchmo—were Socialism! Hitler! Communism! Not Enough Guns! Too
Much Education! Unions! Welfare! The poor are gaming the system! The
rich need more to help create jobs! We need prayer back in school! And
keep government out of my health care!

---

[225] Politico.com, *Glenn Beck*, http://www.politico.com/blogs/
michaelcalderone/0709/Foxs_Beck_Obama_is_a_racist.html

The Christian proprietorship (hell, that's what the word "dominion" means) of the Republican Party has really boiled down to extremely rich people hiring less-rich people to convince working-class idiots to direct their frustration over working longer hours for less pay at poor people.

It's working perfectly. Wealthy people good. Liberal elitists bad. Those who benefit from conservative media couldn't have scripted the results of the Dominionist movement any better.

Brain-Dead Pool

This is their religion. You see, you'll find at the highest
level the atheists aren't really atheists at the higher levels.
They write books. These people worship Lucifer.

—Conservative radio host and paranoid lunatic Alex Jones[226],
who is dire need of both psychiatric help and an education

I have no idea whether or not the unholy trinity of Beck, Ailes, and Limbaugh truly believe the crazy and stupid things they say or whether their motivations are rooted in ideological propensity or capitalism. Nor do I know whether the socially regressive, economically illiterate Christian minions who regurgitate their maniacal ravings are truly as obtuse as they seem. But I do know that the "Conservative Entertainment Complex" (I wish I had thought of that term) is what now drives Republican policy.

The marketplace for crazy and stupid is significant. The cacophony of conservatism that addles radio, television, and the Internet is staggering in its ability to win black hearts and small minds. Worse yet, beyond Beck, Ailes, and Limbaugh is an impressive number of Conservative news-ertainers and political televangelists who appear on radio and television for a living.

---

[226] Allreadable.com, *Alex Jones*, http://www.allreadable.com/091f1UnQ

But understand, as I write this, I do so not as a liberal who gets offended by everything conservatives say. Conservative media can be hilarious … and I do not mean that in an unintentional, Sarah Palin kind of way. I mean that, as well as being fabulous orators, many conservative pundits have actual comedy chops. Many of the politically incorrect things conservatives say—which overly sensitive liberals consistently get their panties in a bunch over—is satire directed at oversensitive tree-huggers. When uber-lefties get defensive over an insensitive remark made by any conservative news-ertainer, they are usually unaware that their politically correct inability to take a joke is the actual punch line.

> *I might be in favor of national health care if it required*
> *all Democrats to get their heads examined.*

—Ann "If You Don't Understand Why That's Funny, You Are the Very Type of Liberal Douche to Whom I'm Referring" Coulter[227]

I get all of that. I despise the way liberals use political correctness as a sociological weapon, and I love cringe-worthy, politically incorrect humor. Al Sharpton is a race-baiting scumbag. Nappy-headed hoes. I get it.

But this segment of this book is not about anecdotal examples of idiocy recited by either party's media representatives.

It is about how conservative news-ertainers use Yahweh as a means to an end. There is no "joke" or double entendre when conservative entertainers invoke Jesus's name. There is no intent other than coercion through piety. This is the distinction between when the Conservative Entertainment Complex makes an effort to entertain and when it betrays the public trust for profit.

As such, conservative talkers have irreparably damaged the GOP by requiring that anyone seeking public office with an (R) in front of their name capitulate to Dominionism, lest they be labeled a RINO and become

---

227 Izquotes.com, *Ann Coulter*, http://izquotes.com/quote/43290

an outcast. This farther-right discourse has moved the center accordingly, and it has taken the Republican party with it. Because of the competition among members of the Conservative Entertainment Complex to out-Jesus one another, what was once the proud party of Eisenhower is now a haven for religious lunatics.

When it all boils down, God is how the new media-driven GOP justifies everything, regardless of whether or not their Yahweh-isms are reflective of the New Testament Jesus of Nazareth. Conservative News-ertainers and political televangelists have redefined and reinvented the Christian savior so as to appease a scripture-ignorant voting base. As such, the cultural anxiety of the tea party easily accommodates a Christian Dominionist worldview. The Conservative Entertainment Complex uses Yahweh as McCarthy did Stalin.

It's such an irrational premise that it's mind-boggling that almost half of the country has bought in.

Twenty-First-Century Schizoid Men

A man full of faith is simply one who has lost (or never had) the capacity for clear and realistic thought. He is not a mere ass; he is actually ill. Worse, he is incurable.

—Equal-opportunity offender H.L. Mencken[228]

When people are chosen for high-profile positions, where lives and livelihoods are at stake, one would think that sanity would be a basic requirement of anyone considered. As such, one would also contemplate that Americans should embrace leaders who are able to keep their wits about them and display reason and intellect during a crisis. That is, unless those would-be leaders are Republicans seeking public office. Then voters on the right apply a completely different set of criteria.

---

[228] Watchfuleye.com, *H.L. Mencken*, http://www.watchfuleye.com/mencken.html

With the Christian conservative media tail wagging the GOP dog comes an interesting crop of elected representatives. The crazy and stupid declarations made by conservative TV and radio hosts has led to an extremely colorful, albeit irrational, cast of characters representing the GOP in local, state, and national office. A pathological sociopolitical incomprehension among those with an (R) in front of their names are all that's left for Republican voters to choose from. And as long as irrationality accompanies the twenty-first-century GOP's "Jesus guided the hands who wrote our Constitution, wanted us to hate Democrats, have lots of guns, and persecute gays" version of Christianity, then Republican voters must rationalize that the delirium is not delirium at all, but rather a valid perspective.

One must extrapolate that crazy and stupid are merely an expression of conservative values.

Which brings us to the state of denial that the "GOP body politic" must be in to mentally reconcile what they want their party to be versus what it actually is: a haven for Dominionist Christian lunatics. For numerous reasons, Republican voters ignore the maniacal "God" ravings of people whom they elect to office, and, more importantly, who write our laws. In what I can only assume is a reflexive disdain for Democrats, the Republican proletariat are able to rationalize—if not justify—their candidates' craziness, no matter how unreasonable or detached from reality it is.

Routinely, GOP candidates and elected officials exhibit what can only be described as a serious misfiring in their synapses, which must allow them to not only experience psychotic delusions but also to proudly speak about them on television. A dangerous combination of crazy and stupid, proudly displayed as a badge of honor. It's as if they're under the misconception that everyone can hear the voices in their heads. Here are just a few examples:

*They (guns) are used to defend our property and our families
and our faith and our freedom, and they are absolutely
essential to living the way God intended for us to live.*

—California Rep. Tim "Sig Sauer" Donnelly[229] (R)

… And lo the Lord sayeth, put a cap in their liberal ass.

*All that stuff I was taught about evolution and embryology and the Big
Bang Theory, all that is lies straight from the pit of Hell. And it's lies to
try to keep me and all the folks who were taught that from understanding
that they need a savior. You see, there are a lot of scientific data that I've
found out as a scientist that actually show that this is really a young Earth.
I don't believe that the Earth's but about 9,000 years old. I believe it
was created in six days as we know them. That's what the Bible says.*

—Rep. Paul "Facepalm" Broun (R)[230]

So sayeth Rep. Broun, of the House Science Committee.

*These are people who are going to have to answer to a much higher power
than me about why they have appealed and appealed and appealed.*

—Ohio Gov. John "Wait 'Till Dad Gets Home" Kasich (R)[231], implying
that critics of his JobsOhio program will have to answer to Yahweh

I don't think Gov. Kasich was talking about Thor when he referred to a
"higher power."

[229] Mediate.com, *Tim Donnelly*, http://www.mediaite.com/online/
gop-legislator-guns-are-essential-to-living-the-way-god-intended/
[230] BrainyQuote.com, *Paul Broun*, http://www.brainyquote.com/quotes/quotes/p/
paulbroun512773.html
[231] Theweek.com, *John Kasich*, http://theweek.com/article/index/239628/
the-10-dumbest-things-republicans-have-said-this-year

One of the things I will talk about, that no president has talked about before, is I think the dangers of contraception in this country. ... Many of the Christian faith have said, well, that's okay, contraception is okay. It's not okay. It's a license to do things in a sexual realm that is counter to how things are supposed to be.

—Rick "Cold Shower" Santorum[232]

Sex is for procreation only. Gotcha. Thanks Rick.

I look at this role in public service really as a form of ministry, and it truly is public service.

—Virginia Gov. Bob "Ultrasound" McDonnell[233]

Constitution, Smonstitution ... the good folks of Virginia were being governed by Minister Bob.

A woman [Terry Schiavo] was healthy. There was brain damage, there is no question. But from a health point of view, she was not terminally ill.

—Rep. Michele "Life Begins at Erection" Bachman[234]

Had it not been for the fact that she was a drooling vegetable being kept alive by machinery, Terry Schiavo might have been an Olympian.

---

[232] Washingtonpost.com, *Rick Santorum*, http://www.washingtonpost.com/blogs/she-the-people/post/rick-santorum-the-idea-im-coming-after-your-birth-control-is-absurd/2012/01/06/gIQAOVy0fP_blog.html

[233] Cbn.com, *Bob McDonnell*, *http://blogs.cbn.com/beltwaybuzz/archive/2010/01/21/gov.-bob-mcdonnells-ministry.aspx*

[234] Msnbc.com, *Michele Bachman*, http://www.msnbc.com/hardball/thanks-the-memories-0

Call me cynical, but I didn't think his (President Obama) views on marriage could get any gayer.

—Rand "Ru" Paul[235]

… And neither could the Republican Party's obsession with ass sex.

Our founders got it right when they wrote in the Declaration of Independence that our rights come from nature, and nature's God, not from government.

—Rep. Paul "Wolfgang" Ryan[236]

Is that why the founders left God out of the Constitution, stupid?

I think even when life begins in that horrible situation of rape, that it is something that God intended to happen.

—Rep. Richard "Quite the Philosopher" Murdoch[237]

A woman's body is God's plaything, and he can't always wait for her to get married. Right.

I think the right approach is to accept this horribly created— in the sense of rape—but nevertheless a gift in a very broken

235 Huffingtonpost.com, *Rand Paul*, http://www.huffingtonpost.com/2012/05/12/rand-paul-obama-gay-marriage_n_1511920.html

236 BrainyQuote.com, *Paul Ryan*, http://www.brainyquote.com/quotes/quotes/p/paulryan412775.html

237 Washingtonpost.com, *Richard Murdoch*, http://www.washingtonpost.com/blogs/she-the-people/wp/2012/10/24/indiana-gop-senate-hopeful-richard-mourdock-says-god-intended-rape-pregnancies/

*way, the gift of human life, and accept what God has given to
you ... rape victims should make the best of a bad situation.*

—Sen. Rick "Ecclesiastic Idiot" Santorum[238]

Maybe for your birthday, God will give you an irascible case of herpes, too.

*God was sending me a clear message to not do things for personal glory or
fame. It was a turning point that helped me in future challenges, helped
me stay focused on the people I was elected to serve, and reminded me
of God's abundant grace and the paramount need to stay humble.*

—Gov. Scott "Anything but Humble" Walker[239],
from his book, *Unintimidated*

Thanks, modest Marvin. But we all know who the people you were elected
to serve are, Scotty, and it's sure as heck ain't the idiots who voted for you.

*You cannot do anything without God. It's a profound and elemental
truth. Not, you cannot do most things without God. You will not be
able to do anything that you want, truly, in fulfillment, without God.*

—Marco "Can I Buy a Vowel?" Rubio[240]

Apparently, Marco doesn't understand the concept of "elemental truth."

*I don't know how much God has to do to get the attention of the politicians.
We've had an earthquake; we've had a hurricane. He said, 'Are you*

238 Huffingtonpost.com, *Rick Santorum*, http://www.huffingtonpost.
com/2012/01/23/rick-santorum-abortion-rape_n_1224624.html

239 Wisconsingazette.com, *Scott Walker*, http://www.wisconsingazette.com/
wisconsin-gaze/critics-blast-scott-walkers-tell-nothing-book-as-shoddy-stunt.
html

240 BrainyQuote.com, *Marco Rubio*, http://www.brainyquote.com/quotes/
quotes/m/marcorubio416119.html

*going to start listening to me here?' Listen to the American people because
the American people are roaring right now. They know government
is on a morbid obesity diet and we've got to rein in the spending.*

—Rep. Michele "Stepford Bimbo" Bachmann[241], suggesting that the
2011 East Coast earthquake and hurricane was a message from God

Apparently, Yahweh is not one for small talk or Post-It notes.

*I am a firm believer in intelligent design as a matter of
faith and intellect, and I believe it should be presented
in schools alongside the theories of evolution.*

—Texas Gov. Rick "Cranial Abyss" Perry[242]

Says Rick Perry, whose solution to a record-setting drought was to gather
a bunch of good Christian folks in a stadium, and pray. It didn't work.

*If it's a legitimate rape, the female body has ways
of shutting that whole thing down*

—Rep Todd "You Do Realize That We Can Hear You, Right?" Akin[243]

… And if it's a legitimate thought, the Republican mind has a way of
shutting *that* whole thing down.

[241] Thinkprogress.org, *Michele Bachman*, http://thinkprogress.org/
climate/2011/08/29/306436/bachamnn-hurricane-message-god/

[242] Theguardian.com, *Rick Perry*, http://www.theguardian.com/commentisfree/
cifamerica/2011/aug/23/rick-perry-creationism-classroom

[243] Slate.com, *Todd Atkin*, http://www.slate.com/blogs/xx_factor/
2012/08/20/todd_akin_s_legitimate_rape_comment_not_a_misstatement_
but_a_worldview_.html

Basic Mental Competency

Say what you will about the sweet miracle of unquestioning faith,
I consider a capacity for it terrifying and absolutely vile.

—Kurt Vonnegut[244]

The tragedy is that there are thousands of these less-than-rational Republican god-quotes spoken within this past election cycle alone. I could copy and paste for hours. And while both Republican *and* Democratic politicians are capable of clumsy verbal faux pas, this is not about bumbled words or even bad politics. This is about electing people to public office who should be given a coloring book between electroshock therapy sessions.

Now, I understand that politicians are by nature culturally awkward, and many even suffer from kind of "social autism" that one might acquire with a zit on prom night. I doubt many of them sat at the cool kids table in high school. Certainly, politicians from either party are capable of saying dumb things. Nancy Pelosi, Barney Frank (who speaks like he has a mouth full of mashed potatoes), and Debbie Wasserman-Shultz have made me shake my head in disbelief on numerous occasions. And let's face it, Vice President Joe Biden is the king of verbal gaffes.

But there is a difference between bumbling politi-speak, differing opinions regarding policy, and psychotic ravings.

For instance, when 2012 Republican nominee for president, Mitt Romney[245], said, "I went to a number of women's groups and said, 'Can you help us find folks?' and they brought us whole binders full of women," it was unfairly harped upon as something that reflected negatively on his opinion of women. The truth is, it was much more likely just a spoken

---

[244] Goodreads.com, *Kurt Vonnegut*, http://www.goodreads.com/quotes/26741-say-what-you-will-about-the-sweet-miracle-of-

[245] Washingtonpost.com, *Mitt Romney*, http://www.washingtonpost.com/blogs/she-the-people/wp/2012/10/17/mitt-romneys-binders-full-of-women/

bungle coming from a guy who was exhausted from campaigning. It was a silly thing to say, but it was hardly reflective of an imbalanced mind.

Likewise when President Obama fudgingly claimed that he visited all "fifty-seven states." These are mere examples of "brain farts"—words that came out of either man's mouth with an awkward lack of eloquence that didn't truly reflect their beliefs. Had Romney's or Obama's postgaffe statements reflected a defense of their imprudent comments rather than offering awkward explanations for their lingual misfires, then maybe one could make a case for idiocy regarding said remarks.

I'm going to go out on a limb and suggest that the above lexical face-plants are not reflective of Mitt Romney being dismissive of women or Barack Obama not knowing how many states there are.

However there is a distinct difference between giving politicians who say silly things a free pass and ignoring insane assertions spoken matter-of-factly, if not consistently. None of the quotes made by Dominionist Republicans is a mere "oopsie;" nor are they mistakes. The irrational assertions about rape culture and Yahweh wanting us to own firearms are how they feel and what they believe. Their convictions regarding creationism, supernatural retribution, and divine intervention are the reflections of disturbed minds.

> *Sex isn't about fun. If you want to have fun, read a book, go to a movie. Sex is about the procreation of children. It's a sacred responsibility that is meant by God to have men and women commit their lifetime to children.*

> —Jerome Corsi[246], tea party activist and sexy beast

The tea/GOP constituency is now willing to vote based upon their candidate's belief in fairy tales. Moreover, they wouldn't consider voting for anyone not publically capitulating to a finely attired celestial monarch.

---

[246] Keystonepolitics.com, *Jerome Corsi*, ://keystonepolitics.com/2013/09/tea-speaker-sex-isnt-about-fun/

Political evangelists tell their voting flocks that they are the stewards of the nation as told to them by Yahweh, and those words are comforting to hear if you're stupid. If not, bat-shit crazy.

But it wasn't always this way. There was a time when the GOP wasn't run by maniacs, and their policies did not reflect a twelfth-century socioeconomic perspective. Here is a reflection of a true conservative Republican, who would undoubtedly be considered a RINO today:

Mark my word, if and when these preachers get control of the (Republican) party, and they're sure trying to do so, it's going to be a terrible damn problem. Frankly, these people frighten me. Politics and governing demand compromise. But these Christians believe they are acting in the name of God, so they can't and won't compromise. I know, I've tried to deal with them.

And:

The religious factions that are growing throughout our land are not using their religious clout with wisdom. … I'm frankly sick and tired of the political preachers across this country telling me as a citizen that if I want to be a moral person, I must believe in 'A,' 'B,' 'C,' and 'D.' Just who do they think they are? … I will fight them every step of the way if they try to dictate their moral convictions to all Americans in the name of "conservatism."

These quotes are from Barry Goldwater[247] (1909–1998), a five-term US senator, Republican Party nominee for president in 1964, Maj. Gen., US Air Force Reserves, and author of *The Conscience of a Conservative.*

As it exists today, one cannot separate the stage-four dementia from the Republican Party, as it has infested its very marrow. Until the GOP voting base recognizes the cancer within their own party, they can never hope to remove it. However, brainwashing is not undone easily. Do tea-voters really

---

[247] Goodreads.com, *Barry Goldwater,* http://www.goodreads.com/quotes/777519-mark-my-word-if-and-when-these-preachers-get-control

hate Democrats enough to want to willfully elect deranged mental cases? If so, what does that say about the Republican electorate?

To live in the 21ˢᵗ Century and to believe in the biblical story of creation, to deny scientific consensus derived from peer-reviewed evidence, and to claim that you hear voices from above guiding your decision making … it doesn't make one pious, godly, or even a decent human being. It makes them certifiably, cuckoo for Coco Puffs, Courtney Love crazy.

… And not-fer-nothin', but a total lack of sanity should prohibit anyone from holding public office.

Tea for Two Million

May we never confuse honest dissent with disloyal subversion.

—Supreme commander of the Allied forces in Europe
during WWII and thirty-fourth president of the United
States, Dwight D. Eisenhower[248], who had a knack of
predicting where this nation would screw up

As the cultural topography of the nation becomes increasingly darker-skinned, the social and racial anxiety over this change can manifest itself in various ways. Using this anxiety to their benefit, extremely wealthy Dominionist profiteers have taken to dividing the segments of the American population along—for the most part—racial and socioeconomic lines. Which is the true impetus of the tea party.

Subversive anti-American sentiments presented as patriotic dissent.

A scam perpetrated on the working-class Republican electorate—engineered by billionaires in order to convince idiots to vote against their own best interests and aid the wealthy in gathering more unto themselves—the tea

---

[248] BrainyQuote.com, *Dwight D. Eisenhower*, http://www.brainyquote.com/quotes/quotes/d/dwightdei149095.html

party helps elect people whose socioeconomic agenda is to create a greater divide between the obscenely affluent and everyone else. As has been true throughout history when the well-to-do want more, religion—in this case, Jesus—is the best way to exploit the masses.

Largely funded by the self-interested and preposterously prosperous, tea party groups have hand-picked politicians and pundits who rally their politically unaware flock—in the name of Jesus and patriotism—to the cause of creating an Orwellian economy. In simpler terms, that means lots for the oligarchy and little for the populace. Indeed, while the tea party has been presented as a "grassroots" movement of like-minded, tri-cornered-hat-wearing, independent free-thinkers, the truth is that they are easily manipulated by their economic oppressors through their Christian predispositions. Tea-compoops are little more than puppets on a Dominionist string.

Hilariously, tea partiers like to refer to nonconservatives as "sheeple." As if it were Democrats being herded by billionaires to rallies like a flock of costume-wearing idiots, and not themselves. This is not simply an example of the pot calling the kettle black. This is an example of the pot calling the kettle a pot. An African joining the John Birch Society. Sheep, who hate sheep, unaware that they *are* sheep. Morons.

But the tea party is the means to an economic end for the financial elite. Indeed, the extremely wealthy—and I'm not talking about your run-of-the-mill millionaire, but rather billionaires who have the ability to influence national policy—need to have their own politicians and judges in place to do their bidding. The Wiki-list of tea-party-approved candidates is staggeringly long, if not united in a twelfth-century approach to governance. An army of Dominionist conformists, all of whom speak about abiding Jesus and the Founding Fathers, as they take direction from their financial donors.

These are not "kookie" birds. Right now the greatest player, the big tent on the political scene in America, is called the tea party movement.

—Former House majority leader and FreedomWorks chairman, Dick Armey[249], who was, ironically, the figurehead for an army of dicks

Multibillionaires Charles and David Koch—who are to America what Emperor Palpatine was to the Galactic Republic—are the puppeteers behind tea party groups *FreedomWorks* and *Americans for Prosperity*, which are among the largest and most influential organizations in the country. But even when tea simpletons are confronted with the truth about who the monetary backers of their movement are, they still don't seem to care. Because it's their bigoted predispositions that drove them to stand before Michele Bachman, Glenn Beck, Sarah Palin, or the myriad of other tea-party-approved lunatics—and applaud when they regurgitate Roger Ailes/ Fox News fact-deficient platitudes—in the first place.

Tea partiers believe billionaire-funded Dominionist lies because it suits their bigoted, willfully ignorant predilections.

However, historically the most effective lies usually contain a hint of truth. It allows for perfidy to be rationalized as something other than what it's intended to be. For instance, paying taxes definitely sucks. There are certainly some unionized teachers out there who should not have a job teaching. So Dominionists add a little truth to their narrow-minded narrative in order to create allies and attract more tea-voters to their cause.

As such, the difficulty in discussing the tea party movement is that of discussing any large group of people. To paint with a broad brush is at best irresponsible and at worst as bigoted as those one hopes to expose. There are, to my understanding, some in the tea party who claim that the movement was brought about by a concern for government overspending

---

[249] Ibid., *Dick Armey*, http://www.brainyquote.com/quotes/quotes/d/ dickarmey412027.html

and a desire to employ fiscal responsibility. These are undoubtedly viable socioeconomic issues to be concerned about.

However, if one looks at the overall tea party message, deficit and budgetary concerns would amount to the hint of truth within the overall lie.

(President) Reagan proved deficits don't matter.

—Former Vice President Dick Cheney[250] in 2002, before
there was a darkie in the White House and a tea party

I understand that there are those in the tea party who claim to adhere to libertarian, free-market principles and who assert that their primary concern is government spending. However, they cannot disassociate themselves from the national tea party message out of convenience. Especially when tea party candidates offer little—if anything—to the cause of fiscal responsibility and typically conflate "free-market capitalism" with rampant cronyism. Being a member of the tea party for "libertarian" reasons would be like claiming that you joined the Klan because you believe that you have a constitutional right to dress in white after Labor Day.

Yet despite the "fiscal responsibility" claims, the tea party message all comes down to Jesus. Tea party representatives elected to office—not to mention voters who show up at rallies—frame their messages within a Christian Dominionist sociopolitical structure. It's Republican Jesus who was against socialized health care and who personally blessed our nation. As such, the biblical savior is the bait on the hook to get the frightened Christian proletariat to hand billionaires more power and influence.

"Prosperity preachers" convince their impoverished flocks that sending them money will in turn allow Yahweh to reward them financially as well; tea party "preachers" do the same. Only instead of multimillionaire evangelists talking idiots into tithing money that they need to feed

---

250 Telegram.com, *Dick Cheney*, http://www.telegram.com/article/20110818/
LETTERS/108189548/-1/mobile&TEMPLATE=MOBILE

themselves—so that said preacher can buy another private jet—tea party speakers ask that you tithe your vote (along with your political donations) so that the extremely wealthy—themselves included—can benefit, politically and financially. Dominionist prosperity will surely trickle down to good, god-fearing tea folks. Vote now, benefit later.

Thus, middle- and lower-middle-class tea-publicans are finding themselves voting at the behest of the uber-wealthy under the guise of patriotism and for the love of Jesus. Oppression framed as "freedom." It's an ethereal pyramid scheme.

P.T. Barnum was right.

The Real RINOs

They used to call me a maverick; now they call me a RINO.

—War hero and 2008 Republican nominee
for POTUS, Sen. John McCain[251]

While it's always been true that our commanders-in-chief have (at the very least) identified themselves as Christians, this has been much more pronounced since the Islamic world made its presence felt in America. The Iranian hostage crisis in 1979 gave America a new Islamic villain to hate. President Reagan responded by inviting evangelical Christian preachers into the White House so as to seek their counsel. And American politicians have been vying for Christian voters and eroding the wall of separation between church and state ever since.

Indeed, shortly after the September 11, 2001, attacks, President George W. Bush claimed to be receiving instructions on how to respond directly from

---

[251] Redstate.com, *John McCain*, http://www.redstate.com/diary/stridentconservative/2013/03/14/john-mccain-and-lindsey-graham-introduce-protection-of-rino-wimps-act-of-2013/

God. Certainly, if Yahweh speaks to George Bush, he must do so using very small words. "Hey, George, I said Iran, not Iraq, you idiot."

But it's gotten even more loony since then. Five Republicans who challenged for the GOP nomination for the 2012 presidential election—Rick Perry, Michelle Bachman, Rick Santorum, Herman Cain, and Thaddeus McCotter—claimed that God had given them personal instructions to run for president. While a sixth—Mike Huckabee—was apparently told by Yahweh *not* to run, and a seventh—Sarah Palin—was patiently awaiting a shift in the odds from the Great Bookmaker, since they both had a lot riding on the outcome. Even if one were to believe that God has a vested interest in our election; clearly either four of these people are lying, or Yahweh doesn't have Sinatra clout and is hedging his bets.

And apparently, God only speaks to Republicans.

Still, perhaps the most laughable thing about the irrational menagerie of Christian fundamentalists vying for the 2012 Republican nomination for President of the United States—including the thrice-married serial philanderer Newt Gingrich constantly rambling about "Christian family values"—was that the eventual nominee, Mormon Mitt Romney felt the need to paint himself as a traditional Christian.

Hilarious, to those who understand the difference between Christianity and Mormonism, was the Romney campaign's pietistic tap-dance around the differences in the two faiths. Understanding that Bible-clutching, Jesus loving tea-voters needed a cognitive cop-out in order to vote for a semi-Christian, Romney—in a conveniently timed coincidence—developed a personal relationship with Jesus Christ. Listening to Tea Party mastodons, sitting in their scooters and gabbling about what a good Christian Mitt Romney was, might just be among the funniest experiences I've had in my life.

Formerly on an evangelical "cult" list, alongside Unitarians, Scientologists, and Jehovah's Witnesses, the sudden removal of Mormonism from that list occurred with Romney's nomination. Once ole' perfect hair had won enough Republican primaries, evangelists who had formerly classified the Mormon religion as a "cult" began defending Romney as a Christian. Oh, the whimsical drollery that political bedfellows can create.

Historically, evangelical Christianity has never embraced Mormonism as a branch of Christianity. Mormonism has always been treated as a cult. In fact, the Southern Baptist Convention, which is the largest Protestant denomination in the world, officially labels Mormonism as a cult.

—Dallas megachurch pastor and Rick Perry supporter Robert Jeffress[252], casually mentioning that the Republican front-runner in the 2012 election was a member of a cult

I never said Christians should not vote for Mitt Romney.

—Pastor Robert "Did I say Cult? I Meant Lovely Group of God-Fearing Christians" Jeffress[253], suggesting, after Romney had gotten the nomination, that being in a cult is no big deal, really

In accordance with the retrospective Mormon-evangelical love-fest was Romney distancing himself from the inanity of Mormon tenets. No-one in the Romney campaign dared mention that Mormons believe that *Elohim* (God) lives on the planet Kolob, or that you can be protected by "Magic Underwear." Never would Team Romney proclaim that their candidate followed the teachings of a polygamist named Joseph Smith, whom he believes is the true prophet of God, as explained through golden plates discovered while Smith was alone in the woods.

---

[252] Christianpost.com, *Robert Jeffress*, http://www.christianpost.com/news/evangelical-baptist-pastor-mormonism-is-a-cult-mitt-romney-is-not-a-christian-57626/

[253] Ibid., http://www.christianpost.com/news/robert-jeffress-calls-romney-lesser-of-two-evils-maintains-mormonism-is-not-christianity-81798

I believe that Jesus Christ is the Son of God and the Savior of mankind.

—Mitt "Joseph Smith Who?" Romney[254]

Indeed, the Mitt-ster was all about Jesus during his campaign. Con man Joe Smith, not so much. Perhaps the Romney family should have waited until after the election to posthumously baptize Mitt's long-deceased atheist father-in-law into the Mormon cult. Not that baptizing someone after they've died is a crazy thing to do, or anything … but you know how the "liberal media" like to twist postmortem religious conversions. Now the old fella can inherit his very own planet, as per Mormon tenets.

Sadly, the 2012 race for the Republican nominee for President came down to Mitt Romney and Rick Santorum. The former believes that he will have his own celestial body to rule over upon his earthly demise; the latter believes that Noah's Ark was a historical event. Even sadder was that arguably the most qualified and lucid Republican running in the 2012 primary, Jon Huntsman, was summarily dismissed from contention after having acknowledged facts derived from science; he was subsequently labeled a RINO for the Republican crime of sanity.

It's too bad; Mary Kaye Huntsman would have been the MILFiest first lady ever. Giggity.

Nevertheless, despite the "Mormon hiccup," the Dominionist strategy is sound. By disempowering Republicans who interpret the Bible metaphorically via the labeling of them as RINOs, the evangelical movement has effectively taken over the GOP. Republicans who do not adopt a position of willful ignorance concerning creation, evolution, stem cells, or an ark full of copulating arthropods are not pliable enough for big-money Republican backers. They require that candidates toe the Dominionist Republican party line, so as to spellbind tea-wits.

---

254 Christiancentury.org, *Mitt Romney*, http://www.christiancentury.org/article/2012-01/are-mormons-christian-its-complicated

… And if Dominionists can turn a Mormon into a Christian, then they have the power to convince Republican voters of anything.

Reverse Traverse

What we have here is our core values as Americans and Christians slipping away into this facade where we should take care of our poor, sick, and disabled.

—Texas Senator Ted "Fuck the Poor, Sick, and Disabled" Cruz[255], in hour nineteen of his 2013 faux filibuster

Just. Wow.

With all of the less-than-rational allegations, declarations, and explanations, there is no greater example of the tea party's departure from sense and sanity than Texas Senator Ted Cruz. I never thought that Republicans could be more smoke-your-own-toenails crazy, or say more astonishingly stupid things than Rick Santorum or Michele Bachman. It seems, apparently, that I was wrong. Since the clown car of tea-party-approved loons set the sanity bar at a new low during the 2012 presidential race, the Republican pathology has only gotten worse.

Heading into the 2014 midterms, Ted Cruz positioned himself as the conductor of the GOP crazy train. Indeed, all tea-publicans and their commitment to Christian delirium are measured against him. Which is why Cruz is loved by conservative media and has managed to amass a significant tea party following. He's carved out a compelling political niche by pushing the boundaries of political discourse further into the realm of crazy and stupid.

---

255 Freewoodpost.com, *Ted Cruz*, http://www.freewoodpost.com/2013/09/25/ted-cruz-jesus-died-to-save-himself-not-enable-lazy-followers-to-be-dependent-on-him/

Amazingly, Ted Cruz is a Harvard graduate and is definitely not weak-minded himself. He does, however, speak the language of puerility fluently. Cruz understands what tea-junkies want to hear, and as such, he's a hero among the cognitively compromised.

> *As believers, we are called to action; not just sitting quietly and hiding our faith under a bushel but to stand and speak no matter what the consequence. Religious liberty has never been more under attack.*

—Ted "Give 'Em What They Want" Cruz[256], speaking
to young, brainwashed Christians at Liberty University
about an imaginary attack on their religion

The lack of rationale it takes to make the above assertion is bewildering. Unless, of course, one feels that trying to maintain a separation of church and state, or not allowing Christianity to circumvent our republic by imposing itself on everyone is an "attack" on Christianity. Marriage equality, for instance, is not an incursion on Christianity any more than repealing slavery was. But tea-psychotics like Ted Cruz easily unsettle Christian sensibilities by regarding "their version of marriage not being forced on everyone" as indistinguishable from persecution.

Indeed, Ted Cruz is correct—insofar as Christianity's freedom to infringe on other people's freedom *is* under attack.

However to better understand Senator Rafael Edward "Ted" Cruz, one only has to gaze upon the psychotic oak from which this delusional acorn fell. Rafael Cruz Sr., Ted's emotionally disturbed father, is not just an evangelical preacher but a conservative political pundit as well. Besides believing that the biblical story of creation is recorded history and that his magical sperm has sired America's next savior, Ralfy is also adept at saying other sensationally irrational and inaccurate things.

---

[256] Forwardprogressives.com, *Ted Cruz*, http://www.forwardprogressives.com/ted-cruz-makes-asinine-statement-religious-liberties/

Karl Marx said it, 'I can use the teachings of Darwin to promote communism.' Why? Because communism, or call it socialism if you think communism is too hard a word, necessitates for government to be your god, and for government to be your god they need to destroy the concept of God. That's why communism and evolution go hand and hand.

—Pastor Rafael "Should Have Pulled Out" Cruz[257]

The amount of farce and falsehood in this quote alone is appalling. But absurdity is not something that ever stopped anyone in the Cruz clan from speaking. Karl Marx never said this. For that matter, neither did Groucho. Nor is evolution a function of communism. I don't mean to insult an older gentleman like R-Cru, here, but Holy Toledo, is he friggin' batty.

So it's not difficult to understand where Ted Cruz's sense of self-important mania stems from. He was raised by a schizoid. Like father, like son. A legacy of lunacy.

With nuts like Ted Cruz at the front of the GOP—and whether one is willing to admit that or not, he is—Republicans have distanced themselves further still from their own consciences as well as the ethics and integrity of a generation ago. Religious lunatics have usurped the party past the point of being able to govern or legislate. Many in the GOP won't make a move without first considering whether it will piss off Ted Cruz.

Veritably, many congressional Republicans would not be so bold as to vote in opposition to Cruz on any prospective piece of legislation. If they dare defy the prevailing far-right wind, the party will find a Christian lunatic in their district who will acquiesce to the next step in Republican devolution. Sanity has become politicized. The GOP is in Cruz control.

It's like having Piper Laurie in the Senate, and everyone else is Carrie.

---

257 Mediate.com, *Pastor Rafael Cruz*, http://www.mediaite.com/tv/ted-cruzs-father-gay-marriage-and-evolution-are-tools-of-marxism-to-destroy-god/

The thing is, those who label other Republicans "RINOs" are themselves the true Republicans in name only. I don't know what the hell Ted Cruz is, but he is no Republican. For the men who built the GOP would never recognize their own party in the midst of all of the irrational Christian platitudes of today.

Yet the closer we come to abandoning the separation between church and state established by our nation's founders—and the greater the chance that biblical law will supplant parts of our constitution—the more we become like the radical Islamic theocracies that prompted these changes in the Republican party in the first place. Ayatollah Cruz.

Truths Self-Evident

As occurred during the sixteenth-century European counter-reformation, the forces of anti-intellectualism are attempting a coup here in America today. Never in the history of this country has there been an assault on reason like we are experiencing now. We are enduring an unprecedented disregard for scientific consensus and a denial of peer-reviewed evidence, to the point where a significant portion of our population truly believes that physics-defying impossibilities are legitimate explanations.

The Earth will end only when God declares it's time to be over. Man will not destroy this Earth. This Earth will not be destroyed by a flood. I do believe that God's word is infallible, unchanging, perfect.

—Rep John "Doesn't Understand Climate Science" Shimkus[258] of the House Energy Committee, claiming that we have no need to worry about the energy industry's negative effect on climate change, because Yahweh promised Noah that his flood would be the last

So drill, baby, drill.

---

[258] Politicalwire.com, *John Shimkus*, http://politicalwire.com/archives/2010/11/12/ shimkus_cites_god_on_climate_change.html

Seriously, an elected Congressman cited a conversation between God and Noah as the reason that people should lay off regulating energy companies. Let's not worry about them dumping toxic chemicals into our drinking water. Who gives a shit if greenhouse gas emissions are increasing the global temperature? Scientists are saying that we're in danger? Humbug! Yahweh told Noah it would all be cool.

It must be nice to be a crazy person who is not concerned with something that's killing you. I actually envy the tea-vangelical mentality in that way. There are purposefully deceptive ideologues who are attempting an appropriation of the United States government, and they really don't care because, well … because Jesus, that's why.

Why else would a simple television show like "Cosmos with astrophysicist Neil DeGrasse Tyson" transcend its role as entertaining education and become ground zero for the battle between ignorance and reason? If not for the evangelical influence in our national zeitgeist, how could giving "equal time" to creationists on a show hosted by a fucking *astrophysicist* even be a consideration? Fundamentalist Christians with no want of understanding feel that their baseless assertions should be aired alongside peer-reviewed science. Indeed, *Cosmos* has become the twenty-first-century Scopes trial.

> *Evolutionary Darwinists need to understand we are taking the dinosaurs back. This is a battle cry to recognize the science in the revealed truth of God.*

—The incomparably incognizant Ken "Incorrect Answers In Genesis" Ham[259]

> *As long as the earth remains, there will be seed time and harvest, cold and heat, winter and summer, day and night, my point is, God's still up*

---

[259] Thinkexist.com, *Ken Ham*, http://thinkexist.com/quotes/ken_ham/

there. The arrogance of people to think that we, human beings, would be able to change what He is doing in the climate is to me outrageous.

—Sen. Jim "Damn It, I'm an idiot, Not a Climate Scientist" Inhofe[260]

The good thing about science is that it's true, whether or not you believe in it.

—Neil DeGrasse "Is Greener on the Sane Side of the Fence" Tyson[261]

The science denial movement is like nothing this country has ever seen before. It's not just that Fundamentalist Christians and tea partiers don't understand science (and they don't) ... but they *hate* it. This is the difference between one who simply doesn't possesses the ability to comprehend and an *anti-intellectual*. Tea-vangelicals fight *against* knowledge so that they might preserve a literal interpretation of religious scripture long ago accepted as metaphor. It is a concerted effort at rationalizing willful ignorance so as to retreat from the scientific age of enlightenment—on which this nation was founded—back into the shadows of Medieval fundamentalism.

Indeed, a frightened, uneducated proletariat is a theocrat's greatest resource. If those who benefit from fear and incomprehension can make an adversary out of science (as well as revise history) for enough people, then the lunatic fringe can become a body politic. Which is why—and how—Dominionists in America have found a political dependent in the tea party.

Regarding Dominionism and evangelical politics, there is also a peripheral ignorance that transcends science denial. Rarely does one repudiate scientific consensus about the origin of our species or the age of our planet and apply critical thinking in other areas. In accordance with the surrendering of one's intellect to biblical literalism, deliberate incomprehension invariably

---

[260]   Righwingwatch.org, *Jim Inhofe*, http://www.rightwingwatch.org/content/
        james-inhofe-says-bible-refutes-climate-change
[261]   Goodreads.com, *Neil DeGrasse Tyson*, http://www.goodreads.com/author/
        quotes/12855.Neil_deGrasse_Tyson

allows for a dismissal of facts regarding a variety of socioeconomic issues. Forming a political ideology that encourages anti-intellectualism—by its very nature—cannot permit reason to permeate its outer defenses.

> *To assert that the earth revolves around the sun is as erroneous to claim that Jesus was not born of a virgin.*

> —Cardinal Robert "Wrong Twice in One Sentence" Bellarmine[262] (1542–1621), saint and cardinal of the Roman Catholic Church during the trial of Galileo

Hence, much of the tea party's socioeconomic policy has abandoned reason in economics and sociology, so as to coincide with its Medieval understanding of science. There are very few Republican candidates that dare defy tea-vangelical precepts, lest they not make it out of their local primaries. So they, too, surrender intellect for votes. Which brings us to the crux of the issue. Our political discourse—on every legislative issue—is infected with fraud, hyperbole, and purposeful deception.

Crazy and stupid.

This is not a problem that will go away if ignored. If America hopes to become the nation it once was—the nation that built giant things, defeated fascists, and sent men into space—we cannot allow the forces of anti-intellectualism to exist in a century where diseases have been cured and science has given people back their limbs. It is patently insane to deny facts derived from the very same peer-review process that permitted these advancements. Contemporary fundamentalists do not have the luxury of their sixteenth-century predecessors. Sane people can no longer blame demons for diseases, or, for that matter, blame homosexuals for their genetic predispositions.

---

[262] Beliefnet.com, *Cardinal Robert Bellarmine*, http://www.beliefnet.com/Quotes/ Christian/S/St-Robert-Bellarmine/The-School-Of-Christ-Is-The-School-Of- Love-In-The.aspx

We cannot allow the pseudo-science of Christian fundamentalists to be placed on the same shelf as real science. For it is peer-reviewed evidence (which survives the trials of scrutiny) that determines viability, not a collection of suppositions derived from a predetermination arrived at via an ancient book of fairy tales. We cannot—must not—allow less-than-sane religious assertions to be placed alongside science and reason in the name of "fairness" or equal time. Giving equal footing to blatant falsehoods spoken in the public square because they are delivered under the guise of religion is not being "tolerant."

Giving science deniers undeserved respect is an asinine, politically correct capitulation to crazy.

Blunt-Force Trauma

You are not entitled to your opinion. You are entitled to your
informed opinion. No one is entitled to be ignorant.

—Writer and curmudgeon Harlan Ellison[263]

However, the way to defeat the march back into the sixteenth century (and beyond) is to caricaturize voluntary stupidity for what it is. Although a true fundamentalist can probably never be made to understand how a rational mind works, others can—and will, under the right circumstances. If the forces of reason push back against anti-intellectualism, some "cultural Christians" will become embarrassed to be a part of what can only be described as a socially regressive movement of crazy people who believe in fairy tales.

Before fundamentalists have the opportunity to infect those around them with anti-intellectualism, they must be ridiculed as the bane of society that they are.

---

263   Goodreads.com, *Harlan Ellison*, https://www.goodreads.com/
quotes/9972-you-are-not-entitled-to-your-opinion-you-are-entitled

Elected officials who hide behind Jesus so as to say and do awful things are crazy, and they are also stupid assholes. We cannot be afraid to say so, and those who are judicious must shame those who prey upon our fellow Americans in the name of Christ. Political correctness must not protect willful ignorance in the name of religion. For if it is allowed to breed unrestrained—like every fear-based ideology—it will flourish in the minds and hearts of the intellectually assailable.

Christians often threaten atheists with eternal torture. But if we say that they're delusional, they will tell us that we're being rude.

—Comedian and political activist Mark Thomas[264]

The lack of curiosity that accords magical thinking is an affront to anyone who ever endeavored to make the world a better place through knowledge. Sadly, there is probably no cure for Christian-inspired scientific illiteracy, other than education. However, chances are that those who dissertate pseudo-scientific platitudes—which disregard the laws of physics, the natural universe, and genetics—have already been exposed to scientific facts. They simply refute them in favor of their psychotic delusion.

It is in the best interests of Christian fundamentalists to repeat the lies long enough and loud enough that others will believe them true. American Christianity is not just dependent upon political influence but recruitment as well. Which is why scientific illiteracy has become so pervasive. Ignorance loves company.

But anti-intellectualism has gotten to the point where people announce their lack of knowledge proudly. They wear it like a badge of honor and shout it to the highest mountaintops. A circular (lack of) logic is employed to undermine scientific truth, and, with a cultlike devotion, anti-intellectuals are unable, unwilling, and too fearful to question their fundamentalism.

---

[264] Godlessgeeks.com, *Mark Thomas*, http://www.godlessgeeks.com/LINKS/Quotes.htm

If you knew what was ahead, you'd be glad to be stepping over tonight.

—Jim Jones[265], moments before killing over 900
people with cyanide-laced Kool-Aid

Where in the past, mentally debilitating cults could easily be written off as sociopolitically inconsequential—in twenty-first-century America, philistinism and cultlike indoctrination is done within the confines of Christianity. As such, it automatically becomes a political force to be reckoned with. This is not a group of morons flying to Guyana to drink some Kool-Aid. This is half of our nation drinking Fool-Aid.

Americans have an intellectual civil war to fight here at home.

There are truths derived from scientific facts that have been proven beyond any reasonable doubt and which must be acknowledged. Virgins cannot give birth. The Earth is approximately four and a half billion years old. Humans have existed as a species for approximately two hundred thousand years, and we share a common genetic ancestry with other primates. Only crazy and/or stupid people deny these things.

Science is the great antidote to the poison of enthusiasm and superstition.

—Economist Adam Smith[266]

These are self-evident truths, facts—and they are undeniable. To allow our political discourse to be influenced otherwise is to base our policy on a lack of sanity. For if we remain too politically correct to confront metaphoric perfidy and allow anti-intellectuals an equal voice in the public square, how can Americans ever hope to find real-world solutions to complex problems?

---

[265] Newsweek, 1979., *Jim* Jones, Volume 93, Issues 10-18, The Washington Post Company

[266] Goodreads.com, *Adam Smith*, http://www.goodreads.com/ quotes/4060-science-is-the-great-antidote-to-the-poison-of-enthusiasm

We have to—*have to*—develop new, better ways to grow food. We must find cleaner, better energy sources. There are diseases that are yet to be cured. Water—and moreover, drinking water—is the world's most precious resource.

America can no longer allow greedy scumbags to screw this all up by manipulating credulous people into believing in magic. Because a sociopolitical movement toward a voluntary capitulation to crazy/stupid affirmations cripples the nation. As such, a progression toward reason is needed, and those who promulgate anti-intellectualism must be ridiculed as a means to counter Christian proselytism.

Americans mustn't permit the likes of Ted Cruz, Rick Santorum, Scott Walker, or any other Dominionist to poison the minds of any more of our fellow citizens without a fight. Rational people need to raise their voices. Dominionists, fundamentalists, evangelicals are saying crazy and stupid things and controlling more of our legislative process than they should. Thus, they are dangerous to our nation.

The Dominionist need to promote fear and ignorance in order to pacify their greed and lust for power is not just un-American—it is anti-American.

CHAPTER 6
Laws of Affliction
(Wonderful Twelfth-Century Ideas Enshrined in Legislation)

Freedom prospers when religion is vibrant and the rule of law under God is acknowledged.

–Original tea partier, voodoo economist, and constitutional illiterate, Ronald Reagan[267]

---

[267]   BrainyQuote.com, *Ronald Regan*, http://www.brainyquote.com/quotes/quotes/r/ronaldreag147687.html

If you are sane, and you read the Bible from Genesis to Revelation, there is a distinct probability that you'll become an atheist. If you are sane, inclined toward Christianity, and only read the New Testament, perhaps you'll become a liberal Democrat. However, if you're just a douche who's more concerned with justifying a departure from morality by bastardizing Christian tenets so they coincide with a bigoted, uninformed, myopic world view … well then, the twenty-first century term that might best describe your sociopolitical outlook would be "conservative Republican."

There are a whole lot of Christian conservative Republicans who vote.

I know that this seems harsh, but how else could one explain the rationale behind the throngs of tea-vangelical voters whose socioeconomic angst is directed at the very same people that Jesus of Nazareth advocated for? How can one claim to be a Christian and vote for candidates who are pro-gun, anti-health-care, and who not only want to cut aid to the poor but who are also tireless defenders of the wealthy? It would be like being a pro-Israel anti-Semite.

In the long run, nothing can withstand reason and experience,
and the contradiction religion offers to both is palpable.

—Sigmund "And the Sea Monsters" Freud[268]

The concepts of political conservatism and Christianity are irreconcilable. What Jesus were Republicans reading about? How does "love thy neighbor" translate into an interpretation of the Second Amendment that warrants the necessity to carry assault rifles in public? When did the meek inheriting the earth come to mean "the rich need tax relief"? Moreover, what part of a sane mind could possibly make routine twenty-first-century Republican sociological determinations in a Christian context?

---

[268] Notable-quotes.com, *Sigmund Freud*, http://www.notable-quotes.com/f/ freud_sigmund.html

The truth is, a rational person can't accommodate both Christianity and political conservatism.

Intercontinental Chump

It's dizzying how many tea party folks who cling to the lowest rung of the middle class—or less—have been convinced by twenty-first-century political televangelists that the source of their economic woes are those farther down the economic ladder. Many of the tea party proletariat, who show up to rallies in their floral-printed Walmart-bought housecoats and tri-cornered hats, are sadly already on some form of government assistance. Yet they are so easily manipulated by conservative media that they've been deluded into thinking that their voting decisions won't affect them.

> I got a letter the other day from a woman. She said, "I don't want government-run health care. I don't want socialized medicine. And don't touch my Medicare."

—President Barack Obama[269], patiently describing
what it's like to deal with tea party idiots

Members of the tea body politic have been conditioned to believe that the Dominionist GOP will protect them from the poor. What they actually need protection from are those whom they vote for. As such, tea party candidates "scapegoat" the indigent for our nation's economic problems, while it is the financial elite who are guilty of undermining our financial system for personal profit and siphoning from the middle class. Flag-waving idiots turn out to support their oppressors in droves—and to vote against their own best interests. And tea-lings are told that it's what Republican Jesus had in mind when he guided the hands who wrote our Constitution.

Irrational is the new patriotism.

---

[269] Huffingtonpost.com, *President Barack Obama*, ://www.huffingtonpost.com/bob-cesca/get-your-goddamn-governme_b_252326.html

The social anxiety directed toward the poor is so powerful that Christian politi-vangelists have also convinced tea partiers who vote for them that they need to help make the rich more wealthy than they already are by lowering their taxes past the record lows that they have been paying. Moreover, they say that it's time for the destitute to stop having it so damn easy. Pretty much the exact opposite of what Jesus of Nazareth preached.

Jesus, looking at him, loved him and said, "You lack one thing; go, sell what you own, and give the money to the poor, and you will have treasure in heaven; then come, follow me." When he heard this, he was shocked and went away grieving, for he had many possessions.

—Mark 10:21–22[270]

Tea-party evangelicals vote to cut Medicare, Medicaid, and school funding, raise the retirement age, and privatize Social Security for dumb shmucks like themselves. If one wants to be a good tea party Christian, one must also oppose poor people having access to public assistance of any kind. Likewise, the tea party demonizes health care and education. Simultaneously, those same individuals want more of their tax dollars going to military allocation, even though the United States already spends more than the next twenty-six countries combined, twenty-five of which are American allies.

Red, the blood of angry men. Black, the dark of ages past.

Like frogs in a kettle, the GOP electorate has been subjected to the economic temperature slowly being turned up over time. A farther-right discourse has been slowly introduced to working-class Republicans over the past thirty years, and many are finding it difficult to realize that their party has moved away from them. The Corporatist/Christian/Dominionist GOP now safeguards the best interests of an elite few.

[270] Holy Bible, *Mark 10:21-22*, Holy Bible. New International Version ®, Copyright © 1973, 1978, 1984, 2011 by Biblica, Inc.®

As it has been throughout history when religion and politics become one, a population is led to believe that a super-amazing space deity is watching over them to make sure that they stay chaste, humble, guilty, and obedient. It is always prescribed that we should follow the example of the affluent, who are thusly rewarded by the supreme cosmic honcho for acts of veneration. Gosh, the exceedingly wealthy are just swell.

As such, every Republican socioeconomic measure of frugality comes at the expense of the poor and the middle class.

I am not for raising taxes in a recession, especially when it comes to job creators that we need so desperately to start creating jobs again.

—Rep. Eric "We'll Just Make the Poor and Middle Class Pay for Everything Instead" Cantor[271]

Sure, Republicans complain about the deficit, but ignore the fact that the "job creators" are paying much less in taxes than when the economy was booming. Of course, those missing revenues gotta' come from somewhere, and it sure as shit ain't gonna be those who donate to Republican Superpacs.

And of course, the Democratic party is flawed, and in many ways, infuriating, too. I get that. But to be a working-class Republican in the twenty-first century, one must disregard reason and self-interest in favor of willful socioeconomic ignorance, if not one's own bigoted predispositions. Concerning sociology, economics, and the mechanisms that made this country great—when the very ideals the twenty-first-century GOP proposes are juxtaposed against the history of how theocracies impact the proletariat—there are no rational comparisons to be made between the blemished Democratic party and the irrational GOP.

---

[271] BrainyQuote.com, *Eric Cantor*, http://www.brainyquote.com/quotes/quotes/e/ericcantor413378.html

People feel like the system is rigged against them, and here is the painful part, they're right. The system is rigged.

—Dem. Sen. Elizabeth "You Can Say *that* Again" Warren[272]

As such, with the rise of evangelism in American politics, policy is affected thusly. When we elect people to public office who are so mentally and emotionally disturbed that they base their decision-making process on the psychotic wishes of an invisible macrocosm commander, then terrible socioeconomic things are bound to happen. History is replete with theocratic atrocities. Yet many Republican Americans are stupid enough to keep repeating those same mistakes and allowing themselves to be suckered by those who speak lyrical "godsmack."

In every country and in every age, the priest has been hostile to liberty. He is always in alliance with the despot, abetting his abuses in return for protection to his own.

—Thomas "Don't Fall for That Job Creator/Jesus/Freedom/ Tea Party Crap" Jefferson[273], in a letter to H. Spafford, 1814

Throughout history, every time religion has been the dominating political force, the aristocracy reigns—and the ranks of the poor swell. Most people suffer and die in needless poverty, while a scant few live in obscene luxury. Yet Christian fundamentalism is the prerequisite in the twenty-first-century GOP.

Alas, the only thing that the tea party proletariat might understand less than the Constitution is the Bible.

---

[272] Quoterature.com, *Elizabeth Warren*, http:// www.quoterature.com/elizabeth-warren-quotes/ people-feel-like-the-system-is-rigged-against-them-and

[273] Nobelifs.com, *Thomas Jefferson*, http://www.nobeliefs.com/jefferson.htm

False Equivalent

I stand for limited government, fiscal responsibility, personal freedom, personal responsibility, so the Republican Party will support me.

—Florida Governor and fiscal hypocrite Rick Scott[274], running through vapid tea party talking points

To the uninitiated, it all might seem the same.

Without a fundamental grasp of economics or sociology, our two-party political system might appear to be two sides of the same coin. Granted, in some ways both the political left and right are similar in their duplicity. However, in most ways, especially regarding the departure from the post-WW2 economic model that built the largest middle class in the history of Western civilization, only the twenty-first-century Republican party and its sympathetic media affiliates represent a fundamental divergence from the socioeconomic ideals that made America great.

With the discourse of the conservative entertainment complex driving the nation's narrative farther and farther right, the political middle has moved accordingly. As such, well-intentioned political centrists—in an effort to be a voice of reason in our nation's vitriolic partisanship—are finding themselves making socioeconomic concessions that just a few years ago would have been considered both irrational and far too extreme.

Today's center was yesterday's far right.

The dismantling of all of the socioeconomic mechanisms established between FDR and Reagan has become rationalized via right-wing/corporatist/theocratic platitudes. Vilifying the economic functions that created postwar America is a singularly Republican phenomenon. Suddenly,

---

274 BrainyQuote.com, *Rick Scott*, http://www.brainyquote.com/quotes/quotes/r/rickscott430976.html

whenever someone attempts to reintroduce legislation that worked prior to Reagan, they are called socialist, anticapitalist, or even un-American.

Yet there remains a concerted effort on the part of well-meaning social diplomats to attempt a political counterbalance. In the interest of fairness, some try to equate socially regressive, economically illiterate ravings routinely blathered from the GOP with whatever imbecilic dolt one can dredge from the left. Republican, Democrat, Toe-mate-toe, Toe-mah-toe.

But these are false equivalents.

For there is no twenty-first-century Democratic equivalent for the tea party and its less-than-sane, not too-bright, socioeconomic affirmations. Virtually every piece of legislation initiated by the tea/GOP during this millennium is designed to create a greater economic disparity between the very wealthy and everyone else. There is a consistent effort on the part of the Christian fundamentalist GOP to subjugate women, punish the poor, and make the working class bear the entire burden of economic cutbacks. The bastardizations of history, scripture, and science of the tea party have become standard talking points within the Republican party.

The "Occupy Wall Street" movement—which is believed by many to be the tea-party equivalent of the political left—not only couldn't get traction within the Democratic Party, it ran no candidates for public office.

What I believe is irrelevant.

—Tea party candidate and perennial punch line Christine O'Donnell[275], after being asked during a debate if she believes evolution is a "myth,"—which, as a creationist, she does, October 13, 2010

Moreover, there is no Democratic equivalent for the irrational ravings of the Conservative Entertainment Complex and its corresponding

---

[275] CBSnews.com, *Christine O'Donnell*, http://www.cbsnews.com/news/ christine-odonnell-my-views-on-evolution-are-irrelevant/

media affiliates. While MSNBC might be a ridiculously partisan public relations outlet for the left, Fox news has no equal in its fact-deficient moral bankruptcy or its unapologetic conjuring of fear-driven nonevents. Indeed, Fox News has an atrocious history of fabrication. It's not just that Fox presents "news" in a partisan fashion; it concocts "news" designed to create panic and paranoia among its viewers. Likewise, right-wing talk radio is inundated with hatemongering lunatics who tout paranoid schizophrenic platitudes. Rush Limbaugh, Mark Levin, Glenn Beck, Ann Coulter, and Alex Jones have no comparable cognitively compromised counterparts on the left.

> *Holocaust? Ninety million Indians? Only four million left?*
> *They all have casinos, what's to complain about?*
>
> —Rush Limbaugh[276]

What an asshole.

And there is no Democratic equivalent for the quasi-celebrities who continually get air time in the conservative talk-o-sphere. Across America, synaptically impaired conservative celebrities like Sarah Palin, Donald Trump, and Ted Nugent have become reality Tea-V stars by blathering irrational, baseless banalities. With a pedestrian socioeconomic perspective (at best), these dullards get regular spots on conservative TV and radio programs, and they get paid to speak at tea party rallies. There is no Democratic example of this.

> *I was in Chicago last week. I was in Chicago and said, "Hey, Obama,*
> *you might want to suck on one of these you punk." Obama, he's a piece*
> *of shit, and I told him to suck on my machine gun. Let's hear it for*

---

[276] Mediamatters.org, *Rush Limbaugh*, http://mediamatters.org/
       video/2009/09/25/limbaugh-on-holocaust-of-indians-they-all-have/155040

him. And then I was in New York. I said, "Hey, Hillary, you might
want to ride one of these into the sunset, you worthless bitch."

—Ted "Charmed, I'm Sure" Nugent[277]

Of course, certifiable right-wing nutcases like Ted Nugent are extreme examples. Obviously, no one elected to our legislature would ever be so irresponsible as to associate with someone like the Motor City Madman. Certainly, every representative of this great nation has enough respect for the Oval Office that he or she would never chum around with a psychotic nut like ol' "Suck on This" Ted, especially after he dishonored the office of the Presidency by menacing our nation's commander in chief.

Well, perhaps not:

I am excited to have a patriot like Ted Nugent joining me in
the House Chamber to hear from President Obama.

—Rep. Steve "Doesn't Really Understand Patriotism"
Stockman[278], from a press release about Nugent being
his guest at the State of the Union address

So I often hear from folks on social media that both Democrats and Republicans are "equally to blame" for our nation's economic woes and that neither party is interested in helping the middle class. But the socioeconomic reality is far from that comparison. I understand the noble intention of neutrality, but in this instance, it is misguided.

Eating vegetables can suck—but not as much as starving to death.

---

[277] Ibid., *Ted Nugent*, http://mediamatters.org/research/2014/02/14/10-misogynist-attacks-from-ted-nugent-greg-abbo/198061

[278] Businessweek.com, *Steve Stockman*, http://www.businessweek.com/news/2013-02-11/pro-gun-rocker-ted-nugent-to-attend-obama-speech

Let Freedom Bling

We say keep your change. We'll keep our God,
our guns, and our Constitution.

—Sarah "Ain't Got Time to Read" Palin[279]

With the historical revision of our founders' intentions regarding where and how Christian fundamentalism should play a part in our legislative process, debates like the ones that America settled years ago with the Scopes trial, or with *Roe v. Wade*, have reemerged.

As with every theocratic approach to governance, a fundamental item is that those in control must convince the proletariat to accept poverty willingly. The twenty-first-century Christian Dominionist approach is no different. The true genius lies in the lies. The most effective method, in the twenty-first-century, media-driven world in which we live, to brainwash Christian folks into accepting a disparity of wealth is presented in the form of tea party patriotism.

At the bidding of the mondo opulent, the conservative entertainment industry acquiesces to the Christian Dominionist philosophy in order to steer the Christian proletariat toward a desired end. A perversion of the meanings of "capitalism" and "liberty" is accompanied by an irrational demonization of "socialism" and "liberalism." And when you add in a side helping of Christian fundamentalism, this cacophony of poorly assembled, misunderstood, oversimplified, incomprehensible sociopolitical ideologies manifests itself as "tea party Libertarianism."

Ha! That's it! Hold it right there! ... Pronoun trouble.

—Daffy Duck[280]

---

[279] Prezi.com, *Sarah Palin*, http://prezi.com/lj-lvfvlq5jm/sarah-palin-great-speaker/

[280] Planetzot.com, *Daffy Duck*, http://www.planetzot.com/cartoon_quotes.php?id=359#.VBdwXRYXPf0

Many in the Dominionist-controlled tea party like to refer to themselves as "Libertarians." However, they are surely not. The tea-vangelical mantra claims to be about "freedom" and "liberty." Sadly, the goal they achieve is more the exact opposite.

America has allowed itself to become so star-spangled stupid that we've changed the political definition of the word *freedom* from "the ability for every American to peruse happiness via intellect, resourcefulness, and opportunity" to "free to be infirmed without the ability to receive proper medical treatment, free to remain impoverished as the mechanisms to establish a livable wage should be abolished, and free to be uneducated and thus cripple our chances for upward economic mobility."

For the record, one cannot be "free" if the statistical likelihood of escaping poverty is so remote that breaking the law is one's best option, nor can liberty be had from under a pile of medical bills. Poverty and the bondage of generational socioeconomic servitude are the exact opposite of freedom.

Moreover, the term *religious freedom* has been bastardized to mean "Christian freedom to usurp everyone else's freedom."

> *Now, the Libertarian Party, is a capitalist party. It's in favor of what I would regard a particular form of authoritarian control. Namely, the kind that comes through private ownership and control, which is an extremely rigid system of domination—people have to … people can survive, by renting themselves to it, and basically in no other way … I do disagree with them very sharply, and I think that they are not understanding the fundamental doctrine, that you should be free from domination and control, including the control of the manager and the owner.*

—Noam "a Fuckload Smarter than Glenn
Beck or Rand Paul" Chomsky[281]

---

[281] Quotes.yourdictionary.com, *Noam Chomsky*, http://quotes.yourdictionary.com/diametrically

For instance, Glenn Beck likes to refer to himself as a Libertarian. As such, he has a large group—those who comprise his cultlike viewership—who do the same. Granted, "Beck-ites" doesn't have much of a ring to it, and "Libertarian" is a much better marketing term than "psychotic, racist hatemonger." But self-identifying as Libertarians without truly understanding the precepts and the philosophies of Libertarianism is a convenient way for the tea party to express its cultural anxiety and ignorance.

How else could one explain the motivations of those willing to aid their economic oppressors achieve an Orwellian disproportion of wealth, as long as gays, poor, and brown people are punished more than they are?

Dumb Broads

All formal dogmatic religions are fallacious and must never be accepted by self-respecting persons as final.

—Hypatia[282]

Long ago, those who hoped to assume authority over the masses realized that he who controls the vagina, rules the world. Once you have dominion over the act of procreation, the process of controlling thought comes easily. Humans are sexual beings, and once religious guilt is applied to our sexuality and the accompanying thoughts that wander through our minds every few seconds, people are forced (subjugated by their Christian upbringing) to be ashamed of their natural inclinations. It's nuts, but it's effective.

As with most religions, Christianity forces women to bear the onus of guilt for carnal desire. Even when men oppose Yahweh's rules for lust—biblically speaking—women are to blame. I know this might come as a shock, but the entire Bible was written by men.

---

[282] Goodreads.com, *Hypatia*, http://www.goodreads.com/
quotes/605903-all-formal-dogmatic-religions-are-fallacious-and-must-never-be

Throughout the Bible, women are depicted as unintelligent, gullible, deceptive, difficult, emotional, sexually wanton, and evil temptresses who are inferior to men. Indeed, scripture asserts that women's sexuality is something to be punished: *"Also the daughter of any priest, if she profanes herself by harlotry, she profanes her father; she shall be burned with fire"* *(Leviticus 21:9)*[283]. It's almost as if the Bible was written by morons who lost their overtime money in a strip club.

The whole biblical shebang starts off with God's first rib-woman, Eve, being gullible enough to allow a reptilian shyster to convince her to eat a piece of forbidden produce. But if that wasn't enough, she coerces poor unsuspecting Adam by way of his raging hard-on to defy God's will as well. Original sin was obviously her fault. If it weren't for Eve's feminine wiles, Adam would have never thought to defy the great Star Lord, and we'd all be living in paradise with free cable and Wi-Fi today.

So it was necessary for Yahweh to establish women's place under male authority: *"To the woman he said, 'I will make your pains in childbearing very severe; with painful labor you will give birth to children. Your desire will be for your husband, and he will rule over you'"* *(Genesis 3:16)*[284]. And men have had biblical justification to reign over women ever since.

To offer an example of a woman who should be a much more prominent figure in history, if not for Christianity's view of her gender: Hypatia (370–415)[285] was a mathematician, astronomer, and philosopher. She was the daughter of scholar and mathematician Theon Alexandricus, and not nearly enough is known about her life. Yet Hypatia's legend is extraordinary, for her, or any age.

However living in the time that she did, intellect and free thought were not the type of Christian-friendly qualities that any woman should have. The

---

[283] Holy Bible, *Leviticus 21:9*, Holy Bible. New International Version ®, Copyright © 1973, 1978, 1984, 2011 by Biblica, Inc.®

[284] Ibid., *Genesis 3:16*.

[285] Lightscience.com, Hypatia, http://www.light-science.com/hypatia.html

Bible is specific in what a woman's role should be in society, and "intellectual with no interest in testosteronic mouth-breathers" ain't it. Thus, she was brutally raped and murdered by a Christian mob—her body violated and torn to pieces—for the crimes of being smart enough to call out men on their bullshit and being dumb enough to be female while doing so.

The story of Hypatia is both tragic and horrifying. But it is not alone in history. The biblical precepts that blame women—and by extension, their sexuality—for the ills of the society are many. Since Christianity's inception, the laws of man have had a significant gender bias. While it's not disputed that in years past, the parameters of the "crime" of female self-expression were more severe, that does not mean that the bias doesn't still exist in American legislation. In this century, it shouldn't exist at all. And with the onset of the Dominionist movement, the lawmaking of the evangelical GOP is replete with misogyny, attempts to control the act of procreation, and an antiwomen bias.

Feminism is a socialist, antifamily, political movement that encourages women to leave their husbands, kill their children, practice witchcraft, destroy capitalism, and become lesbians.

—Pat "He's Not Kidding" Robertson[286]

Since the psychotic examples of female subjugation and sexual blame/guilt in the Bible are many, elected members of the GOP blather twelfth-century sexism with moral vindication. Even Jesus's main squeeze, Mary Magdalene, had to have a moral return to chastity in order to be saved from the pits of hell. Fortunately, she knew a guy. So Christian Republicans—like theocrats before them—have no ethical dilemma when legislating concerning women's vaginas.

It's not like any of these laws will apply to them, anyway.

---

[286] Searchquotes.com, *Pat Robertson*, http://www.searchquotes.com/quotation/Feminism_encourages_women_to_leave_their_husbands,_kill_their_children,_practice_witchcraft,_destroy/178661/

Flintstone

The gals put it (an aspirin) between their knees, and it wasn't that costly.

—Billionaire Republican campaign contributor, and
complete douchebag, Foster Friess[287], explaining how
it's a woman's responsibility to remain chaste

We've seen what happens when men are asked to suppress their natural sexual inclinations. It doesn't usually work out. So the societal onus has been put on women to feel shame for having a libido. The sexual double standard in America is absolutely shameful for a nation that believes it sets the standard to which other nations should aspire.

Sexuality as a means to control the populace is inherently anti-woman. Patriarchy—as a societal trait—is more easily attained than other means of control. Virtually every culture that has contributed to the American melting pot/mosaic has to some degree added to the dynamic of male authority through the religious influences in the places they've immigrated from. Although the United States has made some great strides toward gender equality, we are still very sexually immature.

Surely there is a biblically inspired sexual sanctimony. Women are often "slut-shamed" and made the object of ridicule for promiscuity, whereas men are much more often excused for their predispositions. That is, unless a male indiscretion involves either homosexuality or texting dick pictures to women they meet on Twitter. Otherwise, boys will be boys, and if a woman has sex with more than one guy, she's a whore.

What does it say about the college co-ed (Sandra) Fluke who goes before a congressional committee and essentially says that she must be paid to have sex? What does that make her? It makes her a slut,

---

[287] Politico.com, *Foster Friess*, http://www.politico.com/blogs/burns-haberman/2012/02/foster-friess-in-my-day-gals-put-aspirin-between-their-114730.html

*right? It makes her a prostitute. She wants to be paid to have sex.
She's having so much sex she can't afford the contraception. She
wants you and me and the taxpayers to pay her to have sex.*

—Rush "Has Major Women Issues" Limbaugh[288], because having your
birth control covered by insurance is the same as being a prostitute

Few on the right even bother to mask their chauvinism anymore. Gender
discrimination—if not outwardly expressing disdain for women—has
become tea party policy. Few things are less obvious than Republicans
overcompensating for an inability to achieve an erection. How any woman
in this day and age can align herself with this group of vagina-phobes is
bewildering.

To offer another example of convoluted sexist logic stemming from
the Dominionist right—tea party darling, presidential hopeful, and
fundamentalist Christian Michele Bachman was asked how she could
reconcile the biblical role of "wife" to her effeminate, self-loathing, sissy-
Mary husband, Marcus, with being the person possessing nuclear launch
codes. Biblically speaking, the role of commander in chief and the role
of a wife—and she claims to believe in the Bible word for word—are
diametrically opposed. I mean, we hate to inconvenience Republicans with
their own hypocrisy, but you can't just turn off the crazy when it doesn't
play well on TV.

It's not an unfair question to ask a presidential candidate if we are in
fact, voting for her, or if her lisping, limp-wristed, dough-boy husband/
master would be calling the shots from behind the scenes. Especially when
Congresswoman Bachman had already confessed that her career path as a
tax lawyer was not one that she would have chosen herself. Rather it was
the choice of her butter-ball betrothed, to whom she submitted, as per the
Bible.

---

[288] ChicagoTribune.com, *Rush Limbaugh*, http://www.chicagotribune.com/
entertainment/zap-stupid-celebrity-comments-pics-049-photo.html

Wives, submit yourselves to your own husbands as you do to the Lord. For the husband is the head of the wife as Christ is the head of the church, his body, of which he is the Savior. Now as the church submits to Christ, so also wives should submit to their husbands in everything.

—Ephesians 5:22–24[289]

I'm in love with him. I'm so proud of him. And both he and I—what submission means to us, if that's what your question is, it means respect … I respect my husband. He's a wonderful, godly man, and a great father. And he respects me as his wife. That's how we operate our marriage.

—Michele "Ball Gag" Bachman[290]

I don't think that Michele Bachman understands the difference between the words "submit" and "respect." They are two utterly different words with completely different meanings that, in this context, mean the exact opposite from one another. Just as the words "Bachman" and "rational" are exact opposites of one another.

But submission is what being a good, tea party Christian woman is all about.

---

[289] Holy Bible, *Ephesians 5:22–24*, Holy Bible. New International Version ®, Copyright © 1973, 1978, 1984, 2011 by Biblica, Inc.®

[290] CNN.com, *Michele Bachman*, http://www.cnn.com/2011/OPINION/08/12/martin.bachmann.submission/

Viva la Zygote

People who are willing to stick to a strong pro-life position aren't going to be pushed off a strong antitax position. For people who like to think in ideologically cohesive ways, it makes no sense, but that's the way it is.

—Grover "Then Again, Nothing I Say Makes Any Sense" Norquist[291]

One issue that the current version of the tea party GOP likes to hang its Christian hats on is being "pro-life." Oddly, although a lot of tea party folks like to refer to themselves as Libertarians, the actual stance on the abortion issue from the Libertarian party is pro-choice. Then again, they say "Libertarian," but they really mean "Christian fundamentalist conservative." They say "life," but they really mean something else.

The thing is, "pro-life" policy is a cover for a whole lot of death.

Oh, sure; the goal might seem like something admirable at first glance. A "pro-life" movement of good Christian folks slut-shaming pregnant women to carry their unwanted embryos to term. The pro-life Christian coterie claim to be doing God's work by protecting potentially future humans at the expense of the women whose bodies—according to Christians—are no longer their own. That every sperm is sacred, every life is precious, and that God loves the tiny, unformed, undeveloped, unborn would-be babies.

The thing is, there is no greater abortionist than the Judeo-Christian God of the Old testament. Perhaps Christian Americans have forgotten that Yahweh himself gave orders to abort fetuses. Lots of em' in fact.

---

291 BrainyQuote.com, *Grover Norquist*, http://www.brainyquote.com/quotes/quotes/g/grovernorq613588.html

He sacked Tiphsah and ripped open all the pregnant women.

—2 Kings 15:16[292]

Even if they bear children, I will slay their cherished offspring.

—Hosea 9:16[293]

May the LORD cause you to become a curse among your people when he makes your womb miscarry and your abdomen swell.

—Numbers 5:21[294]

… And the Old testament God-sanctioned abortions just keep on comin'. None of this even takes into account how many children and pregnant women Yahweh drowned in the great flood or in the many military assaults he commanded, or how many human embryos never carry to term every single day in the course of human existence. The Almighty Baby-Killer is unrelenting.

Thousands of pregnant women and babies die every day. Where is Yahweh when this all happens? Is he busy directing the predominantly white male pro-life caucus about unborn Americans while ignoring the thousands of others who perish? And what about miscarriages? Wouldn't they be God's own abortions? Surely if the Cosmic Doctor gave a shit about the unborn, he'd have made uterine malfunctions impossible.

The facts bear out that the pro-life movement is not really about life at all. If it were, it would accompany a legislative push toward health care, education, and all of the things that accord living. Pro-lifers want babies to be born into existence, and after that, it's every infant for themselves.

---

[292] Holy Bible, *2 Kings 15:16*, Holy Bible. New International Version ®, Copyright © 1973, 1978, 1984, 2011 by Biblica, Inc.®

[293] Ibid., *Hosea 9:16*

[294] Ibid., *Numbers 5:21*

The pro-life movement is about enacting punitive measure on the poor, for the crime of being poor. And it's about punishing women for their sex. Just as Christianity has done to women and the poor throughout history.

Indeed, forcing women to give birth is a means to an economic end. The ripple effect of unwanted children is devastating, and it is a primary cause of poverty. The statistical chances of either a young mother or her child escaping economic disadvantage are remote.

But to make the pro-life motives even more transparent, Christian Dominionists also support practices that have been proven to be the *cause* of the very condition they claim to want to prevent. In Christian America, being pro-life also allows one to rationalize anticontraception and anti–sexual education as "encouraging" sexual activity. The reality is—the opposite is true. The Christian legislative position on these issues actually propagates unwanted pregnancies, rather than preventing them.

> *If these young women were responsible people and didn't have sex to begin with, we wouldn't be in this situation.*

> —NC Board of Commissioners Chairman and cutting-edge biological scholar, Ted "Two to Tango" Davis[295]

> *The causes of youth violence are working parents who put their kids into daycare, the teaching of evolution in the schools, and working mothers who take birth control pills.*

> —Rep. Tom "Duck for Cover" Delay[296], displaying a spectacularly obtuse sociological acumen

---

[295] Citizensforchoice.org., *Ted Davis*, http://www.citizensforchoice.org/the-real-cost-of-having-no-contraceptive-coverage-in-healthcare/

[296] BrainyQuote.com, *Tom Delay*, http://www.brainyquote.com/quotes/quotes/t/tomdelay402253.html

But if the hypocrites who call themselves "pro-life" Christians actually gave a shit about the unborn, they would not only support contraception and sex ed, but they would adopt. According to the Congress Coalition of Adoption Institute, in 2013 there are between 400,000 and 540,000 children in the United States without permanent families. About 115,000 of these children are eligible for adoption, today.

Yet to better frame the Christian hypocrisy regarding pro-life, there are approximately 153 *million* orphans around the world. There you go, pro-lifers … they're born. Now what?

And while I do realize that it's important to have a second car or season tickets to the Astros, I'm thinking that according to what American Christians claim as the tenets of their faith, maybe they should put their pro-life money where their mouths are. If Republicans truly cared about life, they would adopt some of these actual, born-into-this-world children. But they rarely do, because ultimately, most American Christians are full of shit.

Unless they adopt the rest of the liberal policies that give children a fighting chance to pursue the American dream, pro-life Republicans are Christians only insofar as they can justify sanctimony and self-righteous indignation through their faith. Many of these children will die. Many more will live in poverty. Tough luck. But at least pro-life Christians made sure they were born.

So sure, call the pro-zygote movement whatever you want. But it's surely not about preserving life. It's about making sure that as many economically disadvantaged people as possible will be born. Insuring generational poverty is a function of preserving the disparity of wealth, subjugating women, and keeping the proletariat uneducated and clinging to their religion. Claiming to be pro-life like calling McDonald's "pro-health" because they offer you a salad with your seven-hundred-and-fifty-calorie double quarter pounder with cheese.

Here kid, have a gun.

Righteous Copulation

I hate the word homophobia. It's not a phobia.
You are not scared. You are an asshole.

—Morgan Freeman[297]

Another very "un-Libertarian" social stance is the tea party/Christian view of gay marriage. But the Dominionist twist allows for the irrational assertion that somehow gay Americans asking for the same rights and privileges that heterosexual Americans have in some way diminishes the rights of straight people. If you test crash helmets for a living, this should make perfect sense.

But we get it. The Judeo-Christian Yahweh hates when the same kind of genitals interact. It's made perfectly clear in the Bible. As such, it is incumbent upon good Christian folks to enact God's penis phobia. Being gay is against nature, even if there are examples of same-sex relationships throughout nature. However, shrubbery that dispenses life-coaching instructions is a perfectly natural occurrence.

If a man has sexual relations with a man as one does with a
woman, both of them have done what is detestable. They are to
be put to death; their blood will be on their own heads.

—Leviticus 20:13[298]

But although the Bible specifically says gays are bad, this is becoming a tougher sociological position to defend on a daily basis. Most people in the twenty-first century know people who are gay and have figured out that the genetic suppositions of Bronze Age goatherds is not a viable way

---

297   Newnownext.com, *Morgan Freeman*, http://www.newnownext.com/
      morgan-freeman-twitter-homophobia-gay/08/2012/

298   Holy Bible, *Leviticus 20:13*, Holy Bible. New International Version ®,
      Copyright © 1973, 1978, 1984, 2011 by Biblica, Inc.®

to establish social policy in modern Western civilization. It's fairly obvious that gay people are among us, and, shockingly, we have not crumbled as a society.

It (same sex marriage) not only is a complete undermining of the principles of family and marriage and the hope of future generations, but it completely begins to see our society break down to the extent that that foundational unit of the family that is the hope of survival of this country is diminished to the extent that it literally is a threat to the nation's survival in the long run.

—Rep. Trent "Hyperbole" Franks[299]

Anything else you care to toss in there, Trent?

As for the acerbic rhetoric that Christian Dominionists try to use to mask gay-hating bigotry, none of the anti-equality assertions appeal to anyone with the slightest sense of logic. Not one of the reasons Christians offer as a basis for denying same-sex couples equal rights and privileges under the law stands up to the simplest tests of logical scrutiny. Which is why invariably, good, hate-filled Christian folks revert to their default setting of "Because God says so" when confronted with civil rights as it applies to the Constitution.

Of course when doing so, Republicans expose themselves as Dominionist propagandists, intolerant, bigoted, and with little concern about Jefferson's and Madison's wall of separation between church and state. Each rationalization for wanting to deny same-sex couples equal rights under the law is as unconstitutionally lame as the next. Morgan Freeman is right. They are assholes. And it's becoming apparent to more people every day.

---

[299] Rightwingwatch.org, *Trent Franks*, http://www.rightwingwatch.org/content/rep-trent-franks-calls-marriage-equality-threat-nations-survival

*In every society, the definition of marriage has not ever
to my knowledge included homosexuality.*

—Rick "Puts the 'Dick' in Dictionary" Santorum[300]

For instance, the "We don't want to change the definition of marriage" argument is utterly inane. First of all, in America, marriage is defined by a commitment of love, not Yahweh. No one is changing the *definition* of marriage, merely who is allowed to marry. The definition remains the same; the only thing that changes is the exclusion of certain Americans from equal rights under the law.

In Christian terms, the simple fact that, despite biblical precedent, we do not require a woman to marry her rapist, and we no longer allow that a man can sell his daughter for a milk cow, means that we've already changed the "definition" of marriage. The fact that women have rights means that we've changed the definition of marriage. Just that it's become a felony to hit your wife means that we've changed the definition of marriage.

And all for the better.

We have changed the definition of marriage much in the same way that we've changed the definition of "freedom" as it applies to person ownership. Americans are no longer "free" to own slaves, because, as it turns out, that is a slight imposition on the freedom of the person who is enslaved. So we figured out that societal redefining is not such a bad thing when the existing definition unconstitutionally discriminates against some of our fellow Americans.

Yet, according to biblical precepts, divorce is also a no-no in the eyes of God. *"'I hate divorce,' says the LORD God of Israel" (Malachi 2:15)[301]*.

---

[300] ABCNews.go.com, *Rick Santorum*, http://abcnews.go.com/blogs/
politics/2012/01/rick-santorum-in-the-hot-seat-again-for-gay-marriage-stance/

[301] Holy Bible, *Leviticus 20:13*, Holy Bible. New International Version ®,
Copyright © 1973, 1978, 1984, 2011 by Biblica, Inc.®

Thou must remain married and miserable for eternity. However many hetero-Christians are damned if they're going to make these lifelong commitments for life. We're sure that Yahweh gives good Christian straight folks a few passes when defying biblical percepts—as long as they're not playing heinie hockey.

> *Or do you not know that wrongdoers will not inherit the kingdom of God? Do not be deceived: Neither the sexually immoral nor idolaters nor adulterers nor men who have sex with men.*

—Corinthians 6:9[302]

Adulterers? Idolaters? Then again, why take biblical passages so literally when they affect heterosexual males? Even though Yahweh specifically denounces anyone who has been married more than once, cheated on his or her spouse, or has ever knuckle-shuffled to Baywatch reruns as also having defied his wishes, the important thing is to focus on the gays. Because Christian Dominionism is a male-dominated sociopolitical dynamic, and just look at the tits on Pam.

But the psychological denial of Christian bigotry as it pertains to coded douche-baggery goes even farther …

For neither does the "morality" argument make sense to anyone who has the slightest grasp of what actually constitutes morals. By attaching a moral implication to the manner in which consenting adults fornicate—let alone whom they love—the "morality" argument attempts to mask bigotry by bastardizing the concept of morals, it changes the premise of the discussion from one that is based on civil rights under the Constitution to one that must tether to ethereal, third-party oversight. Indeed, if people's morals are dependent upon an intrusion into people's bedrooms in order to establish that sexual activity be in accordance with the Judeo-Christian God's carnal ideals, then their morals suck.

---

[302] Ibid., *Corinthians 6:9.*

*If we cannot have moral feelings against homosexuality, can we have it
against murder? Can we have it against other things? I don't apologize
for the things I raise. … I'm surprised you aren't persuaded.*

—Supreme Court Justice Antonin Scalia[303], during
Princeton University appearance, 2012

In fact, gay people are no more, or no less, moral by the nature of their
sexual predispositions than anyone else. How we treat our fellow human
beings is what truly defines morality. And on that basis, Christian
fundamentalists fail miserably.

Another bit of sensational gay-hating stupidity is the Christian axiom of
"Don't hate the sinner; hate the sin." Well, gee willikers, thanks a diaper-
load, good Christian folks for not actually hating gay people, but just their
genetic makeup. Christians don't hate gays, they just hate who they are.
Right. Gotcha. Now go fuck yourselves.

Yet Christian bigots rarely recognize themselves as such, and thus these
rationalizations make sense to them. By comparing consensual adults
engaging in same-sex marriage to pedophilia and bestiality, fundamentalists
bare themselves as homophobic dullards. But because bigotry and stupidity
are subjective, they don't see it that way. For anyone who needs an
explanation of why those comparisons are not only invalid but hateful is
truly beyond reason. Yet these are the types of arguments continually made
by Dominionist members of the Republican Party.

---

[303] ABCNews.go.com, *Justice Antonin Scalia*, http://abcnews.go.com/
Politics/OTUS/justice-antonin-scalias-provocative-comments-gay-issues/
story?id=18791020&page=2

Then why not have three men and one woman, or four women and one man, or why not somebody has a love for an animal? There is no clear place to draw the line once you eliminate the traditional marriage.

—Rep. Louie "Sharp as a Bowling Ball" Gohmert[304], who apparently doesn't understand the meaning of the word "consent"

Sadly, these were the same retrospectively ignorant arguments made against interracial marriage in 1967. When the Supreme Court ended all race-based marital restrictions in the now-famous *Loving v. the State of Virginia* case, where Richard Loving, a white man was sentenced to a year in prison for marrying Mildred Loving, a black woman. These same arguments were made by those who hoped to deny interracial marriage. Today we mock those ignorant, racist assertions, just as we will those making the case against same-sex marriage years from now.

Truly, the only impact the gay couple down the street has had on my hetero-marriage is that their superior landscaping has undoubtedly raised the property value of my home.

DOMA and the GOP

AIDS is not just God's punishment for homosexuals; it is God's punishment for the society that tolerates homosexuals.

—Rev. Jerry "Cuddles" Falwell[305]

Today, the Republican Party finds itself in a difficult circumstance regarding same-sex marriage. The GOP has backed its members into a corner: they can either try to defend the indefensible or dissent from

---

[304] NyDailyNews.com, *Louie Gohmert*, http://www.nydailynews.com/news/politics/texas-rep-compares-gun-limits-animal-sex-article-1.1306602

[305] Theholyatheist.com, *Rev. Jerry Falwell*, http://www.theholyatheist.com/great-quotes

party-line bigotry. It is an unenviable choice. But nevertheless, it is what the Dominionist influence on the party has left them.

The "Defense of Marriage Act" (DOMA) more accurately should have been titled the "God Hates Fags Act" since it wasn't actually *defending* any heterosexuals' rights. It was designed specifically to deny gay Americans the same rights and privileges that heterosexuals have. But more specifically, *Section 3* of DOMA codified the nonrecognition of same-sex marriages for all federal purposes, including insurance benefits for government employees, Social Security survivors benefits, immigration, and the filing of joint tax returns. It was written into legislation that same-sex couples had different rules applied to them.

In case anyone is wondering what applying a different set of standards to selected segments of society is more commonly referred to as, it's called discrimination. Hence the Supreme Court's 2013 decision to overturn Section 3 of DOMA.

Since then, the Dominionist, evangelical wing of the GOP has come out in force to denounce the SCOTUS decision, allowing for no pretense of church-state separation while renouncing marriage equality as defying the will of the Judeo-Christian God. Sadly but predictably, the evangelical right is forcing the party's discourse toward rationalizing Medieval predispositions and reciting bigoted platitudes. Congresswoman Michele Bachman and former governor of Arkansas and now Fox News pundit Mike Huckabee—to name just two—were both defiant, and adamant about their disapproval of marriage equality. The former erroneously asserted that *"Marriage was created by the hand of God"* (Um, no, stupid, it wasn't), while the latter offered the supposition that *"Jesus wept."* Ugh.

This is the sociological quandary that the GOP finds itself in. Do members capitulate to the Dominionist base and their less-than-rational assertions, or do they acknowledge that every American citizen is entitled to equal rights under the law? Is it possible for some within the GOP to articulate that denying equal rights is not a right unto itself? Do they allow the bigoted predispositions of their lunatic fringe to dictate policy to the party's detriment? Or does this become a wedge issue *within* the Republican party?

Ironically, before it became law in 1996, DOMA was a bipartisan bill engineered by House Republicans led by then-speaker (R) Newt Gingrich and signed into legislation by none other than (D) President Bill Clinton. Hilariously, the thrice-married Gingrich and the convicted marital-vow-breaker Clinton were the key figures in protecting the cherished institution of matrimony. An institution, which by all statistical accounts, long ago had its reverence forsaken by heterosexuals like Clinton and Gingrich.

> *I did not have sexual relations with that woman.*

—Bill "Chubby Chaser" Clinton[306], lying about having received
a blow job from Monica Lewinsky in the oval office

> *She (Jackie Gingrich) isn't young enough or pretty*
> *enough to be the president's wife.*

—Newt "Three Times a Charm" Gingrich[307], talking
about his first wife after divorcing her

The truth is that, despite the rhetoric about the sanctity of marriage needing to be preserved, traditional marriage was always based upon patriarchy. Of course, by "traditional," the evangelical right means that, in biblical terms, a wife is to be obedient to her husband. In a "traditional" marriage, women have a subservient role to play, as defined by the scriptures, which is what's implicated when the Christian right harkens back to "better days." Cooking, cleaning, and baby-making.

---

[306] Washingtonpost.com, *Bill Clinton*, http://www.washingtonpost.com/wp-srv/
politics/special/clinton/stories/update0126.htm

[307] Huffingtonpost.com, *Newt Gingrich*, http://www.huffingtonpost.
com/2012/03/21/newt-kayne-quotes-who-said_n_1369829.html

The reality is that the Christian right's assault on same-sex marriage has a collaterally negative effect on women as well.

But the hypocrisy from the so-called traditional marriage purists runs deeper than their bias against women and gays. The denial of how traditional marriage has failed in the post "women should be barefoot and pregnant" world is matched only by the ignorance it takes to defend an institution that boasts a dismal 50 percent divorce rate as something "wholesome." An even more alarming fact is that, like Gingrich's and Clinton's poor excuses for traditional marriages, many hetero-couplings that survive a litigious end are replete with extramarital indiscretions.

For a more detailed analysis of how and why traditional marriage is obsolescent and an exposition of secular relationship viability, see my book, UnLearn Vanilla Marriage.

—Rich Woods

However, since the signing of DOMA into legislation, the Democratic Party has wisely modified its position on same-sex unions to coincide with the zeitgeist. Which is what a government by the people and for the people is *supposed* to do. While their motives may be politically feckless, Democrats have nevertheless acquiesced to reason regarding the lack of constitutionality regarding marital discrimination. Likewise, today Republican voters are faced with a choice: side with bigots and homophobes or defy their party.

Still, the GOP is defending the Defense of Marriage Act the way that racists in 1967 defended the Racial Integrity Act. Both sets of arguments against operate from the premise that who and how we love is not germane to the precepts of liberty, and moreover, are subject to Christian doctrine. Thankfully, the Supreme Court disagreed on both accounts. Regardless of whatever excuse one uses for wanting to deny certain Americans equal marital rights and privileges due to their sexual orientation, the American consensus no longer allows for such rationalizations constituting a "different opinion."

The only reason why anybody would want gay people to not marry is either they're dumb or they're secretly worried that dicks are delicious.

—Joe Rogan[308]

In the second decade of the twenty-first century, it is generally understood that making antigay assertions defines one as a bigoted asshole. But despite everything leading up to, and including, the striking down of Section 3 of DOMA, there is a much more important issue, and one that should never have allowed the debate to get this far.

The striking down of Section 3 of DOMA is what separates us from the backward, twelfth-century xenophobes we're at war with in the Middle East. Just as America improved itself when we abolished slavery, gave women the vote, and allowed Richard and Mildred Loving to marry, so we did on June 26, 2013, when the Supreme Court struck down Section 3 of DOMA.

However it is inherent within the nature of humanity to forget the travails from eras past—those who suffered, sacrificed, and even died so that their children's children might lead a better life—and give back to our former oppressors that which we've fought so hard to gain.

Thumbless Mitts

We need to stop being simplistic, we need to trust the intelligence of the American people and we need to stop insulting the intelligence of the voters.

—Gov. Bobby "But You Can't Insult the Intelligence of Idiots" Jindal[309]

Following the 2012 pasting that the Republican Party took in the national elections, Louisiana Governor Bobby Jindal's instinct for political

---

[308] Favstar.fm, *Joe Rogan*, http://favstar.fm/users/joerogan_quotes
[309] Politico.com, *Bobby Jindal*, http://www.politico.com/news/stories/1112/83743.html

self-preservation cajoled him into publically proclaiming that the GOP had to stop being the "party of stupid" (his words). It is an admirable sentiment. Governor Jindal is, in fact, an exceptionally smart guy, and that comment was most probably prompted a crisis of conscience. How long can smart people like B-Jin dumb-down their vernacular to court votes? Especially when doing so keeps costing his party national elections?

Except that despite Governor Jindal's proclamation about the GOP's relationship with willful ignorance, he continued to capitulate to his evangelical overseers by supporting the teaching of creationism alongside evolution *as science* in public schools. In consecutive breaths, the Republican governor makes an urgent call for reason within his party, and then contradicts himself by defending a purposeful misrepresentation of science, and more importantly, the scientific method.

Stupid is, as stupid does, Governor Jindal.

Repackaging Bible stories as "intelligent design" is part of a collaborative Christian endeavor to undermine the very process by which we garner knowledge. It's not just that Christian Republicans are crazy and/or stupid enough to believe the biblical story of creation, they want to *legislate* that it be taught in science class. Throughout the predominantly fundamentalist Christian South and Midwest, school board members attempt to hijack curriculum with an obtuse paranoia. Apparently, a bunch of godless smart people have conspired to fool good Christian folks with "science." Very crazy, very stupid people are trying to determine what children should be taught.

> *The Bible teaches that God made land animals on day six, alongside of Adam and Eve.*

—Ken "Needs an Instruction Manual to Breathe" Ham[310], who must've not understood the sarcasm in chapter two of this book

---

[310] CBSnews.com, *Ken Ham*, http://www.cbsnews.com/news/design-vs-darwin/

Christian fundamentalists continue to reintroduce the fact-deficient notions of creationism. Rejecting the scientific consensus about the age of our universe and indisputable proof of common genetic ancestry, these scientific illiterates claim that it's all just made-up nonsense. It is with pride that they assert that the fairy tale in the Old Testament about a six-thousand-year-old earth created in six days by an erstwhile thumb-twiddling Yahweh deserves equal time in our children's science classrooms. For some inexplicable, rationality-defying reason, this debate—long thought settled—is still continuing in the twenty-first century. It would be like teaching that Narnia is a real place in geography class.

And for every one of these school districts that have raving loons promoting (un)intelligent design, there are elected officials who are in agreement.

I believe that dinosaurs are not only in the Bible, but they have lived with man all through his six-thousand-year history.

—Kent "Rock Pile" Hovind[311], in his unintentionally hilarious dissertation from an unaccredited academic institution

I don't believe that the earth's but about nine thousand years old. I believe it was created in six days as we know them. That's what the Bible says.

—Rep Paul "Straight from the Pit of Hell" Broun[312]

The thing is—and if you don't already understand this, please shoot yourself—evolution is a determination arrived at through years of research and gathered evidence that has exponentially increased in the years *since* Darwin's death. The embodiment of the scientific community—through

---

[311] Believersnonbelievers.wordpress.com, *Kent Hovind*, http://believervsnonbelievers.wordpress.com/2014/01/10/top-10-quotes-from-kent-hovinds-doctoral-dissertation/

[312] Mediate.com, *Paul Broun*, http://www.mediaite.com/online/gop-house-science-committee-member-evolution-big-bang-%E2%80%98lies-straight-from-the-pit-of-hell%E2%80%99/

peer review and authoritative scrutiny—have come to embrace these theories, and some elements of Darwinian law only remain categorized as "theory" because we cannot physically travel back in time. To offer some perspective, gravity (also once opposed by the church) is also still a scientific theory.

Well, the jury is still out on evolution, you know.

—George W. "Not Crazy, Just Stupid" Bush[313]

Actually, the jury on evolution came back a long time ago. The earth is approximately four and a half billion years old. Human beings share a common genetic ancestry with other mammals. These are not suppositions or vaguely formulated hypotheses. These are peer-reviewed facts supported by millions of pieces of genetic, geological, astronomical, and biological evidence. They are indisputable for anyone who is not either a complete lunatic, or too stupid—like George W. Bush, Ken Ham, Paul Broun, or any of the myriad of religious fundamentalists—to admit that basic science is beyond their ability to understand.

How the first president of the twenty-first century was elected despite not having achieved basic scientific literacy is a staggering indictment of how Dominionism has affected our political process.

Moreover, Dominionist Christians only want *their* version of creation taught to the impressionable blank slates occupying public school classrooms. No one promoting this drivel is also suggesting that along with the biblical story, the similar tale written in the Koran also be taught. Nor do they suggest that the stories of origin of our species in the book of Mormon or Scientology be taught.

Nope, because *that* would be crazy.

---

[313] iWise.com, *George W. Bush*, http://www.iwise.com/L5pf3

With satellites orbiting our planet, the Dominionist-led Republican party is attempting to disregard the scientific method and retry the Scopes trial without having garnered any evidence since. This is possible because the Dominionist steering of the Republican thought process has discouraged rational people from remaining tethered to a party that doesn't seem to know the difference between delusion and reality. Lunatics and ignoramuses are what now comprises the GOP base, and they want a fairy tale taught in public schools as science.

What was that you were saying about the *"party of stupid,"* Gov. Jindal?

Demonizing Academia

*All truths are easy to understand once they are
discovered; the point is to discover them.*

—Galileo Galilei[314]

What Kepler and Copernicus theorized, Galileo proved. The sun—not the Earth—was the center of our solar system. For his efforts in discovering this truth (which every grade school child understands today) Galileo was rewarded by the Pope with being forced to denounce his work publically, under threat of torture, and spending the remainder of his life under arrest. Discovery that conflicted with scripture was considered blasphemous, regardless of truth.

And so it is in certain parts of America today. The fight against knowledge doesn't begin and end with trying to teach creationism to impressionable young people. It continues through every level of academia.

---

[314] BrainyQuote.com, *Galileo Galilei*, http://www.brainyquote.com/quotes/quotes/g/galileogal136976.html

Those who control the access to the minds of children will set the agenda for the future of the nation and the future of the Western world.

—Dr. James "Get Kids Hooked on Jesus While They're Young, Because They'll Never Believe This Bullshit Once They Grow Up" Dobson[315]

As the tea-vangelical movement takes over total control of the Republican Party, there has been a concerted effort to impose a sixteenth-century-style suppression of academics via policy. Thanks to a barrage of antieducation platitudes—worded so as to convince the tea party proletariat that higher education is more accurately labeled liberal propaganda designed to disinform the masses by using science and liberalism to steer good Christian folks away from biblical truth—there is now a rationalization among GOP voters that allows for a whole bunch of intellectual concessions.

A significant portion of our country now denounces higher-level academics as a matter of party-line protocol, which is explained via conservative, monosyllabic diatribes on cable news.

(Teachers are) inculcating students in the precepts of the Socialist Party of America—as understood by retarded people.

—Ann "Ironic That She Should Mention Retardation" Coulter[316]

But the motivations behind these attacks on education are much more sinister than one might think. Just as during the Medieval Inquisition, the constraining of knowledge is being portrayed as something other than what it is. Since evangelical Christian politicians can't come right out and say, "we want to keep you less educated so you'll be more easily manipulated, and therefore easier to control," they attack the institutions of higher learning under the guise of "fiscal responsibility." As if there is

---

[315] Newsvine.com, *Dr. James Dobson*, http://ttruth3829683.newsvine.com/_news/2012/05/21/11783432-the-religious-right-is-the-american-taliban
[316] Godless The Church of Liberalism, *Ann Coulter*, http://www.randomhouse.com/book/32459/godless-by-ann-coulter

anything fiscally responsible about reducing the earning potential of the populace by denying or distorting their education. Academics (or, more accurately, educating people) within the Republican economic stratagem is simply not worth the investment.

Well, the world needs ditch diggers too. Lots of em'. Because ditch diggers tend to go to church.

To make educational matters worse in the predominantly Christian, red-state South, there are no laws to mandate that medically accurate information be taught in sexual education classes. The results have been significantly higher teen pregnancy rates than in the blue-state counterparts. In fact, the top ten states for unwanted teen pregnancies in 2013 were Mississippi, New Mexico, Texas, Arkansas, Oklahoma, Arizona, Louisiana, Kentucky, Tennessee, and South Carolina ... which are all Christian red states. But the Christian tea party can't allow reality to seep into its method of counter-education when it defies their pedestrian interpretation of biblical precepts.

I will tell you, it is three agencies of government when I get there that are gone. Commerce, Education, and the ... what's the third one there? Let's see.

—Gov. Rick "Oops" Perry[317], in the presidential debate moment when
he became a national punch line by forgetting his own platform,
stating that he would eliminate—along with the departments
of Commerce and Energy—the Department of Education

For the record, Gov. Perry's state of Texas has below-average math and science scores.

Yahweh apparently wants abstinence through blind obedience, not via choices made through understanding reproductive facts. However, crippling education is really a means to steer the zeitgeist. The Dominionist

---

[317] CBSnews.com, *Rick Perry*, http://www.cbsnews.com/news/
rick-perry-fails-to-remember-what-agency-hed-get-rid-of-in-gop-debate/

endeavor—as has been the case throughout history when Christianity vies for political power—is to create poverty and sociological strife among the masses. It is not (as they are claiming) in the instance of abstinence-only education, to avoid unwanted pregnancies, or, in the example of Christian-based charter schools, to offer more learning options.

Amazingly, the Republican education strategy is working perfectly. With the easy access to media in the twenty-first century, the most effective method of deriding education has proved to be convoluting the meanings of sociopolitical terminology. In some cases, it is to apply an ignominious insincerity to these terms and mean the exact opposite of what one says.

Inverse terminology is how Dominionists can sell the attack on education to the red-state Americans who need it most. For instance, teaching children facts about science and history in public school is now being referred to by the Christian proletariat as "indoctrination," whereas actually indoctrinating them with factually inaccurate versions of these same subjects is being referred to as "freedom." Freedom to remain ignorant, I guess.

But in order to control the masses, one must keep them not only uneducated—but wary of those who are. Republicans have even gone so far as referring to academics as "elitists" and "snobs" in order to create hostility between middle America and institutions of higher learning. There is actually a pervading sentiment in the tea party that—in twenty-first-century America—there should be no reasonable expectation for college graduates to find employment. How dare they.

> *President Obama once said he wants everyone in America to go to college. What a snob.*

—Rick "the Bible Is Better Than College" Santorum[318]

---

[318] Newsfeed.com, *Rick Santorum*, http://newsfeed.time.com/2012/03/01/class-notes-rick-santorum-college-snobs-and-more-education-news/

We've seen what happens when people become educated. The middle class and the economy grow. Generations prosper. The wealth gap is significantly more equitable. The quality of life is appreciably better. That is the socioeconomic opposite of what any theocracy in history has endeavored to create.

Indeed, an appropriate monetary distribution is the theocratic ruling class's worst nightmare. So the tea-vangelical GOP has rebranded its educational policy to equate to: *Lack of knowledge is power.* By vilifying scientific and sociological edification, Dominionists can keeps facts away from those who vote for them. The march backward, toward a twelfth-century sociological power structure, requires nonthinking, unquestioning, uneducated, easily manipulated Christian soldiers.

The Kin-yun So-sha-list wants ta destroy 'Murrica.

The very basis for Christian fundamentalism is derived from the story of what happens when one seeks knowledge. In the book of Genesis, Adam and Eve's fall from grace occurred when they defied God by eating fruit from the *forbidden tree of knowledge of good and evil.* Despite this particular topiary being denominated like it was named by Kim and Kanye, it stands as a warning to Christians that comprehension defies Yahweh. Fear of knowledge is the very premise from which Christianity operates.

Those signs carried by Christian hatemongers should more accurately read "God hates facts."

To further this anti-education madness in the middle of the second decade of the twenty-first century, interest rates on college tuition loans have doubled. Universities are becoming more out of reach, for more Americans. And even if one can attain a tuition loan, there's a distinct possibility that financial ruin awaits.

He who opens a school door, closes a prison.

—Victor *"Les Miserables"* Hugo[319]

Despite the direct correlation—both individually and communally—between education and prosperity, there has been a tea-vangelical-inspired socially conservative movement in America to circumvent the process by which we garner knowledge. It begins with teaching grade-school children that women were created from the first man's rib, and it ends with denying entrance to the institutions where they might learn otherwise. It is nothing short of Christian right-wing social engineering.

There is a reason why scientists, and intellectuals—AKA "smart people"—tend to shy away from the Christian-led GOP. Academics stand for everything that those who would profit from an uneducated nation are afraid of. Because socioeconomic fairness, empowering women, scientific literacy, and general knowledge are to Christian fundamentalists what sunlight is to vampires.

As such, being afraid of the dark, while irrational, is one thing. But being afraid of the light is quite another.

Behind the Curtain

It's easier to fool people than to convince them they have been fooled.

—Mark Twain[320]

When one considers how, despite the economic reality that the wealth gap between the top 1 percent and the rest of the country is wider than at any time in America's history, even while tea/GOP voters are under the

[319] BrainyQuote.com, *Victor Hugo*, http://www.brainyquote.com/quotes/quotes/v/victorhugo104893.html

[320] Dailyatheistquote.com, *Mark Twain*, http://dailyatheistquote.com/atheist-quotes/2013/09/25/mark-twain-easier-fool-people/

inurbane impression that our nation is becoming more and more "socialist," I would venture to guess that most probably don't realize what their lack of understanding has gotten our nation into. Since the merging of the Republican Party with Christian fundamentalism, there has been a slow, but systematic, dismantling of Thomas Jefferson's and James Madison's wall of separation between church and state. Rather than be the nation born of the Enlightenment, the Christian-led GOP is—among other things—revisiting the 1925 Scopes trial and making sure that women make babies. But as bigoted and backward as GOP domestic policies are, there is certainly an even more wicked intention to their madness.

All of this socially regressive Christian legislation is a means to an economic end.

While subjugating women, discriminating against gays, attacking science, demonizing academia, and the myriad other twelfth-century GOP social policies are Dominionist goals unto themselves, they are also part of an overall socioeconomic plan that ultimately leads to a preponderant amount wealth going into fewer hands.

> *By cutting wasteful spending, strengthening key priorities,*
> *and laying the foundation for a stronger economy, we have*
> *shown the American people there's a better way forward.*

—2012 Vice Presidential nominee, Rep. Paul "Good Catholic" Ryan[321], explaining how cutting Medicare, Medicaid, Social Security, food stamps, education, medical research, and student loans, while increasing defense spending and drastically lowering taxes for the wealthiest 1 percent of Americans, amounts to the cacophony of banal hyperbole in his idiotic, morally indefensible budget

What part of anyone's sensibilities allows them to believe for one second that the same group of Christian theocrats who promote such regressive

[321] Paulryan.house.gov, *Paul Ryan*, http://paulryan.house.gov/news/documentsingle.aspx?DocumentID=374793#.VBigPRYXPf1

social policies are concerned with anyone's economic interests but their own? What kind of detour through one's synapses does a thought have to take in order to formulate the failed logic that tea-vangelicals will be different from every other group of Christian fundamentalists throughout history? All through mankind's recorded past, an aristocracy was created every time religion has been the political standard bearer. Every fucking time.

> *As believers, we are called to action, not to sitting quietly*
> *and hiding our faith under a bushel, but to stand*
> *and speak no matter what the consequences.*
>
> —Ted "Less Jefferson, More Jesus" Cruz[322]

Indeed, the Dominionist legislative agenda goes beyond the issues themselves. It's easy to be distracted when fighting individual battles for reason against overtly ignorant religious fundamentalists, but Christian Dominionism is ultimately about establishing a theocracy—and the power that it accords—here in the United States. They say Jesus, but they mean money and control.

So it's easy for a casual Christian or someone who identifies with the Republican Party to disagree with the policies of the lunatic fringe and mistakenly determine that a Christian monument on public property is not a big deal. But it is, because it's never just about the monument. The fight is for maintaining the wall of separation between church and state—and against religious incursion into our legislative process.

This might even seem paranoid. Heck, What's the big deal if you can't buy liquor before noon on the Lord's day? So what if we teach creationism alongside evolution in science class? Who cares if gays can marry? The big deal is that all of these issues transcend themselves and are a part of a greater body politic.

---

[322] Christianpost.com, *Ted Cruz*, http://www.christianpost.com/news/ ted-cruz-to-liberty-u-students-defend-your-religious-freedom-117292/

All of these Christian-based legislative issues are germane to the more important political goal of how a theocracy works. Sure, gay marriage and a woman's right to choose are important civil rights issues in and of themselves, but they become more important when juxtaposed against the economic and power division that accompany a theocracy. Ultimately, the goal of any church-run state is to own everything—including you. Dominionists—as Christian theocrats before them—begin by trying to control thought via "nationalism" and an irrational hatred of the government.

A sense that, with the blessings that God bestowed upon this land, came the responsibility to make the world a better place.

—Marco "Yahweh Likes America Best" Rubio[323]

And before you mistakenly think to yourself that a theocracy could never happen here in America, realize that most of the South and Midwest of the United States are already under Dominionist legislative control. The gaggle of intellectual oafs that constituted the 2012 Republican primary was wrought with Christian fundamentalism. Elections are won by Christian politicians who say things that should warrant them having supervision when they eat their pudding.

And legislation is affected thusly.

Moreover, theocracies exist all over the Middle East today. Entire nations oscillate back and forth between the twenty-first and the twelfth centuries, for no other reason than the people who live there have been convinced that an all-powerful overseer demands that they capitulate to his will as explained through the Koran. Those at the top of the religious aristocracy live in obscene wealth. Poverty and ignorance are used as the tools to keep the population in place.

---

[323] BrainyQuote.com, *Marco Rubio*, http://www.brainyquote.com/quotes/quotes/m/marcorubio418966.html

A tea party tidal wave is coming.

—Rand "That's the Problem, Stupid" Paul[324]

Realize that the only differences between an American and some poor Islamic slob who has been taught to believe that fresh and salt water don't mix because it says so in his holy writ, are geography and the name they calls their god. And the only way that the Dominionist Christian Republican Party can get so many people to willingly support theocratic legislation that defies the Constitution, discriminates against their fellow Americans, and promotes an Orwellian economy, is to psychologically manipulate them into hoping for a payoff after they are dead.

And God blessed them. And God said to them, "Be fruitful and multiply and fill the earth and subdue it, and have dominion over the fish of the sea and over the birds of the heavens and over every living thing that moves on the earth."

—Genesis 1:28[325]

Allahu fucking akbar.

---

[324] Ibid., *Rand Paul,* http://www.brainyquote.com/quotes/quotes/r/randpaul446147.html

[325] Holy Bible, *Genesis 1:28*, Holy Bible. New International Version ®, Copyright © 1973, 1978, 1984, 2011 by Biblica, Inc.®

CHAPTER 7
Ethical Schizophrenia

(Exactly What You Think Will Happen When Maniacs Provide a Moral Compass)

When you say "radical right" today, I think of these moneymaking ventures by fellows like Pat Robertson and others who are trying to take the Republican Party and make a religious organization out of it. If that ever happens, kiss politics good-bye. Every good Christian ought to kick Falwell right in the ass.

— Barry Goldwater[326] in response to Moral Majority founder Jerry Falwell's opposition to the nomination of Sandra Day O'Connor to the Supreme Court, of which Falwell[327] had said, *"Every good Christian should be concerned."* …

---

[326] Liberalslikechrist.org, *Barry Goldwater*, http://www.liberalslikechrist.org/about/Goldwater.html

[327] Reason.com, *Jerry Falwell*, http://reason.com/archives/2007/07/31/jerry-falwells-paradoxical-leg

Many on the political right speak of morality, but alas, very few understand its meaning. That just might be because the moral standard-bearers for Christian America consistently exhibit an utter lack of morality, and do, in fact, bastardize the concept to coincide with their twisted sense of right and wrong. And it's accomplished via a convenient conflation of Old Testament Yahweh and New Testament Jesus.

The concept of the Holy Trinity brings about a seamless moral merging. So when one's idea of morality stems from a supreme being who gives orders to cut open the stomachs of pregnant women, rape virgins, own slaves, and wipe out entire populations, it can be easily justified through the exalted Bambino. Truly, the concept of morality—in the name of "family values" Christian conservatism—has been hijacked by people with none.

It is long past the time that the word *morality* be taken back by people with actual morals.

Puppeteers

A while back, leaders of the Republican Party decided that it was in their best interest to court the voting sensibilities of Americans who fill stadiums to hear obscenely wealthy evangelical preachers editorialize the wishes of Yahweh via carefully chosen biblical passages. Short term, it was a good idea. Long term, who knows? But now, the craziest of the Christian crazies not only lobby the White House in attempts to erode the wall of separation between church and state, conservative Republicans are forced to lobby *evangelical preachers* for *their* endorsements. The relationship between the GOP and the evangelical lobby has gotten so turned upside-down that it's become like parents asking their spoiled child for approval before making a decision.

It's fucknut kooky.

Although there have always been Christian fundamentalists trying to impose their will on our nation, in the twenty-first century, fanatics are exerting more political influence over Republican legislators than ever before. However, the evangelical beast has become too big for the GOP to control. Sure, there are ratings to be had on conservative TV and radio, regional elections to be won by touting Christian platitudes, and donations to be pocketed from a fearful Christian proletariat ... but the political cost has been that the according irrationality and incomprehension have become impossible to contain.

Now, lunatics on the pulpit make and break GOP party leaders. In order to be a twenty-first-century Republican politician, one is not only forbidden to speak of science, one is also barred from exhibiting his or her own conscience if it doesn't abide fundamentalist precepts. Instead, they are confined to the depraved version of morality—as it is applied to social legislation as defined by the evangelical lobby.

As an example, there is no longer such a thing as a "pro-choice" Republican. In the conservative lexicon, the word "moderate" is usually followed by the word RINO. The kicker is that it's not the morals of New Testament Jesus that steer the conscience of the GOP, but rather the economics of theocrats, the business of religion, and the disproportionate division of wealth and power they accord.

> *I will preserve and protect a woman's right to choose and am*
> *devoted and dedicated to honoring my word in that regard.*

—Mitt "I'm Not So Bad for a Republican" Romney[328], in a 2002 gubernatorial debate in the very blue state of Massachusetts

---

[328] Politifact.com, *Mitt Romney*, http://www.politifact.com/ truth-o-meter/statements/2012/may/15/mitt-romney/ mitt-romney-evolved-significantly-his-position-abo/

Do I believe the Supreme Court should overturn Roe v. Wade? Yes, I do.

—Mitt "So Much for Dedication and Honor" Romney[329],
trying to keep up with the far right nuts he was running
against during the 2012 Republican primaries

It's undeniable that the evangelical lobby has become the driving sociological force behind how the tea/GOP legislates. However, the Republican electorate seem blind to this, as their concepts of politics and morals have become distorted to fit with their own biases.

As such, Christian Americans are provided with biblical sound-bites to help them justify very "un-Christ-like" behavior from GOP leaders. For even if one is inclined to excuse the socioeconomic nonsense that pours from the pie-holes of elected lunatics like Scott Walker or Ted Cruz as "political conservatism"—or from Glenn Beck or Sean Hannity as "fair and balanced journalism"—they'd still have to downshift their cognitive Edsels into an entirely new delusional gear in order to rationalize the psychotic ravings from multimillionaire evangelical preachers as having any connection to the New Testament Jesus.

Yet that's what the cycle of conservative psychosis has yielded.

And if they're (Native Americans) not going to negotiate with things like the Geneva Treaty or other rules of civilization, you still have to secure the life and the property and the protection of your citizens.

—Evangelical Christian political powerhouse and revisionist
historian David Barton[330], explaining why the mass killing

[329] Rollingstone.com, *Mitt Romney*, http://www.rollingstone.com/politics/news/what-president-romney-would-mean-for-women-20120515

[330] Rightwingwatch.org, *David Barton*, http://www.rightwingwatch.org/content/david-barton-explains-just-war-theory-we-had-destroy-indian-tribes-until-they-became-civiliz

of American Indians was kosher in the eyes of the Christian God … because sometimes wars are righteous

Mega-churches the size of auditoriums are filled with emotionally needy believers who've been indoctrinated into subjugation. These are not your typical Christmas/Easter church-goers. Ruthless profiteering occurs at the expense of mega-church attendees who are simply trying to cope with the frightening world around them by putting their trust in celestial real-estate salesmen. And as bad as the financial toll on these gullible slobs is, the intellectual and emotional tolls of allowing one's self to submit to cultlike piety are even greater.

The Christian Dominionist rhetoric from both the political and church pulpits has become virtually identical. The evangelical Christian and political conservative doctrines have departed little, if at all, from one another. Yet the cognitive dissonance of Republican voters rarely makes that correlation.

However, many Republican voters outside of the Beltway *do* realize that evangelical preachers are (at best) insincere, if not incapable of comprehending a literary metaphor. Yet, when it comes time to pull the voting lever, most ignore the similarities between Republican politicians and televangelist shysters. It has become common practice within the GOP to conflate biblical law with the Constitution.

Freedom of religion doesn't mean freedom from religion.

—Texas Governor and intellectual giant Rick Perry[331]

---

[331] Examiner.com, *Rick Perry*, http://www.examiner.com/article/
gov-rick-perry-freedom-of-religion-doesn-t-mean-freedom-from-religion

We would create law based on the God of the
Bible and the ten commandments.

—Former Alaska Governor Sarah "Conservative Snooki" Palin[332]

I don't know that atheists should be considered as citizens, nor should
they be considered patriots. This is one nation under God.

—Former President, and he of the mighty sperm,
George Herbert Walker Bush[333]

Jesus died for our freedom, and Jesus destroyed Satan
so that we could be free and that is manifested in what
is called the Constitution of the United States.

—Former house majority leader and *Dancing*
with the Stars contestant Tom Delay[334]

As such, Dominionists in both the public and private sectors no longer have to pretend that their political goal is anything less than totalitarian. Many on the conservative right come right out and state their intentions as such. The GOP talk-o-sphere is replete with public and private sector conservatives proudly stating that the United States should adopt "biblical law."

Those predisposed to abide the conservative entertainment complex are not inclined to consider the consequences of Christian Sharia.

---

[332] Huffingtonpost.com, *Sarah Palin*, http://www.huffingtonpost.com/2010/05/10/sarah-palin-american-law_n_569922.html

[333] Positiveatheism.org, *George Herbert Walker Bush*, http://www.positiveatheism.org/writ/ghwbush.htm

[334] ABPnews.com, *Tom Delay*, http://www.abpnews.com/culture/politics/item/8977-tom-delay-says-he-s-on-divine-mission

Religious factions will go on imposing their will on others unless the decent people connected to them recognize that religion has no place in public policy. They must learn to make their views known without trying to make their views the only alternatives.

—Barry "Rolling Over in His Grave" Goldwater[335]

One-time conservative standard-bearer, and retroactive RINO, Senator Goldwater warned the Republican Party about the very political dynamic of the fundamentalist Christian theocrats usurping the party of Lincoln. Now the GOP is being dictated to by crucifix-wearing racketeers who demand that anyone who runs for office with an (R) in front of their name must be willing to deny basic history and science. That they must—in the name of "Christian morality"—do everything they can to prevent women from obtaining birth control, deny gays equal rights, and restrict the ability of many children to have adequate access to education health care and food—that is, once they've already made sure that said children have been born into poverty.

However, just as historical and scientific reality is not what evangelical Christians say it is, neither are their morals. For that matter, neither are their economics. But that's what the Republican Party has become. An evangelical-like selling of an invisible product and the promise of prosperity. Certainly, Dominionists don't give the God-fearing electorate the truth, rather merely what they want to hear.

Indeed, if conservative media and politicians are intertwined in reciprocal cycles of fact deficient, irrational socioeconomic assertions, then the Christian evangelical lobby is the source from whence the crazy and stupid came.

---

[335] Motherjones.com, *Barry Goldwater,* http://www.motherjones.com/politics/2004/09/faith-system

West Shied Story

If a man has sexual relations with a man as one does with a
woman, both of them have done what is detestable. They are to
be put to death; their blood will be on their own heads.

—Leviticus 20:13[336]

There is one particular Dominionist bedfellow that has created a revulsion
within the GOP, to the point where it's like they've awoken to a regrettable
romantic interlude after a rough night drinking.

On a public relations front, sometimes a political message can become
inadvertently equated with an undesired element. Unintentional
socioeconomic associations—when made by the public—can be
embarrassing when one is trying to create a winning political brand. Still,
"image" comparisons between political brands are often easy enough to
make when there is a distinct similarity in tone, and terminology.

However, despite a few semantic discrepancies, or variations in willingness
to employ discretionary vernacular, the evangelical-fundamentalist-
Christian message is synonymous with the GOP brand. Which is why,
throughout the conservative lexicon, it is rare when the moral imperatives
of Christianity are debated *within* the Republican Party. Routinely, those
who reside on the political right support one another when assigning
biblical precedence while legislating. Fearing "moral" retribution from
within their own party, no one of political significance in the tea/GOP
differs from those who espouse Christian fundamentalism.

But there is one hilarious exception.

Unless you've recently arisen from cryogenic stasis, you might have heard
of a delightful group of good Christian folks whose tiny church resides

---

[336] Holy Bible, *Leviticus 20:13*, Holy Bible. New International Version ®,
Copyright © 1973, 1978, 1984, 2011 by Biblica, Inc.®

on the west side of Topeka, Kansas. Founded by a grandfather-like fella, the late Pastor Fred Phelps—and presently led by his charming daughter, the ever-engaging Shirley Phelps-Roper—this church and its members are dedicated to bringing the message of divine superintendence through a literal interpretation of the Bible. Better known as the Westboro Baptist Church, they have become famous for their firebrand method of saving Christian souls, their brand of morality, and their unique patriotism. And en masse, the GOP rebukes the WBC, for all the wrong reasons.

The across-the-board castigation of the Westboro Baptist Church from the political/Christian right is moral hypocrisy at its side-splitting best. Although evangelicals, Republicans, and conservative media denounce the Westboro Baptist Church for its acerbic hate speech, or for picketing tragic events as a means to express Yahweh's anger at America for allowing secularism, the overall Christian message from the church and from the rest of the Christian right is virtually the same. Sure, the folks who made "God Hates Fags" so right-wing chic are more vitriolic in their speech than most biblical purists. But if it weren't for Fred and Shirley's unwillingness to be tempered by political correctness and the lack of diplomacy they use when speaking their minds, the majority of the things that they say, and what the twenty-first-century GOP says, are virtually identical.

> *These fags are going to hell, and instead of squawking like crybabies, they ought to be so thankful that at no expense to them, we've dedicated time and resources to preach to them.*

—Pastor Fred Phelps[337]

---

[337] Huffingtonpost.com, *Pastor Fred Phelps*, http://www.huffingtonpost.com/joshua-kors/god-hates-fags-qa-with-pa_b_689430.html

Homosexual conduct is, and has been, considered abhorrent, immoral,
detestable, a crime against nature, and a violation of the laws of nature
and of nature's God upon which this Nation and our laws are predicated.

—Alabama Supreme Court Chief Justice Roy "Makes
Fred Phelps Seem Tolerant" Moore[338]

From the literal interpretation of the Bible, to the condemnation of gays, to the irrational disdain for President Obama, to blaming tragedies on divine retribution, to the denial of science in favor of what the Bible says, the WBC and the tea/GOP have no moral departure from one another. But the good folks at the Westboro Baptist Church won't play according to the rules of American politics. They don't bother to mask their hate speech with conservative code. Neither do they make overtures to disguise the crazy and stupid moral assertions that blab from their vapid traps.

So the tea/GOP mustn't allow its voting base to make the legitimate correlation between themselves and the WBC. Because it might allow the more Christian-casual members of the Republican body politic to realize that they've been voting for xenophobes and lunatics. Indeed, the Westboro Baptist Church has unwittingly exposed how crazy and stupid one has to be in order to reference the Bible for science, history, or morality. And doing so has become part of the tea/GOP platform.

But in a way, you gotta love the Westboro Baptist Church—via an unintentional satire of the fundamentalist Christian tea/GOP—its members have managed to shed light on the psychosis of twenty-first-century conservative politics.

---

[338] Au.org, *Justice Roy Moore*, https://www.au.org/church-state/
march-2002-church-state/editorial/alabamas-mullah-moore

One Card Monte

(In the universe it may be that) Primitive life is very common and intelligent life is fairly rare. Some would say it has yet to occur on Earth.

—Stephen Hawking[339]

There are scam artists who separate people from their money all over America. Self-proclaimed "psychics" who convince desperate, grieving people that they can communicate with recently deceased loved ones, for a price. Online scammers, gold-diggers, con artists, astrologers, and pyramid-schemers all manage to take money from people by promising things that they have no chance of (or in some cases, no ability) to deliver. And while a fool and their money are soon parted, not all those who are taken advantage of are fools. Some simply have their trust betrayed.

There were very bright people who had their savings taken from them by Bernie Madoff.

However, there is a name for taking money from people under false pretenses. It's called fraud. That's why Madoff went to jail. He promised financial returns that he knew that he had no chance of delivering. But there are many schemes where the false pretenses under which money was stolen are not as readily acknowledged by the law.

Such is the case with televangelists and big-money evangelical preachers. The thing is, for some reason, religion—and Christian evangelicals in particular—get a pass where bullshitting people out of money is concerned. For that matter, they seem to get a legal free pass regarding child molestation, too. If rampant kid touching by Catholic priests doesn't warrant criminal prosecution, conning people—tax free—out of money sure as shit won't raise any legal red flags. The obvious fraud of religion is

---

[339] Goodreads.com, *Stephen Hawking*, http://www.goodreads.com/author/quotes/1401.Stephen_Hawking

distinguished from other types of criminal misrepresentation in the eyes of the American legal system.

Those of you who do not give up everything you have cannot be my disciples.

—Jesus "Blond and Blue" Christ, Luke 14:33[340]

Filthy rich "prosperity" preachers who convince financially struggling people to send them money, while they shamelessly display their wealth, are replete within the evangelical preach-o-sphere. Prosperity evangelists promise that Yahweh will reward those who donate toward helping make themselves limo-riding, Lear-jet-flying, Ric Flair opulent. According to the "prosperity" contingent, it is the will of Jesus "moneybags" Christ that all decent, gun-owning, liberal-hating Christians have a nice car, a lovely home, a big TV, and a mattress full of money. All they have to do to cash in on Jesus bucks is display their faith by forgoing education and health care—and sending their favorite preachers what little money they have.

Then, for that small investment, the promised return will be enormous. If not in this life, then the rewards will come in the next one. Tough luck if you didn't survive long enough to collect your earthly payoff. But thanks for the donations.

As you use your faith, God is going to wipe out your credit card debts.

—Zillionaire Televangelist Mike Murdoch[341], telling his viewers that for a donation of a mere $1,000, the Lord will take care of those pesky credit card bills

---

[340]   Holy Bible, *Luke 14:33*, Holy Bible. New International Version ®, Copyright © 1973, 1978, 1984, 2011 by Biblica, Inc.®

[341]   Christianpost.com, *Mike Murdoch*, http://blogs.christianpost.com/ridiculous-reads/10-crazy-quotes-from-televangelists-17444/

Some people get mad when I talk about money. They says
"Whenever I see Dollar, he's talking about money!" That's
because you ain't got none, I ain't talking to you!

—The aptly named Rev. Dr. Creflo Dollar[342], explaining that
if you can't help him pay for his jet, his mansion, his Rolex, or
his limo, he can't be bothered with your sorry, tired old ass

However, as the message of a celestial reward system via bribery not only
defies biblical scripture, but would also be impossible to facilitate, one
can reasonably determine that prosperity preachers are lying, fraudulent
scumbags. Yet many of these hustlers share a stage with Republican
candidates in the hopes of helping them garner votes. It's like being
endorsed by Tony Soprano.

Contrary to what evangelical preachers would have you believe, morality
cannot exist when one believes in an eternal punishment and reward
system. If one does good deeds out of a belief that he or she will be
rewarded—either in this life, or the afterlife—there is nothing moral
about those deeds. Rather, they were done selfishly. True morality stems
from one's inner sense of empathy, propriety, and willingness to make the
world a better place through one's own understanding of right and wrong.

As such, religion and morality are incompatible. When a people of faith do
something moral, they do so despite their faith, not because of it. If they
only reason that you don't act like an asshole all the time is because you
believe that a transcendental Jiminy Cricket will send you to the celestial
toolshed if you don't obey his boss's divine wishes, then those very same
voices in your head can also make you rationalize terrible things in the
name of that same religious morality.

---

[342] Safeguardyoursol.com, *Dr. Creflo Dollar*, http://jesus.safeguardyoursoul.com/
html/creflo_dollar.html

So, although the common misconception is that only idiots can be conned, the truth is that few, if any, of us are above falling prey to someone who betrays our trust. Where Christian evangelism is concerned, considering the sheer number of Americans who identify themselves as "Christians," the seeds of betrayal were planted from when we were all children by our parents, as they were planted by their parents before them. So by the time Christian Americans reach voting age, many are predisposed to being hoodwinked by amoral, evangelical con men.

But these are *magic* beans.

Superstar

Beginning the parade of preaching-from-the-pulpit scumbags who have influenced national policy is evangelical elder statesman, the mad-as-a-March-hare Rev. Billy Graham. Since the moment that the elder Graham was invited into the White House by then-President Ronald Reagan in order to court morons for their votes, the Republican Party has never been the same. Indeed, Rev. Billy Graham was not only among the first to use television to make the revival tent from which he preached cover a national audience, he was a pioneer in using the pulpit for political propaganda.

In fact, many believe that the not-so-right Reverend Graham set the intolerant tone for the Bible-bashing predators who followed him:

> The word "tolerant" means "liberal," "broad-minded," "willing to put up with beliefs opposed to one's convictions," and "the allowance of something not wholly approved." Tolerance, in one sense, implies the compromise of one's convictions, a yielding of ground upon important issues. Hence, our tolerance in moral issues has made us soft, flabby, and devoid of convictions. We have become tolerant about divorce; we have become tolerant about the use of alcohol; we have become tolerant about delinquency; we have become tolerant about wickedness in high

places; we have become tolerant about immorality; we have become tolerant about crime and we have become tolerant about godlessness.

—Rev. Billy Graham[343], from his book, *The Sin of Tolerance*

Indeed, Reverend Graham makes an excellent point. People with the ability to reason, and who wish to aid those needlessly suffering around the world, should no longer tolerate the hate-filled bigotry of those who claim they're doing the will of God. Graham speaks of morals, yet he—and the rest of the conservative Republican Christian club—display none. Intolerant bigots like the Reverend Billy Graham should be condemned, vilified, and publically embarrassed for the routine lack of compassion and empathy they display, as well as their willfully ignorant denial of science. Evangelical Republicans need to be exposed for their propensity to favor the wealthy in an extremely un-Jesus like manner.

True *morality* demands that voluntary incomprehension, backward social policies, and the inequitable division of wealth condoned by the twenty-first-century GOP be denounced. However, I doubt that Reverend Graham—in his self-righteous myopia—ever considered that his words could, and should, be applied to his own bigoted worldview as well.

The same sensationally obtuse sense of actuality holds true for the "other" Reverend Graham, Superstar Billy's runt of the litter, Franklin. They say that certain traits skip a generation. Apparently, a talent for perfidy and monetarily capitalizing on the misplaced trust of others is not one of them. For if it was Rev. Billy Graham who set the bar for evangelical preachers to influence national policy, his shit-for-brains son Franklin Graham is the acorn fallen from the mighty dope.

---

[343] Billygraham.org, *Billy Graham, The Sin of Tolerance,* http://billygraham.org/story/the-sin-of-tolerance/

> *But the more you listen to him (Donald Trump), the*
> *more you say to yourself, you know, maybe this guy's right*
> *(for the office of president of the United States).*

—Rev. Franklin Graham[344], displaying his razor-sharp political acumen

Still, with a net worth of tens of millions of tax-free dollars, Rev. Billy Graham has sat at both the right hand of Yahweh and whatever Republican president was in office during the height of his celebrity. The same can be said for his witless spawn. Those at the top of the GOP food chain claim to have relied on the counsel of both Grahams. However the reality is, by "counsel," I really mean instructions. For no Republican politician seeking national office makes a move without first getting the approval of, if not directions from, the Evangelical lobby. And those who suffered the presence of the Graham crackers were no different.

... And with a lifetime audience that exceeded two billion Jesus-lovin' dolts, who could blame them?

Cashews, Pistachios, and Almonds

> *I distrust those people who know so well what God wants them to*
> *do because I notice it always coincides with their own desires.*

—Susan B. Anthony[345]

After the Graham patriarch established a prosaic Christian presence in the GOP, the crazy train into the White House went full steam ahead. In the years following his holiness, Saint Reagan, more and more evangelical leaders found themselves being sought after for their public endorsements.

---

[344] ABCnews.com, *Rev Franklin Graham,* http://abcnews.go.com/Politics/franklin-graham-trump-candidate-choice/story?id=13437543

[345] BrainyQuote.com, *Susan B. Anthony,* http://www.brainyquote.com/quotes/quotes/s/susanbant403780.html

The merging of evangelism and the Republican Party is what gave rise to Christian Dominionism.

But the Dominionist movement, in its early stages, had a lot of help. Coinciding with the advent of the personal computer and most Americans' obtaining Internet access, and cable news creating an entertainment venue out of politics, evangelism became a political force to be reckoned with. Groups of Jesus-lovin', liberal-hatin' Christians from all over the country started to communicate in chat rooms (and now on Facebook) about Jesus, our "Christian founders," and whom to hate and whom to vote for.

Of course, as it has been whenever religious fervor and zealotry dominate the discussion, things became acrimonious and fearful rather quickly. The Internet helped allow the Christian conservative discourse to spiral out of control. The darkness of Medieval fundamentalism came back with a vengeance. And in 1996, a fledgling media organization called Fox News capitalized on a growing Christian fanaticism and further amped up the Jesus mania.

To the surprise of no one, the market share for crazy and stupid was significant.

So, with the help of the Internet and the conservative entertainment complex, the ensuing departure of the Republican Party from sanity and toward evangelism was evident. Men like Liberty University founder, the Reverend Jerry Falwell—once considered the lunatic fringe—became mainstream Republicans.

The idea that religion and politics don't mix was invented by the Devil to keep Christians from running their own country.

—Liberty University founder and carbohydrate
lover, the late Jerry Falwell[346]

---

[346] Ibid., *Jerry Falwell*, http://www.brainyquote.com/quotes/quotes/j/
jerryfalwe389309.html

Invented by the devil? In case you are wondering, this was not said in jest. This maniac spoke these words with a straight face, and with the intention of communicating how those who oppose tearing down the wall of separation of church and state are in league with Satan. The above statement should make perfect sense, provided one's mother and sister are the same person.

But of course, a ponderous clod like Falwell felt like he had to say crazy-assed shit like this in order to convince idiots that they were voting on the side of righteousness. It meant more money in his pocket, more power over his flock, and more influence in the Republican Party. And once evangelicals were able to tap into new revenue streams via the GOP, it meant that to a person, it was in their financial, and political best interest to give Thomas Jefferson and James Madison a postfactum kick in the 'nads.

The competition to out-Jesus one another for national attention is fierce:

> *The Lord had some very encouraging news for George Bush.*
> *What I heard (from God) was that Bush is now positioned*
> *to have victory after victory and that his second term is going*
> *to be one of triumph, which is pretty strong stuff.*

—Televangelist Pat Robertson[347], displaying his impressive Kreskin skills

In this fabulous quote, the televangelist tells his audience about a private conversation he had with Yahweh, where he was told by the great space kahuna that George W. Bush was going to have a kick-ass second term. It was to be smooth sailing for the Bush-ster, as guaranteed by the voices in Pat Robertson's head. Apparently the Christian God forgot to mention that the economy would collapse in 2007. Oops, forgot about that one, did we lord?

---

[347] Au.org, *Pat Robertson,* https://www.au.org/church-state/february-2005-church-state/people-events/god-tells-pat-robertson-expect-a-good-year-for

But nevertheless, George W. Bush was the kind of good Christian leader that the evangelical lobby liked to have sitting in the big chair.

God has called us to be His representatives in our nation and in our world. Select candidates who represent your views, and work for their election.

—James Dobson[348], founder of Focus on the Family,
Time Magazine's "most influential evangelical leader,"
and big-time SpongeBob SquarepPants fan

Few White House evangelicals have had as much political clout as James Dobson. he is a White House regular. Although perhaps not as outwardly psychotic (and as a result, slightly less famous) as some of his Christian brethren, his fundamentalism makes him no less irrational. Dobson has simply not been as prone to as many "WTF" moments as most of his fellow science denying associates. He has rarely said the outrageous things, that say, Robertson or Falwell have … unless of course you count this:

My observation is that women are merely waiting for their husbands to assume leadership.

—James Dobson[349], who obviously associates
with different women than I do

Really J-Dob? Not-so coincidentally, it's been my observation that you are a misogynist douche bag. One might think that Mr. Dobson—being a psychologist—would have the presence of mind to compensate for an inability to achieve erection with more subtlety than this. Then again, that seems to be another Republican staple.

---

[348] BrainyQuote.com, *James Dobson*, http://www.brainyquote.com/quotes/quotes/j/jamesdobso182577.html

[349] Ibid., http://www.brainyquote.com/quotes/quotes/j/jamesdobso182573.html

Long for Yesterday

*The greatest tragedy in mankind's entire history may
be the hijacking of morality by religion.*

—Arthur *"2001: A Space Odyssey"* C. Clarke[350]

When one needs to defend the morally indefensible, a third party in the form of a supreme being is required. Being chosen by one's god to enact earthly discipline has been the rallying cry for dictators and tyrants throughout history. This simple scam has gotten humans to do morally reprehensible things to one another for thousands of years.

How else could one justify horrible acts of violence as morality? How else—for instance—could an entire culture celebrate when a young man straps a bomb to himself and kills a mall full of people? How else could any nation decide to invade a foreign land? How could anyone morally defend such barbarism, if not for it being the will of God?

This blessed attack revealed the real hypocritical face of the West.

—Ayman al-Zawahiri[351]

Christians, like slaves and soldiers, ask no questions.

—Rev. Jerry Falwell[352]

---

[350] Ibid., *Arthur C. Clarke,* http://www.brainyquote.com/quotes/quotes/a/arthurccl141085.html

[351] NWsource.com, *Ayman al-Zawahiri,* http://search.nwsource.com/search?offset=20&topic=Nation&from=stnv2&similarto=STEvents%3A2018313000

[352] BrainyQuote.com, *Jerry Falwell,* http://www.brainyquote.com/quotes/quotes/j/jerryfalwe382343.html

While the immoral precepts of American evangelism don't conjure the visceral reactions we experience when we see body parts strewn across a market, the net effect is not as different as one might think. Until the socioeconomic mechanisms of the latter part of the twentieth century were woven into legislation, millions died needlessly. Many Americans, impoverished and without the proper health care, or the education to know better, or decent working conditions, or without retirement savings, suffered and died prematurely.

Both poverty and bombs kill children.

Yet the economic mechanisms legislated after the Great Depression—which gave rise to America's middle class—are the very same socioeconomic precepts that the Christian Dominionist movement has already begun dismantling in the years since Reagan. So, while the inhumanity of a dead child on the evening news at the hands of terrorists is indeed horrifying, the loss of the lives of American children who die in poverty is no less tragic. Both are preventable. Both occur at the hands of others, and both are the net result of rationalizing God's morals.

> *It's no wonder, with that kind of intense training and disciplining,*
> *that those young people are ready to kill themselves for the cause of*
> *Islam. I wanna see young people who are as committed to the cause*
> *of Jesus Christ as the young people are to the cause of Islam. I wanna*
> *see them as radically laying down their lives for the Gospel as they are*
> *over in Pakistan and Israel and Palestine and all those different places,*
> *you know, because we have ... excuse me, but we have the truth!*

—Becky Fischer[353], Pentecostal minister and Harry Potter
hater, musing about how great it would be for Christian kids
to have the same commitment as Muslim kids who blow
themselves, and innocent people around them, to bits

---

[353] Mustwatchfilms.com, *Becky Fischer*, http://www.mustwatchfilms.com/videos/jesus-camp/

Morally speaking, twenty-first-century Republicans are much different from their twentieth-century predecessors. Which to say that Republicans used to exhibit the kind of morality that sane people do. At one time, the GOP would have never thought to unilaterally cut domestic programs and burden the working class with economic austerity while extracting capital from general welfare and giving it to the top fiscal 1 percent. They would have never done so on moral principles. There was a time when Republicans thought Social Security and Medicare were good ideas.

Sure, Republicans—real Republicans—feel that there are too many social programs that are mired in red tape and amount to an ineffective application of our tax dollars and that responsible government spending should be reflected in a judicious tax application, not a burdensome one. Republicans have always been a voice of reason when addressing the bloated bureaucracy of government. But there was a time when the ideas of abandoning the impoverished, neutering the federal government, and handing control of our legislature and economy to the wealthy elite would have been considered ludicrous within the GOP.

The ideological and moral disparity prior to Ronald Reagan was not such that Republicans and Democrats were so irrationally diametric. However, since the Dominionist movement has taken root in the GOP, basic human rights of food, shelter, and clothing—which have always been understood to be the moral foundation of a country that guarantees life, liberty, and the pursuit of happiness—have been supplanted in the minds of the Republican electorate with the right to carry automatic weapons in public, the right to not have health care, or the right to work longer hours for less money. However, the right to be a jackass is apparently still intact.

No rational person with any sense of history would think that postdepression, pre-Reagan Republicans would have cut food stamps for the poor while they gave tax breaks to the obscenely wealthy. Indeed, there is nothing less Jesus-like than abandoning the poor. And there is nothing less moral than evangelical morality.

*The minister of the Gospel is really the yardstick by
which the nation measures its morals.*

—Jimmy Swaggart[354], discussing morals between visits with hookers

The thing is, if you are a Republican and a Christian, you are doing at least one of those two things very badly. The GOP platform is about as far away from the teaching of New Testament Christ as one can get. Somehow, the evangelical movement has managed to extrapolate that helping the rich, and not helping the sick and impoverished, were the core messages of Jesus of Nazareth. It is more accurately the life philosophy of Ebenezer Scrooge.

And although I do realize that Republicans invoke the name Jesus an awful lot, for the life of me, I cannot figure out how a group of assholes who have the same ethical instincts as George Costanza during a fire have managed to claim the political moral high ground.

Cosmic Dots

As much as the screw-the-poor, go-fuck-yourself approach to health care flies in the face of Christ's teachings, there are several other moral perversions that are right in line with the divine psychopath's doctrine. Indeed, there are more than a few affronts to actual morality that the GOP can rationalize with biblical precepts. For instance, the conservative orifice obsession regarding men's heinies and women's coochies—although only moral indiscretions when one can invoke the Bronze Age ruling of a divine arbiter—actually have ecclesiastical precedence.

---

[354] BrainyQuote.com, *Jimmy Swaggart*, http://www.brainyquote.com/quotes/quotes/j/jimmyswagg178021.html

*I know one man who was impotent who gave AIDS to
his wife and the only thing they did was kiss.*

—Pat "Best Comedy Writer on TV" Robertson[355]

For it is the Christian fundamentalist version of right and wrong that allows for the corruption of the Republican moral code. The same way that Islamic fundamentalism has attenuated enough people's sensibilities to permit stoning women to death as a moral righteousness as decreed by Allah; so too do Dominionists rationalize antigay, antiwomen, antipoor, antihealth-care, anti-education, anti-all-the-shit-that-would-actually-help-people legislation as morally dutiful via Jesus. It's what happens when large groups derive their morality from a divine power that kills and tortures those who offend him, and who exhibits petty, base human emotions that rational humans recognize as adolescent.

Evangelical morals is how the Republican party has gone from this:

*Every gun that is made, every warship launched, every rocket
fired, signifies in the final sense a theft from those who hunger
and are not fed, those who are cold and are not clothed.*

—Dwight "Kicked Hitler's Ass" Eisenhower[356]

---

[355] BrainyQuote.com, *Pat Robertson*, http://www.brainyquote.com/quotes/
quotes/p/patroberts381715.html

[356] Brainyquote.com, *Dwight Eisenhower*, http://www.brainyquote.com/quotes/
quotes/d/dwightdei112029.html

To this:

> *You cure poverty eye to eye, soul to soul. Spiritual*
> *redemption: That's what saves people.*

—Paul "What's Up With Those Eyebrows?" Ryan[357]

Now, to be fair, I doubt that Paul Ryan is really this nutty. He appears, by all accounts to be otherwise sane. But he does have to say things like this if he wants to remain viable in the GOP. So the whole "Poor folks need Jesus, not food stamps" narrative is simply another trite Christian bromide spoken in order to help enable cerebrally disadvantaged voters acquiesce to the greater Dominionist message. Which is "More for the wealthy; fuck you and your aspirations." Frankly, I don't know whether Paul Ryan would feel compelled to engage in overt dip-shittery if it were not for the evangelical lobby.

But I do know that the evangelical lobby is why crazy and stupid are predominant components in the twenty-first-century conservative discourse, of which Rep. Paul Ryan is a part.

Communing Via Disaster

Since his holiness Ronald Reagan performed the miracle of being regarded as the small government, antitax, conservative standard-bearer thirty years after his administration raised taxes seven times—and increased both government spending and the national debt—the systemic neutering of Republican intellect has been dramatic. And you thought that walking on water was a neat trick. However, the divorce from reason that was once spoken only by evangelical preachers has now blended into the overall conservative lexicon and is spoken by anyone in the tea/GOP with shameless abandon.

Really, it's staggering that there are large enough groups of knuckleheads who vote for people who, in all seriousness, blame disasters—natural or

---

[357] Motherjones.com, *Paul Ryan*, http://www.motherjones.com/
kevin-drum/2013/11/paul-ryan-continues-pretend-he-wants-fight-poverty

otherwise—on gays, abortion, or women's lib. The synaptic dot-connecting of morals as they apply to Yahweh and those who piss him off induces bounteous crazy/stupid assertions. According to Christian evangelicals—elected or otherwise—whenever anything bad happens to people who seem distant, foreign, or naughty, it is the Lord's way of communicating his displeasure with their actions. A cosmic reprimand.

Mass annihilation is God's preferred method of teaching morality. Not-so-great floods, delivered twenty-first-century style. Like a father spanking his child, this is the big fella upstairs way of saying "This is gonna hurt me more than it hurts you, junior."

Forty years ago, the United States Supreme Court sanctioned abortion on demand. And we wonder why our culture sees school shootings so often.

—Rep. Kevin "Cuckoo for Cocoa Puffs" Cramer[358]

… Of course, the increase in school shootings has nothing to do with the easy access to guns, the cuts to education, or the increase in poverty. It's Yahweh sending us a message that he is angry at us for legalizing abortion by killing other children. Good point, Lord. Way to make sense.

Washington, DC—you'd think by now they'd get the message. An earthquake. A hurricane. Are you listening? The American people have done everything they possibly can. Now it's time for an act of God and we're getting it.

—Rep Michele "Five-Mile Stare" Bachman[359]

---

[358] Huffingtonpost.com, *Kevin Cramer,* http://www.huffingtonpost.com/2013/05/16/kevin-cramer-school-shootings_n_3285328.html

[359] Enterprisenews.com, *Michele Bachman,* http://www.enterprisenews.com/x1698394532/Today-in-the-news-Another-hurricane-on-the-way?template=printart

Yeah Michele, we're listening. How can we not? You're more fun than a schizophrenic off her meds. Which begs the question: Are you off your meds?

> *When a nation does something bad, it gets judgment or it gets blessing (from God) right now in the present.*

—Tea party candidate and dirt roads scholar David Barton[360]

Gee, Dave I wouldn't mind getting a little of that Hugh Heffner judgment. But I could counter your baseless assertion with, "Did you ever see what a beautiful city San Francisco is? That must be God's way of saying that he loves gay people ... and how 'bout them 49ers?"

> *I do believe that God punishes us for things that are against his word. I believe that with all my heart.*

—Rep Tony "Sinking" Shipley[361]

The Tennessee congressman said this while defending a quote where he likened California to Sodom and Gomorrah and suggested that God might "slide it into the sea" as punishment for not being as awesome and smart as the state that wisely chose to elect him. Perhaps Rep. Shipley simply forgot about the devastation occurring on December 22, 2008, when the walls of a dam holding 1.1 billion gallons of coal ash crumbled, spilling a toxic concoction into the town of Kingston, Tennessee, and creating the largest industrial spill in US history. Yahweh had nothing to do with that one, I'm sure.

[360] Rawstory.com, *David Barton,* http://www.rawstory.com/rs/2013/10/possible-senate-candidate-david-barton-climate-change-is-gods-judgement-for-abortion/

[361] Nashvillescene.com, *Tony Shipley,* http://www.nashvillescene.com/pitw/archives/2009/03/19/the-wrath-of-god-is-coming-beware-rep-tony-shipley-explains-his-doomsday-message

*God is angry. We are provoking him with abortions
and same-sex marriage and civil unions.*

—Republican congressional candidate with the
worst hair in politics, Susanne Atanus[362]

The crazy that poured out of Ms. Atanus's mouth more accurately seemed like it emanated from the place described by last four letters of her name. She also blamed the polar vortex, tornadoes, and autism on gay marriage. Now to be fair, I doubt that she will ever amount to much politically. However, the local Republican Party decided that this raving loon was the best candidate they could find.

*(The Columbine shootings happened)because our school systems
teach our children that they are nothing but glorified apes
who have evolutionized out of some primordial mud.*

—Former house majority leader and legal-bullet dodger, Tom Delay[363]

This quote was actually entered into the Congressional Record. It's nice to know that two-step Tom can—from the comfort of his office—bypass CSI and solve the case. It's not that blaming murdered children on teaching actual science being taught in schools is irresponsible or anything. By the way, Rep. Delay … "evolutionized" is not an actual word, you dim-witted simp.

[362] Huffingtonpost.com, *Susanne Atanus,* http://www.huffingtonpost.com/2014/01/23/susanne-atanus-gop_n_4652255.html

[363] The congressional record 145., *Tom Delay,* June 16 1999 h4366. Consequences for Juvenile Offenders Act of 1999.

*(New Orleans has) always been known for gambling, sin and wickedness. …
It is the kind of behavior that ultimately brings the judgment of God.*

—Alabama State Senator and deep thinker Henry E. Erwin Jr.[364]

Hey Hank, I'm not sure if you noticed, but the French Quarter in N'awlins—the area where most of the "sin and wickedness" occurs—was not very damaged by Hurricane Katrina. Yahweh must have shitty aim. They were back to titty flashing in no time. The good Lord set his sights on Bourbon Street and hit a bunch of poor black folks instead.

Do you think that maybe Yahweh hasn't noticed that little desert town in Nevada? Nah. Me neither.

Amazingly though, when a disaster befalls a mostly white, Christian community, we never hear these "hand of God laying the smackdown on your heathen asses" kinds of explanations from Bible Belt Republicans. Instead we get the "God works in mysterious ways, and it is not for us to judge" line of bullshit.

For instance, no Republican politicians or their evangelists cronies credited the tornados that ravaged the mostly white Christian town of Joplin Missouri in consecutive years to Godly discipline. Obviously, those were just natural disasters that the Lord was just testing the decent people of Joplin with. Sorry 'bout them dead kids, though.

The cruel and misguided Republican comments that capitalize on people's postdisaster suffering can fill a book by themselves. The gall it takes for a politician or an evangelist to glean rapturous retribution in the wake of people having lost their loved ones or their homes—out of political opportunism—is *morally* reprehensible. But after-the-fact discernment is an evangelical Christian's best trick. Because they sure as hell can't predict anything.

---

[364] NBCnews.com, *Henry E. Erwin, Jr.*, http://www.nbcnews.com/id/9731623/ns/us_news-katrina_the_long_road_back/t/apocalypse-now/#.VBik3hYXPf1

And one might think that, if evangelical Christian preachers and politicians have so many personal chats with the supreme omnipotent creator of the universe, that Yahweh might let a couple of these assholes know when a tornado is coming.

Awe Inspiring

Beware of false prophets, which come to you in sheep's clothing, but inwardly they are ravening wolves.

—Matthew 7:15[365]

The usurping of American morality by evangelical preachers and politicians—in conjunction with the conservative entertainment complex—has yielded a really interesting dynamic. It seems that the keepers of the moral code can do as they wish. When Republican politicians and evangelical preachers are guilty of violating their own quasi-moral standards, it's rationalized as human frailty and dismissed as mere "mistakes."

However, whenever those who are not "evangelical approved" engage in libertine copulation, well then, they're just shit out of luck. Within the conservative public relations machine, Jesus-folk can get away with almost anything, and it's those damned gay-tolerant, condom-wielding liberals who need Jesus to guide them. The hypocrisy is awe-inspiring.

For example, 2012 presidential candidate and former speaker of the house—"she turned me into a" Newt Gingrich—while calling for the impeachment of President Bill Clinton over that now-famous extramarital indiscretion where the executive schmekel found its way into Monica Lewinsky's festering gob—and the ensuing errant money-shot—"El Gingro" was at the time boning an all-too-eager congressional aide twenty-three years his junior. Ole' toddler body Gingrich did so while married

---

[365] Holy Bible, *Matthew 7:15*, Holy Bible. New International Version ®, Copyright © 1973, 1978, 1984, 2011 by Biblica, Inc.®

to his second wife, Marianne. This would be no big deal, and no one's business, except for the "family values" hypocrisy that Speaker Gingrich, and every other sanctimonious spunk dumpster on the right, invokes every time a biblically nonsanctioned act of procreation occurs.

And while the ambitious young Callista Bisek would eventually become so enamored with the undulating love machine known as Newt Gingrich that she would eventually become his *third* wife, the two of them carried on this affair for years. Eventually, the Newtster ended his second marriage much as he did his first, after having found a better piece of ass. But to be fair to Speaker Gingrich, he is way too much sexy for one man to not share.

> *The Democratic Party has been the active instrument*
> *of breaking down traditional marriage.*

> —Newt "You Gotta Be Shittin' Me" Gingrich[366]

Oh but the right-wing moral hypocrisy gets even more cringe-worthy hilarious. The cacophony of carnally compromised Christian conservatives who reside at 133 C Street, a Washington, DC, gathering spot for Dominionist Republican legislators, equates to a "who's who" of "what the fuck."

South Carolina Governor and C Street resident Mark Sanford disappeared from the office to which he was elected—literally—to go shack up with his mistress in Argentina. Before Gov. Sanford returned from his good-will South American spooge exchange to a speculative, albeit incredulous, gathering of media, his staff had explained his unannounced departure as having been a spontaneous hiking of the Appalachian Trail. If by "hiking," Sanford's staff meant "fucking," and by "Appalachian Trail" they meant "Latin American trim," then by all means, blame the media.

---

366   Thinkpress.org. *Newt Gingrich*, http://thinkprogress.org/
yglesias/2009/04/20/192618/thrice-married-former-house-speaker-charges-
democrats-with-breaking-down-traditional-marriage/

I don't know how this thing got blown out of proportion.

—Mark "Leavin' on a Jet Plane, Don't Know
When I'll Be Back Again" Sanford[367]

I know this sounds like a bullshit story, but it actually happened. After his clandestine affair had been exposed, a teary-eyed Sanford blubbered, "I have been unfaithful to my wife."—As if admission after discovery means anything. And as always, Christian politicians only admit wrongdoing after they've been caught. Then expect forgiveness that they don't accord legislators across the aisle.

But in 2013, as only tea-publican gullibility will permit—just a few years removed from "hiking the Appalachian trail"—the good (mostly) Christian citizens of South Carolina forgave Mark Sanford for his international trespasses and elected him to Congress. Sanford claims to have been "saved" by God's grace. Along with the credulousness of voters and some Argentinean coochie, no doubt.

But the "C Street" fornication train just keeps on rollin':

*Last year, I had an affair. I violated the vows of my marriage.
It is the worst thing I have ever done in my life.*

—C Street resident Sen. John "Clinton Should Resign" Ensign[368]

Former Nevada Senator John Ensign is another wonderful example of a "family values" Christian conservative who has the morals of slumlord. Hardcore Christ enthusiast that Ensign is, his minor doctrinal transgression involved banging the wife of his friend Doug Hampton while touting Christian ideals with his fellow C Street fundamentalists. It's one thing

---

[367]   Politico.com, *Mark Sanford*, http://www.politico.com/news/
stories/0609/24146.html

[368]   ABCnews.go.com, *John Ensign*, http://abcnews.go.com/blogs/
politics/2009/06/sen-ensign-to-acknowledge-affair-with-campaign-staffer/

to cheat on your wife; it's another thing still to do so with someone else's wife. Yet marital infidelity degrades into an entirely new moral bankruptcy when it is done with the wife of a friend. John Ensign's feckless, moral duplicity was such that he would look his pal Doug Hampton in the eye, shake his hand, engage in small talk, and pretend that he wasn't creating miniature works of modern art on the small of his wife's back.

So somehow, despite his solemn after-the-fact confession—based on John Ensign's ability to betray his friend so easily—I doubt that this was the "worst thing" this scumbag has ever done. But let's keep going:

I still believe it is in the best interest of our five boys if our differences are resolved privately and before the appropriate court and not in the media.

—C Street resident Rep. Chip "Can't Get More Caucasian" Pickering[369]

Mississippi congressman Chip Pickering is yet another perfidious Christian sack whose wife divorced him for putting the Pickering pecker where it did not belong. But in a true display of Christian forgiveness, the love-scorned Mrs. Pickering then sued his mistress—the married and uber-wealthy Elizabeth Creekmore Byrd—for alienation of affection. Both marriages crashed and burned.

Way to go, Chip. You've made your bunkmates proud. The easy-on-the-eyes Leisha Pickering also charged that this affair occurred on the 133 C Street premises, enabled by none other than Congressman Pickering's C Street Christian pals. "Hey, Chip, can you keep it down in there? We're trying to watch the 700 club."

Frankly, I've seen better displays of morality at three in the morning on Amsterdam Avenue and 168th Street, during transactions occurring out of the back of a car trunk, than I have at 133 C Street in broad daylight.

---

[369] Huffingtonpost.com, *Chip Pickering,* http://www.huffingtonpost.com/2009/07/17/chip-pickerings-wife-clai_n_237429.html

Hey, Hanrahan!

Of all religions, the Christian should of course inspire the most tolerance, but until now Christians have been the most intolerant of all men.

—Voltaire[370]

But not all Republican sex scandals are so traditional. I mean, you would think that a group of xenophobic, fear-mongering, gay-hating ideologues who tout "traditional marriage" would also have "traditional" extramarital affairs. And by traditional, I mean a little too much Aqua Velva and a slap on a bimbo secretary's ample rump, leading to an office supply closet romp. Good old-fashioned heterosexual, imbalance of power, quasi-prostitution, "sure, I'll help your career" sex.

Yet as Christian Republicans go, some simply cannot resist phallic allure.

Although the conservative movement in general seems preoccupied with man-on-man butt-sex, according to them, they do so out of concern for the gay community's immortal souls. Don't hate the sinner; hate the sin. Which is Christian-speak for, "I don't hate you, but I do hate the embodiment of who you are." It is the moral mandate of Christian conservatives to discriminate against gays for their own damn good.

Yet, according to anyone with the slightest bit of psychological acumen, it's apparent that many are trying to keep their own closet door shut. Me think thou doth protest too much, you bunch of right-wing homos.

"I am not gay. I never have been gay," Senator Larry "Wide Stance" Craig[371] said in response to the 2007 guilty plea for disorderly conduct, which he signed after having been arrested by an undercover police officer for lewd

---

[370] BrainyQuote.com, *Voltaire*, http://www.brainyquote.com/quotes/quotes/v/voltaire402245.html

[371] Foxnews.com, *Larry Craig*, http://www.foxnews.com/story/2007/08/28/senator-larry-craig-am-not-gay/

conduct in a public restroom. According to the police report, an officer sat in a bathroom stall as part of an undercover operation investigating complaints of sexual activity. Covert toilet temptation tactics.

The officer had observed Senator Craig lingering outside and frequently peeking through the crack of the door on the stall. Then ole' love-handle Larry entered the stall next to the officer, and engaged in "Hey, big boy, what's a nice fella like you doing in a men's room like this?" incursions into the officer's stall with his foot. This is a maneuver well known in the gay community as a "come hither" invitation. Unfortunately for Sen. Craig, the would-be power bottom in the adjacent alcove was a cop, at which time the jig—among other things—was up.

But of course you're not gay, Larry. Everyone believes you. You simply enjoy trolling public men's rooms for gentlemen's companionship now and again. That's what all of us "family values" straight guys do when we have no one to watch the game with.

But as pole-smoking hypocrites go, there is no shortage in the GOP:

> *It's vile. It's more sad than anything else, to see someone with such potential throw it all down the drain because of a sexual addiction.*

—Rep. Mark "Glass House" Foley[372], speaking of Bill Clinton's affair

Florida Congressman Mark Foley is a staggering example of the Christian Republican double standard machine at work. The temerity of Foley's actions is impressive, even by C-Street standards. As a Republican legislator, Foley voted along party lines against gay marriage, as well as committing other moral contradictions, while he, himself was taking it in the keister and batching to Honcho magazine. But that isn't even the whole story.

---

[372] Washingtonpost.com, *Mark Foley*, http://www.washingtonpost.com/wp-dyn/ content /article/2006
/10/13/AR2006101301418.html

Co-founder of the Congressional Missing and Exploited Children's Caucus, Foley was also in the public spotlight for his alleged desire to protect children from sexual predators. As such, he had a chance to exhibit true morality by helping kids. Despite the hypocrisy of being a Christian conservative while also being a closeted homosexual, it seems that one who co-founded a group designed to protect children would understand the asymmetrical relationship of underage people and adults whom they confide in. Certainly, a person's sexual orientation has no bearing on their ability to understand that adults taking advantage of children is the worst betrayal of trust there is.

When he made the following quote, Rep. Foley sure seemed to get it:

> *They're sick people. They need mental health counseling. They certainly don't need to be interacting with children.*
>
> —Rep. Mark "Would Have Made a Terrific Priest" Foley[373], speaking about pedophiles in 2002

Tragically, the above statement was made prior to him being caught for having made sexual advances, via instant messenger, to a young boy. That's right, Congressman Mark Foley's crime isn't just that he is a hypocritical, two-faced jizz-licker who condemned gays while he, himself is gay. I mean, he *is* that. But beyond being a Christian Republican who derives sexual gratification from having other men breach his back gate, Foley is an even bigger hypocrite for co-founding a group to help protect kids from people just like himself.

Here's a little excerpt from the cringe-worthy instant message exchange—all of which you can find online—that Congressman Foley had with a sixteen-year-old male page from his own office:

Mark Foley: "Do I make you a little horny?"

---

[373] Democracynow.org, *Mark Foley*, http://www.democracynow.org/2006/10/3/calls_increase_for_hastert_to_resign

Teen: "A little."

Foley: "Cool."

I am deeply sorry, and I apologize for letting down my family and the people of Florida I have had the privilege to represent.

—Rep. Mark "Stone Thrower" Foley[374], after he was caught

Go fuck yourself, Foley, you sick bastard.

Not as I do

By the pricking of my thumbs, something wicked this way comes.

—William Shakespeare[375]

But to be fair to Christian conservative Republican legislators, many of those who find it difficult to behave as they preach are merely following the moral examples of Christian conservative preachers.

The founder of the politically powerful New Life Church, Pastor Ted Haggard, is what us satirists like to refer to as a "real gem." A man who was a part of weekly evangelical conference calls with President George W. Bush and was once on *Time Magazine*'s list of the twenty-five most influential preachers, the livin' *la vida loca* pastor was a national figure. The natural successor to aging evangelical lunatics Jerry Falwell and Pat Robertson, T-Hag was set to be among the most powerful men in the nation.

---

[374] Washingtonpost.com, *Mark Foley*, http://www.washingtonpost.com/wp-dyn/content/article/2006/09/29/AR2006092901574.html

[375] Goodreads.com, *William Shakespeare*, http://www.goodreads.com/quotes/2816-by-the-pricking-of-my-thumbs-something-wicked-this-way

That is, right up until the time that Pastor Ted Haggard—high on methamphetamines—had a homosexual romp with a male escort named Mike Jones.

Of course, like the perfidious putz that Haggard[376] is, at first he vehemently denied "breaking gay": *"I did not have a homosexual relationship with a man in Denver ... I am steady with my wife. I'm faithful to my wife."*

Going on to say that he had also never done drugs, ever. Of course not, Ted. We won't be swayed by your creepy demeanor or the fact that you make Jim McGreevey look like Chuck Norris. You preach the gospel of Jesus. So of course we trust you.

At first, the evangelical community came out in force to support Ted Haggard. Not only was he one of their own, he was also among their most wealthy and politically influential.

> *It is unconscionable that the legitimate news media would report a rumor like this.*

—James "Got Your Back, Even If It Has Dried Jizz on It" Dobson[377]

But then the voice mail left by Pastor Haggard to Jones confirmed both his involvement in what he was denying and that he was a deceitful sack of shit.

Ted Haggard's[378] "humana humana humana" moment went like this: *"I bought it (meth) for myself but never used it. I was tempted but I never used it."*

376 About.com, *Ted Haggard*, http://marriage.about.com/od/infamous/p/tedhaggard.htm

377 Newson6.com, *James Dobson*, http://www.newson6.com/story/5626002/dobson-criticizes-media-for-reporting-haggard-allegation-focus-chairman-calls-coverage-of-unsubstantiated-rumor-unconscionable

378 ABCnews.com, *Ted Haggard*, http://abcnews.go.com/GMA/story?id=2626067

Of course, Ted. I receive naked massages and buy crystal meth from male escorts all the time, just to fill my candy dish.

And like Saint Peter before them, Ted's evangelical pals all bailed on the once mighty pastor:

Our investigation and Pastor Haggard's public statements have proven without a doubt that he has committed sexually immoral conduct.

—Pastor Ross Parsley[379] (Haggard's successor at the New Life Church)

Apparently, the cock crowed three times. And by crowed, we mean a biblically forbidden expenditure of DNA. Yep. Ted Haggard is a man's man. Literally.

But, concerning the Bible Belt proletariat and their favorite evangelical preachers, it's like they're all suffering from supernatural Stockholm syndrome. No matter what these evangelical scumbags do or how badly they violate the trust of those who put their immortal souls in their hands, evangelical preachers just smile, say a few platitudes about forgiveness, and get right back to taking money from the same indoctrinated dolts as before.

I have sinned against you, my Lord.

—Televangelist Jimmy Swaggart[380], after he was caught fornicating with a streetwalker in his limousine

The fear-inspired brainwashing has gotten so obvious to those with the ability to think, that even after the Pastor Ted Haggard/male prostitute/ methamphetamine scandal, even after Rev. Kent Hovind was sent to jail for tax fraud, even after televangelist Jimmy Swaggart was caught

---

[379] Cnn.com, *Pastor Ross Parsley*, http://www.cnn.com/2006/US/11/03/haggard. allegations

[380] ABCnews.com, *Jimmy Swaggart*, http://abcnews.go.com/US/video/ jimmy-swaggart-affair-apology-9876022

with a hooker, even after Pastor Jim Bakker did jail time for fraud and made a B-list celebrity out of Jessica Hahn, and even after the litany of other purposeful wrongdoings where priests, politicians, and evangelical ministers were literally caught with their pants down or were arrested for misappropriating money—the Christian masses still keep coming back for more.

The Lord told me it's flat none of your business.

—Jimmy "Go Fuck Yourself" Swaggart[381], explaining to unwashed masses who send him money why his violation of the gospel, which he preaches, is none of their damned beeswax

Perhaps the psychological reconciliation is that if churchgoing folks forgive these lying, stealing, fornicating, kid-touching hypocrites, then Yahweh might give them a pass on a few of their own not-so-Christian indiscretions as well. Hey, if all one has to do is ask Jesus for forgiveness after stealing money intended for sick children and swallowing spunk in the back of a limo, then cheating on one's taxes and jerking off to tranny porn must equate to a divine misdemeanor. *Sorry for hitting my wife, Lord. Now can I still get into heaven?*

But hey, maybe I'm being too cynical about evangelical morality. Perhaps the Reverend Creflo Dollar actually does believe that the best way for you to get into heaven is to help pay for his Lear jet. Maybe Pat Robertson is speaking from his heart when he suggests that poverty-stricken people should tithe more than they already do. It is conceivable that Jerry Falwell didn't just blather absurd, hate-filled things in order to build his ministry, make more money, and acquire more political influence. It is within the realm of possibility—however remote—that all of the Christian conservative Republicans who have taken up residence at 133 C Street, and who actively try to legislate toward erasing church-state separation, to a man, had become temporarily possessed by the forces of evil.

---

[381] Fmh-child.org, *Jimmy Swaggart,* http://www.fmh-child.org/S6.19.11.html

Then again … Maybe they're all just greedy, bloodsucking, licentious, evil bastards with the morals of a serial pedophile. I know where I'd place my bet.

Sorry 'bout That, Chief

To err is human; to forgive, divine.

—Alexander "Not That Kind of" Pope[382]

Here's the thing about preachers, politicians, or anyone else who steals money or who puts his penis where it doesn't belong: after they get caught, they will invariably apologize, claim that they made a "mistake," and ask for forgiveness.

However, there is a common misconception about the word "mistake" and, more to the point, how it applies to undertakings such as theft and fornication. When one premeditates, and then follows through on his objective, that is not how one commits a mistake. When a person tries to do something and then accomplishes his intended task, neither is that a flub, a gaffe, or a blunder.

A mistake is what happens when one achieves a different outcome than expected. Not when one's ambition is realized.

For instance, unintentionally misplacing a decimal point during long division is an example of a mistake. Becoming distracted while making breakfast and burning toast is a mistake. Drunken karaoke is usually a tragic mistake.

But to commandeer an observation from my last book, sex is never a "mistake." There is no possible way for a phallus to accidentally find its way inside a woman's vagina (or, in some conservative evangelical

---

[382] BrainyQuote.com, *Alexander Pope*, http://www.brainyquote.com/quotes/quotes/a/alexanderp101451.html

Republican instances, another gentleman's inviting sphincter). In the history of mankind, there has never been an example of happenstance intercourse that occurred via the same type of spontaneous collision that created Reese's Peanut Butter Cups.

The actual "mistake" is getting caught, not misappropriating funds or violating Yahweh's rules about fornicating out of wedlock. The thievery and copulation are done on purpose.

So when so-called men of God—be they Republican politicians or evangelical preachers—try to weasel out of their premeditated actions by claiming that they made a mistake, they are completely full of shit. It is, every time, a willful act made in defiance of what they claim to hold most dear—the divine behavioral doctrine of the biblical God.

> *The deadliest bullshit is odorless and transparent.*

—Writer and inventor of the term "cyberspace" William Gibson[383]

To offer some perspective, in case you might be thinking that I am neglecting the hypocrisy that also occurs on the political left ... Democratic Congressman Anthony Weiner did not accidentally take pictures of his mule and send them to women online under the mistaken impression that he was to be return-tweeted a prostate evaluation. Neither was it a matter of random kismet that guided Governor Elliot Spitzer into a hotel room where a prostitute just happened to be sleeping spread-eagle-naked as he stumbled atop of her in the dark. President Bill Clinton did not blow an errant load while his chunky intern was fixing his broken zipper. And lowlife extraordinaire and Democratic Senator John Edwards did not father a child out of wedlock in order to harvest stem cells to treat his wife's cancer.

---

[383] Goodreads.com, *William Gibson*, http://www.goodreads.com/quotes/38357-the-deadliest-bullshit-is-odorless-and-transparent

None one of these wayward penis excitations was a mistake. Each of the above examples of Democratic adultery was done on purpose. They were all committed as acts of willful deception. And they are all deserving of our vociferous scorn.

However, the difference in instances of Democratic and Republican would-be illicit extramarital copulation is that Democrats don't go around yelling "Jesus!" as a means of political marketing every chance they get. The hypocrisy, while still significant, is much more evident when one claims to have been spoken to directly by the Christian space deity. One's duplicity is magnified when he engages in willful acts that contradict the very moral premise from which they operate.

And legislating according to supposed biblical morality—in American politics—is a singularly Republican precept.

So when a fundamentalist/evangelical Christian inserts his wrinkly, semi-flaccid trouser tuna into someone who isn't his wife, and then tries to cover it up with "Oops, I made a mistake," there is an entirely different dynamic to their bullshit, compared to that of a businessman whose wife finds lipstick on his collar. When an evangelical Christian preacher or politician—especially one who is in the public eye and who is actively trying to circumvent church-state separation—purposefully puts his putz where he knows he shouldn't, he doesn't just betray his oath of office, but according to his own beliefs, he betrays *God*.

I cannot speak to the sincerity of evangelical preachers and politicians, as far as what might travel through the vast wasteland of their delusional minds. That would be speculation on my part. But would anyone who was as devout as they claim to be willingly defy God? If evangelical morals are what they assert, are there reasonably mitigating circumstances that can explain why so many alleged men of God might find themselves in contempt of their own beliefs? The list of evangelical cocksuckers—and I use that term as those who suck cock, not as an Al Swearengen aphorism—is hilariously long.

I know that if I were convinced that not being tortured for an eternity in a fiery hell depended on keeping my shvantz in check, then I'd put the lil' fella in a lock box. I sure as hell wouldn't purposefully solicit prostitutes, hop on a plane to Argentina, text message an intern, or fornicate with my friend's wife. And if the morals of the Christian Republican Party are so pathetically easy to abandon, how can anyone who is not either less than sane or not too bright trust the word, let alone the legislation, of its members?

So I'll end this chapter with this:

I have a zero tolerance for sanctimonious morons who try to scare people.

—Pat Robertson[384]

Neither do we, Pat. Neither do we.

---

[384] Brainyquote.com, *Pat Robertson*, http://www.brainyquote.com/quotes/quotes/p/patroberts381714.html

CHAPTER 8
The Big Reveal
(A Final Plea for Reason—and Beer)

Christians have an obligation, a mandate, a commission, a holy responsibility to reclaim the land for Jesus Christ—to have dominion in civil structures, just as in every other aspect of life and godliness, but it is dominion we are after. Not just a voice … It is dominion we are after. Not just equal time … World conquest.

—George Grant[385], former executive director of Coral Ridge Ministries, presently known as Truth in Action Ministries, which must be code for "Holy Shit These People are Crazy" Ministries

---

[385] Dailykos.com, *George Grant*, http://www.dailykos.com/ story/2012/06/02/1096273/-Why-We-Fight-Christian-Dominionists-Are-Dead-Serious-About-Overthrowing-Democracy

When one speaks of Christian Dominionism in our political system, there is a distinct possibility that many will dismiss it as some sort of conspiracy theory. I get that. Such assumptions are not unwarranted. People make grandiose, speculative, and seditious claims all the time.

But it is important to understand that, when I speak of the Christian influence in American politics eventually hoping to gain *Dominion* over the nation, I am not hoping to paint a portrait of some sort of half-assed illuminati maniacally planning how to take control of our government. Religion in American politics is only different from religion in theocratic nations insofar as the United States of America has had a defined separation of church and state since Thomas Jefferson and James Madison wrote it into the Constitution. That separation has endured until recently.

History has proven that *whatever* religion breaches the church-state wall is of no consequence. The results will always be the same. A totalitarian regime will invariably and undeniably supplant the existing political structure. Civil laws will be replaced by an orthodox authority. *Every time.*

So, as American Dominionists hope to impose biblical doctrine on our system of law, it is incumbent upon rational people to stop them. There is a *moral* mandate to do so. As it has been the case throughout history, the more that one's government resembles a pure theocracy, the fewer one's liberties, and the greater the disparity of wealth between those at the very top of the economic food chain and everyone else. With unfailing consistency, religious fundamentalism masks socioeconomic bondage as godly virtuousness, and the faithful get in line to willingly accept their chains.

Whatever one's religion in his private life may be, for the officeholder, nothing takes precedence over his oath to uphold

the Constitution and all its parts—including the First
Amendment and the strict separation of church and state.

—John F Kennedy[386], Interview, *Look*, March 3, 1959

In twenty-first-century America, we can see this dynamic at work within the tea party: a lack of historical and economic comprehension expressing itself as a "return" to an America that never existed. Cries for liberty from the beleaguered tea-proletariat as they campaign for those actively working to remove those very same liberties. "Keep government out of my Medicare!" It would be hilarious, if not for the consequences.

The "big reveal" is that this book is not actually about Christian Dominionism, crazy, stupid people, or why we need Jesus out of politics. I mean, it is … but it's not *just* about those socioeconomic developments on the cover. This book is more accurately about a wealthy, powerful few using Christian Dominionism as a means to an economic end.

Indeed, Christian Dominionism—the usurping of the Republican Party by the Christian evangelical right, the creation of the conservative entertainment complex, and the consequent fear, paranoia, irrationality, and incomprehension—is merely the medium by which some aim to create an economy in which very few people have an incommensurate amount wealth and power. It is merely a financial abandonment of the masses, held in place by the fear of an ethereal, postlife dictator. As such, Christian Dominionism is less about Christianity than it is about the wealthiest people in our nation becoming the "inner party" elite; a small group of socioeconomic and political "Orwellians" whose purpose—once they've attained their status—is to maintain their repugnant abundance.

Big Brother Jesus is watching.

---

[386] Wordsfitlyspoken.com, *John F. Kennedy*, http://www.wordsfitlyspoken.org/gospel_guardian/v11/v11n4p13a.html

So, if it is difficult to fathom a bunch of religious nuts planning the Christian takeover of our country, contemplate what the best method to acquire and maintain wealth and power would be. Think to yourself, *if I were rich enough to have senators and congressmen kissing my ass, how would I best control the economic, and political environment?*

Church states are how hierarchies have been achieved and preserved since mankind has first stood upright and wondered what that big orange ball in the sky was. It is what keeps most people in the Middle East living in the twelfth century, while a few obscenely wealthy sheiks get to drive Rolls Royces, screw harem girls, and fly in private jets on a whim to eat lemon tarts baked by some little old lady in Venezuela. In America, our sheiks wear custom-tailored twenty-thousand-dollar suits.

Christianity is merely the vehicle that sociopathic domestic enemies of our nation—who have amassed an unfathomable amount of wealth—use to deliver the virus of socioeconomic illiteracy to the population. With reason and comprehension being founding precepts of our nation, introducing their opposites into the American zeitgeist is therefore a deliberate attempt to undermine our Republic. For terrorists need not be Islamic or use bombs to deliver fear into the minds of those whom they hope to mentally incapacitate. Some are natural-born, absurdly wealthy American citizens who advance dread and loathing via institutional poverty—and Jesus.

It's happened before, and it doesn't require a master's degree in political science to see that it is the intention of some to influence policy toward that end in America now. Really, what we've been experiencing in the years since President Reagan misguidedly fed a group of strays known as the evangelical lobby, is a circumvention of our Constitution and economy through Christian political propaganda. They should have been neutered before they were allowed inside, because—by their very nature—they have sought to take control.

Give then an inch, and they'll take the White House.

Big Valley

Those who do not remember the past are condemned to repeat it.

—George "You Got a Point There" Santayana[387]

But there is no need to believe anything this atheist tells you. The correlation between the tea/GOP, the evangelical lobby, conservative media, and the opulent elite aren't difficult dots to connect. Unless, of course, you're inclined toward a Glenn Beck-esque equating of Social Security to Hitler. If so, then: Benghazi!

The correlation between Orwellians and Christian Dominionism is illustrated in that the merging of religion and politics accompanied a decimation of the wall between commercial and investment banking. The Glass-Steagall Act—put in place after the financial collapse of 1929 to protect people's pensions and savings from sharing the same fate as risky stock investments—was repealed in 1999. Since the Glass-Steagall rescission, people's personal savings accounts, pensions, and retirement investments were all allowed to be under the same corporate umbrella as much more speculative investments. So, if an investment bank failed, as did many during the financial crisis of 2007, more than just a few douche-bag stockbrokers' Ferrari were on the line.

Dominionists wanted access to your net worth, and now they have it.

Simply follow where the money has gone since the collapse of our economy in 2007. Since President Obama has taken office—as I write this—the DOW Industrial Average has more than doubled. So whether you understand what that means or not, just try to grasp that a shit-ton of money has been made, and—statistically speaking—probably not by you.

---

[387]   BrainyQuote.com, *George Santayana*, http://www.brainyquote.com/quotes/quotes/g/georgesant101521.html

Traditionally, a significant increase in the stock market is reflected in our nation's economy. A rising DOW is normally indicative of capital flowing toward business interests, translating into employment and wages. But not so with the most eminent stock market escalation in American history. The money went up, and it never came back down.

In a September 2013 interview with President Barack Obama, the host of ABC's *This Week*, George Stephanopoulos [388] spoke to the president about how, despite record gains in the DOW, the economy is remaining virtually stagnant. *"Ninety-five percent of the (monetary) gains (have gone) to the top 1 percent (of income earners). That is so striking."*

To which President Obama responded, "It is." [389]

Thank you, President Obvious. Striking … gotcha.

The percentage of DOW gains going into so few people's pocket means— among other things—that the wealth disparity between those at the very top of our economic food chain and the vast majority of Americans has reached an unprecedented level of partition. Not only has the nation as a whole not benefitted from the Republican promise of a "trickle-down" economy, we are undeniably moving toward an Orwellian economic reality. A whole lot for very few, and not much for the rest of us. Striking.

If you've ever used the word "socialist" to describe the economy under President Obama, I beg of you … do your patriotic duty and never vote ever again. What the United States is experiencing since 2007 is the *opposite* of socialism. And if the convoluting of "isms" by conservative media has allowed you to blame President Obama for the wealthiest of the wealthy becoming increasingly wealthy with only a promise of more wealth

---

[388] ABCnews.com, *George Stephanopoulos,* http://abcnews.go.com/blogs/ politics/2013/09/full-transcript-president-obamas-exclusive-interview-with-george-stephanopoulos/

[389] Ibid., *President Barack Obama.*

to come as being a socialist endeavor, consider these public statements as they apply to policy:

Anybody who thinks that we can move this economy forward with just a few folks at the top doing well, hoping that it's going to trickle down to working people who are running faster and faster just to keep up, you'll never see it.

—Barack "the Kenyan, Marxist, Muslim Freedom-Hater Who Is Out to Destroy America" Obama[390]

And this:

The top 1 percent of wage earners in the United States pay 40 percent of the income taxes (despite that number being significantly less of a percentage than their actual income) ... The people he (President Obama) is talking about taxing are the very people that we expect to reinvest in our economy.

—Speaker of the House of Representatives John "I Can't Believe They Make Me Say This Bullshit" Boehner[391]

The reality is that the top 1 percent—those whom speaker Boehner and the Republican Party are so eager to protect—have a larger percentage of national wealth in their hands than at any time since the preorganized labor industrial age. They have the money, and they are not creating jobs with it. Yet, despite that reality, and despite the assertions that trickle-down "job creators" are being hampered by an imaginary radical president, the Dominionist-controlled GOP continues to blame the Democratic administration for the stagnant economy.

[390] BrainyQuote.com, *President Barack Obama*, http://www.brainyquote.com/quotes/quotes/b/barackobam412574.html

[391] Dailykos.com, *John Boehner*, http://www.dailykos.com/story/2011/05/15/976328/-Boehner-says-what-s-good-for-the-top-1-is-good-for-all-Americans

In case anyone at home is keeping score, the economic spiral actually began during George W. Bush's presidency, with the biggest losses in the DOW since 1929 stock market crash and the ensuing Great Depression. As I write this, the United States economy has had five years (under President Obama) of slow, but steady, economic growth. It takes neither an economics major nor a math whiz to know that Boehner's statement is utter bullshit.

Then consider—on top of the tightly coiled, steamy pile of "job creator/ trickle-down tea party crap" that is regularly served as economic acumen by twenty-first-century Republicans—that the most prominent tea party organizations are bankrolled by the very same scumbags that the Republican Party refers to as "job creators." Tea organizations such as FreedomWorks, the Tea Party Patriots, and the Tea Party Express, among others—which have created the gun-loving, health-care-hating Christian base upon which the twenty-first-century GOP has become dependent— are nothing more than pep rallies for the wealthy elite to propagate their selfish agendas.

Regular, frolicsome, seal-clubbing Orwellians like Charles Koch, David Koch, and Rupert Murdoch are the marionettes for tea party puppets, socially engineering society away from its own self-interest and toward their own.

We've got a country that the poverty level is wealth in 99 percent
of the rest of the world, so we're talking about woe is me, woe is
us, woe is this. The guy that's making, oh my God, he's making
$35,000 a year, why don't we try that out in India or some countries
we can't even name. China, anyplace, the guy is wealthy.

—Multibillionaire Bud "Let Them Eat Cake" Konheim[392],
expressing his view that impoverished Americans should
stop whining about not having enough to eat or a roof over
their heads because folks in Burundi have it worse

---

[392]   CNBC.com, *Bud Konheim*, http://www.cnbc.com/id/101410955

Great logic, Bud. Thanks a diaper load.

> *I've never been to a tea-party event. No one representing the tea party has ever even approached me.*

> —David "I'd Like to Buy the World a" Koch[393]

Of course not, Dave. You hire people to mingle with commoners.

Seriously, who else would pay big money to have Sarah "Shill Much?" Palin[394] get up in front of a crowd of would-be tea-party-voters and say inane things like: *"The Republican Party would be really smart to absorb as much of the tea party movement as possible."* Have any of the America-loving tea-folk ever wondered how events that charge no admission can pay such high-salaried speakers, as well as tea party CEOs and staff? Is anyone in the tea-tribe the least bit curious about the corporate structure and revenue sources of these institutions? Have they ever considered any of this? Do they even want to?

Or are the Glenn Beck-watching morons sitting in lawn chairs, clutching their Bibles, and waving their made-in-China American flags content in having no idea how badly they're being exploited?

False Idols

> *When it is a question of money, everybody is of the same religion.*

> —Voltaire[395]

---

[393] Nymag.com, *David Koch*, http://nymag.com/news/features/67285/

[394] BrainyQuote.com, *Sarah Palin*, http://www.brainyquote.com/quotes/quotes/s/sarahpalin411694.html

[395] Ibid., *Voltaire*, http://www.brainyquote.com/quotes/quotes/v/voltaire106818.html

People have always idolized those with a lot of money. I get that. To be honest, and to the extent that there are a myriad of admirable qualities that go into making one financially successful, I do too. Nice car, dude.

Certainly there is something admirable about one who acquires wealth from an idea and hard work. Beyond admirable, it is awesome. That is the economic premise of our nation. And it is a good premise. Hula Hoops, iPods, and handheld melanoma detectors … where would we be without them?

Moreover, most people—even over-the-top liberal party bottoms—aspire to live more comfortably than they already do. We all want a nice house, a swimming pool, and a new car. I am certainly hoping to make enough money from writing this book to fly first-class to Vegas and engage in enough debauchery to make a Marcus Bachman/Ted Haggard soiree look like an AA meeting. A boy can dream.

But calling out the *1 percent of the 1 percent* for undermining our nation's economy and manipulating legislation to favor their psychotic appetites and vainglorious ambitions is not the same as saying that *all rich people are evil*. Nor can such claims warrant accusations of being *anticapitalism*. It's really just a call for economic common sense.

> *I get called 'controversial' all the time.*

—Michal Moore[396], who gets called a lot of other things, most of them not very nice, and who, I admit, is a self-indulgent contradiction to what I just stated above

All right, I get it. Personally, I'd love for this Twinkie-loving egomaniac to shut the hell up too. But the well-moneyed, out-of-touch list of celebrity hypocrites aside, appealing for social and economic justice is hardly an indictment of the post-WWII American economic model. Even though

---

[396] Ibid., *Michael Moore,* http://www.brainyquote.com/quotes/quotes/m/michaelmoo580159.html

"celebri-libs" like Michael Moore and Alec Baldwin are obnoxious jerks, the core of what they say is nonetheless valid. What they fail to articulate, as the self-absorbed prick-digglers that they are, is that there is a significant departure between being *Elmer Fudd-millionaire* enough to have a mansion and a yacht—and being able to manipulate legislators and Supreme Court justices.

Even the *Occupy Wall Street* dolts—despite being a rudderless group of uber-idealistic hipsters who most probably all got participation trophies in soccer camp—were more of an "antitheft via collusion" movement than they were an "all money is evil" movement. Granted, most of them needed to bathe, but they were not entirely wrong. Just sensationally bad at articulating why their panties were in a knot.

Ironically, the fella in the funny hat summed up what OWSters were trying to say between dropping acid and public fornication, rather nicely:

> *Some people continue to defend trickle-down theories which assume that economic growth, encouraged by a free market, will inevitably succeed in bringing about greater justice and inclusiveness in the world. This opinion, which has never been confirmed by the facts, expresses a crude and naïve trust in the goodness of those wielding economic power and in the sacralised workings of the prevailing economic system.*

—Pope Francis[397], courageously stating the obvious and denouncing rigged economic principles that cause mass, institutionalized poverty

However, the misconception propagated by conservative media is that any suggestion for a return to the pre-Reagan economic model that brought about the greatest period in American history is viewed as an attack on the wealthy and a declaration for a socialist monetary distribution among the citizenry. Even so, since the culture of deregulation began under Reagan, wages have virtually stagnated, while inflation hasn't. The

---

[397] Washingtonpost.com, *Pope Francis*, http://www.washingtonpost.com/blogs/post-politics/wp/2013/11/26/pope-francis-denounces-trickle-down-economics/

conservative reaction to economic reason is not befitting the facts, and it is unwarranted, if not for political motivations. No more wire hangers!

What the political right infers from the term "redistribution of wealth" is that the middle class is suffering because poor folks are getting so much free stuff. "See that uppity single mom buying KFC with food stamps? It's her fault that you can't go on vacation. Just look at her shuckin' and jivin'. I bet she has six kids and doesn't know who their fathers are."

The reality is that the majority of money being siphoned from the middle class has gone into the pockets of the extremely wealthy. The Republican Party has become a shill for—not just the wealthy—but the corporate and the criminally wealthy. "See that WASP hedge fund manager buying a Lear jet with nontaxed 'carried interest'? Just look at that Dolce suit. I bet his great grandkids will never have to work a day in their lives."

Redistribution of wealth is the wrong term. The more appropriate phrase for a return to the pre-Reagan economic model would be a "reclamation of wealth."

The truth is, from FDR to Reagan—when we defeated the Nazis, grew the largest middle class in history, built our nation's infrastructure, ushered in the civil rights era, began Social Security and Medicare, gave Miles Davis and Bob Dylan to the world, and put a man on the moon and a computer in everyone's home—the United States of America was a capitalist/socialist hybrid. We tempered the runaway greed and ruthless profiteering that devastated our nation in 1929 by legislating socioeconomic safeguards. We regulated the banking industry so that it would be protected from itself. And it all worked.

Before Ronald Reagan, Democrats and Republicans alike understood the need for education, pensions, health care, retirement, and an honest day's wage for an honest day's work. Both parties understood the necessity for a socioeconomic structure that helped Americans provide for their families. Now we get horseshit like this from the Dominionist right and its media shills:

*Like Obama, (Pope) Francis is unable to see the problems that
are really endangering his people. Like Obama, he mistakes the
faithful for the enemy, the enemy for his friend, condescension
for respect, socialism for justice, and capitalism for tyranny.*

—Adam Shaw[398], news editor for FoxNews.com and
personal testicle cleaner for Roger Ailes, criticizing Pope
Francis and conflating capitalism with corporatism for
tea-twits who don't understand the difference

I see pedestrian socioeconomic comprehension reflected in stupid social media comments posted by fiscal ignoramuses all the time. The Republican psychological de-evolution has gotten particularly evident with the election of President Obama. The tea-rabble actually believe that the billionaire Dominionists—whom they do the bidding of—are victims. There is even a complete lack of understanding that there is a difference between wealthy billionaires like Warren Buffet, George Soros, and Bill Gates who work *against* their own self-interest by calling for more economically fair legislation, and oligarchs like Rupert Murdoch, Sheldon Adelson, or the Koch Brothers, who use their money and influence to manipulate the political process to abide their bidding. Surely, if people cannot make that distinction, then they would truly had to have been brainwashed.

My Mother the Car

I buy expensive suits. They just look cheap on me.

—Warren Buffett[399]

The thing is, the United States of America during the post–World War II era of prosperity allowed for many to achieve a vast degree of wealth. There

---

[398]   Foxnews.com, *Adam Shaw*, http://www.foxnews.com/opinion/2013/12/04/
pope-francis-is-catholic-churchs-obama-god-help-us/

[399]   BrainyQuote.com, *Warren Buffet*, http://www.brainyquote.com/quotes/
quotes/w/warrenbuff102760.html

were plenty of rich people, along with the healthy middle class. But there were also government intercessions preventing the conditions that created the Great Depression in the first place.

However, the *Citizens United v. Federal Election Commission* ruling of 2010 granted corporations and labor unions a form of "personhood" insofar that it gave them the green light to spend unlimited sums on ads and other political tools. Essentially, the Supreme Court's 5-to-4 decision said that it is okay for corporations and labor unions to dole out as much as they want to convince people to vote for or against a candidate. Vote for Pedro.

This ruling was great for Dominionists, since corporations were making record profits and would undoubtedly fork over big money to elect (Republicans) who would serve their best interests. Moreover, since organized labor is at its weakest point since the Depression and is actively being destroyed by (Republican-sponsored) "right to work" legislation, Dominionists really didn't have to give a shit about union political contributions. Conservative Christian Republicans definitely have the better end of this deal, by far.

And in a country where the candidate who spends the most money wins more than nine out of ten elections, Citizens United is a huge piece of legislation.

Corporations are people, my friend.

—2012 Republican nominee for president Mitt Romney[400], saying something so crazy that, before Dominionism infected our nation, no politician would dare assert for fear of being laughed out of an election

Yet prior to the Citizens United vote, two Supreme Court justices (Scalia and Thomas) attended a "retreat" held by the most active pro-Citizens

---

[400] Washingtonpost.com, *Mitt Romney*, http://www.washingtonpost.com/politics/
mitt-romney-says-corporations-are-people/2011/08/11/gIQABwZ38I_story.
html

United sponsors (the Koch Brothers) in the country. Amazingly, neither felt the need to recuse himself, despite having cavorted in Palm Springs on the Kochs' dime. So, naturally, when it came time to vote on legislation regarding who and how money could be thrown at Super PACs (multimillion-dollar political action committees), it was deemed that corporations, were, kind of, sort of, "people." Make it so, Mr. Data.

Circumvention of our highest court via collusion? Nah. But those Pina Coladas were fantastic.

> *I see in the near future a crisis approaching that unnerves me and causes me to tremble for the safety of my country … corporations have been enthroned and an era of corruption in high places will follow, and the money power of the country will endeavor to prolong its reign by working upon the prejudices of the people until all wealth is aggregated in a few hands and the Republic is destroyed.*

—Republican President Abraham Lincoln[401], November 21, 1864, in a letter to Col. William F. Elkins

Still, until Citizens United, a huge, multinational corporation had never been a metaphor for a fat guy who likes to travel. But now they are the same, inasmuch as their ability to donate to political organizations is concerned. Since 2010, corporations and billionaires can donate tens of millions of dollars to benefit whomever candidate they see fit. Of course, so can the traveling fatso, providing he has fifty or sixty million to spare, in case he needs to get the zoning on his block changed to accommodate his hedge line.

In the meantime, we'll all have to pretend that our fifty-dollar donation, and a corporation's $50 million donation, are the same fucking thing. Perhaps Goldman Sachs can invite Justices Scalia and Thomas on a Vegas junket before petitioning the court to grant it Second Amendment

---

[401] Goodreads.com, *Abraham Lincoln*, http://www.goodreads.com/quotes/tag/lincoln

personhood protecting it from a hostile takeover. I can see the gun turrets atop 85 Broad Street already.

Yet, regardless of any legal interpretations, corporations remain corporations in all the ways selling widgets can turn a profit, and people remain people in that they bleed when they skin their knees. Simon and Garfunkel were neither a rock nor an island. But at least that song was intended as symbolism, and not to infer that they should be granted special rights under the National Historic Preservation Act of 1966. Corporations feel no pain, and a business never cries.

And if you understood the above parody, you, too, are probably past your prime.

Buzz Cuts

Please sir, I want some more.

—Oliver Twist[402]

The sad reality is that not enough Americans understand the difference between an investment bank and a commercial bank. Therefore, not enough people were concerned when the Glass-Steagall Act was repealed. Moreover, not enough Americans grasp how the democratic process is undermined when the outcomes of elections can be disproportionately influenced by a wealthy few. Therefore, not enough people seemed to appreciate the importance of the Citizens United ruling, as it pertained to them and their individual voice.

But they should have been. In fact, they still should be.

Austerity—when used as an economic term—describes policies implemented by governments to reduce deficits. With the financial

---

[402] Ibid., *Charles Dickens' Oliver Twist*, https://www.goodreads.com/quotes/188796-please-sir-i-want-some-more

collapse of 2007 causing high unemployment, occurring in the midst of two unpaid-for wars (Afghanistan and Iraq), and with taxes for the wealthiest 1 percent unsustainably low, something had to be done to get our fiscal house in order. We have budget problems that need fixing. So how do we go about tightening the nation's belt?

Dominionist Republicans claim that we should ignore the economic reality that the wealthiest of the wealthy are more copious in their plentitude (thanks in part to the repeal of Glass-Steagall) since their grandfathers' factories were working eighteen-hour days. We should also overlook that they now had senators and congressmen kissing their posteriors for campaign contributions (thanks, in part, to the Citizens United ruling). So the most prosperous among us sure aren't going to kick in to help solve the problems they caused in the first place.

The mondo-opulent are financing Dominionist interests—from Republican politicians to media affiliates to evangelists—so as to indoctrinate tea party voters on their behalf. They invest a modest (by their standards) few million to insure that they won't have to contribute at the same tax rate as a working stiff with two jobs. Why would Orwellians "chip in" to help the nation, when their primary motivation is personal profit—and not the state of the union?

So, in direct opposition to the method that we used to escape the Great Depression, the burden of economic austerity has fallen on the working class. The Orwellian mantra is "Ask not what you can do for your country, ask what your country can do for you." They broke it; we pay to fix it. Seems perfectly fair. I believe that the economic term is "We got ours, so fuck you."

According to conservative TV and radio, the economic and budgetary problems of our nation have nothing to do with ostentatious shit bags earning more than ever while paying disproportionately low taxes. Apparently, we need to lower their taxes more. Nor are any of our fiscal woes due to corporate welfare or any of the other capitulations to lobbyists representing wealthy right-wing interests.

Apparently, the nation's problems are completely independent of—and can only be fixed by—Dominionist Orwellians. So if we elect Christian Republicans, Jesus-on-high will smile on our nation.

It seems that the real fiscal dilemmas emanate from selfish Americans who feel entitled to too many luxuries. Fortunately, we have Fox News and the bevy of other right-wing abettors to explain that the actual drains on our economy are "entitlements" like Medicare, Medicaid, health care, Social Security, retirement, organized labor, food stamps, unemployment insurance, disability, and the rest of those *socialist* programs that have been successful for decades. Not surprisingly, this clumsy sleight of hand actually works on tea-cretins because it is done with Jesus's blessing.

So, after 2007, we started to hear about *entitlement reform* from the right more than ever.

> *Back in the day of slavery, slaves were kept in slavery by denying them education and opportunity while providing them with their basic needs ... Not by beating them and starving them. (Although there were isolated cases if course.) Basically slave owners took pretty good care of their slaves and livestock and this kept business rolling along.*

> —Arizona tea party candidate Jim Brown[403], likening modern day "entitlements," like education and food stamps, to slavery

Because he is fucking crazy. Isolated cases? Took pretty good care? Really dude?

---

[403] Rawstory.com, *Jim Brown*, http://www.rawstory.com/rs/2014/03/arizona-gop-congressional-candidate-slavery-wasnt-so-bad-kept-business-rolling/

The entitlement state has driven us into insolvency.

—Would-be Alaskan tea party senator Joe "Close but No
Cigar" Miller[404], utilizing his H&R Blockhead accounting
skills to determine the cause and effect of personal vs. corporate
entitlements as they pertain to budgetary matters

The problem—it would appear—is that working-class Americans—like
spoiled children—feel "entitled" to a fair day's wage for a fair day's work.
We feel "entitled" to see our retirement. We feel "entitled" to not have to go
bankrupt due to medical bills. We feel "entitled" to educate our children.
We feel "entitled" to want the opportunity for home ownership. Who do
we think we are, the wealthy? The poor rich folks are finally due their day
in the sun, and who are we to deny them that?

Indeed, Conservatives hate entitlements … until they benefit from them.
When the rich receive government handouts or are able to influence laws
to their advantage, they believe it to be deserved. It's like a revisionist
manifest destiny, where the rhetoric of *American exceptionalism* is redefined
to equate to an Orwellian wealth disparity. The sense of entitlement among
the wealthy is as astonishing as it is infuriating.

*Writing from the epicenter of progressive thought, San Francisco,
I would call attention to the parallels of fascist Nazi Germany
to its war on its "1 percent," namely its Jews, to the progressive
war on the American 1 percent, namely the rich.*

—Multibillionaire venture capitalist Tom Perkins[405], explaining
that being asked to pay the same percentage in taxes as the woman
who cleans his office is just like murdering six million Jews

---

[404] BrainyQuote.com, *Joe Miller,* http://www.brainyquote.com/quotes/quotes/j/
joemiller412545.html

[405] Wsj.com, *Tom Perkins,* http://online.wsj.com/news/articles/SB1000142405270
2304549504579316913982034286

The duplicitous self-martyrdom is staggering. The Orwellian mind-set is so insufferably selfish—if not insane—that they feel "entitled" to hold Dominion over our legislature—and play the victim when they are inconvenienced. The economic top 1 percent in the United States have more than ever. The elite *within* the 1 percent have become unprecedentedly stratospheric. Yet when the working class ask that we return to the economic standard prior to deregulation, we are unduly "entitled" in their eyes. It's nuts.

The reality is that there are none who feel more "entitled" than the wealthy. Dominionists, Orwellians, cocksuckers—whatever you want to call them—are like some spoiled brat on "My Super Sweet 16." And like an annoying, overindulged whining teen, the uber-rich find themselves feeling that they are due special "princess" treatment. But the United States of America is not like a Mercedes for these brats to complain about the color of. It is our sovereign nation, which guarantees life, liberty, and the pursuit of happiness to *all* of its citizens.

Not just a few aristocratic oligarchs.

Looking Glass

Republicans and Democrats can barely do what they're supposed to do, and they sure can't do math.

—Lewis Black[406]

The dismantling of post-Depression economic bulwarks, along with corporate and banking deregulation, have created an economic condition where the typical American CEO makes almost four hundred times what the average worker in his or her employ earns. Not the lowest-paid worker, but the average worker. That does not include incomes from capital gains,

406 BrainyQuote.com, *Lewis Back,* http://www.brainyquote.com/quotes/quotes/l/lewisblack583559.html

trust funds, carried interest, stock gains, etc. That's just salary. The actual wealth disparity is significantly greater.

The tea-misconception is that twenty-first-century fiscal segregation is the result of "capitalism," and not the result of a rigged, corporatist "crony" system. Many feel that the growing monetary disparity is something easily overcome with hard work and dedication. Those socialist Democrats are vilifying patriotic prosperity.

Part of the problem in trying to wrap one's mind around wealth inequality is that many perceive the numbers as allegorical rather than trying to understand what they really mean.

There is a tribe of people living in the Brazilian jungle called the *Piraha*, who have words for "one" and "two"; "few" and "many"—but that is all. From accounts I've read, the *Piraha* people seem unable to distinguish between piles of ten and fifteen stones. In their lives, they have no need for numerical specifics. It doesn't mean that the *Piraha* are stupid; it simply means that their life experience has integrated no algebraic requirements. I bet they almost never get sunburned.

Regarding the tea party and working-class Republican voters, as it applies to their perception of economic or capitalist principles, the lack of understanding does not differ all that much from the *Piraha* tribe. Most Americans have no algebraic requirements beyond cashing their paychecks and perhaps balancing their checkbooks. That isn't an indictment; that is a tragic fact. Most Americans live paycheck to paycheck.

Therefore, conceptualizing how and why this economic disparity occurred, let alone what it means to have a million, or a billion of anything—let alone dollars—is inconceivable to many Americans. To offer a little perspective:

A *million* minutes equates to just under *two* years. Maybe you've gained a little weight, got a little grayer, but in the grand scheme of things, you'd have to wait twice that long for the next Olympics. You remember two years ago. New York Jets fans have been waiting *twenty five* million minutes, and counting.

A *billion* minutes ago was around *one thousand, nine hundred* years ago. Columbus wouldn't discover America for another one thousand, four hundred years, give or take. That Jesus fella in the New Testament was dead less than a hundred years. The Bible wouldn't be pieced together for another two-hundred-plus years.

So consider that, if you have a net worth of less than a million dollars (and most of you do), and the Koch brothers have—according to *Forbes* magazine—an estimated *fifty billion* dollars, think of it this way: Your net worth in minutes is less than two years ago. Their net worth, converted to minutes, is roughly around the time homo sapiens began walking upright. Or as Christians like to say, ninety-four thousand years before Yahweh created the Earth.

> *Some Americans I have spoken with (who were otherwise of quick and rational parts enough) could not, as we do, by any means count to 1,000; nor had any distinct idea of that number.*

—English philosopher John Locke[407], in 1690

Get the picture? So putting your own capacity for rational thought to the test, whom do you think your congressperson gives more of a damn about? You, or the guy who can finance his election and give awesome jobs to his wife and kids as easily as you can order a pizza?

The concepts of tens of billions of dollars is mind-boggling, even to those with an economic background. It is more than a shit-ton of money. Regarding what ten, twenty, or fifty billion dollars of net worth is like, most Americans are like the *Piraha*. Most people have a difficult time distinguishing between a millionaire entrepreneur and a nation-raping

---

[407] An essay., *John Locke*, Concerning Human Understanding Book II: Ideas by John Locke

billionaire. From a working-class perspective, both are unfathomably wealthy and beyond one's scope.

And this is why the "class warfare" bullshit works so well on working class-Fox-News-watching Republican voters. The Dominionist GOP has combined gall and guile to convince voters that people with billions of dollars—making more than ever—are victims of a socialist regime's class war. Conservative media makes it seem that Democrats decrying multibillionaires manipulating legislation is the same as trying to prevent us from ever being able to afford a BMW. And that Jesus wants the wealthy to have more, for everyone's benefit.

The thing is, the "class war" is already over. The game has been rigged. The outcome, predetermined. The financial elite have won. The poor and the middle class have lost.

Funky Bunch

When the rich wage war, it's the poor who die.

—Jean-Paul Sartre[408]

There is a certain type of pathology that accords discontented billionaires. It's a hoarder-like compulsion that can never be satisfied. Indeed, acquiring money for acquisition's sake is more than just a sickness. It involves a lack of empathy and lack of concern for human suffering that can best be described as sociopathic.

Anyone who has ever raised children knows about when toddlers go through their "mine!" phase. It's when a child believes everything is due to him or her. For instance, if a three-year-old has a collection of marbles, and he sees another kid with a couple of marbles, the first kid wants the other kid's marbles too. You have it; he wants it—so it's rightfully his.

---

[408] BrainyQuote.com, *Jean-Paul Sarte*, http://www.brainyquote.com/quotes/quotes/j/jeanpauls108422.html

Because, in a child's still-developing mind, he doesn't yet comprehend—among other things—what having "enough" is. The little brat must have dominion over all the marbles. Mine!

Thus, in pursuit of better understanding the mentality of a billionaire sociopath, I submit a whimsical channeling of the fictional, albeit brilliant, Hannibal Lechter. Who else would one reference after a toddler analogy? We must ask that of each particular thing: What is it in itself? What is its nature? What do they do, these Dominionist Orwellians?

Is the primary ambition of the Dominionist, Orwellian monetary acquisition? Is it to spread Christianity? Or foremost, do they hope to influence legislation? No Clarisse, they are all incidental.

They control.

> *Access to water is not your right. Believing you have a right to water—is an extreme belief. Water is a raw material and a "foodstuff" that should be privatized and commercialized.*

—Nestle CEO, sociopath, and potential Bond villain, Peter Brabeck[409]

> *I want my fair share—and that's all of it.*

—Charles "Classic" Koch[410]

The end games, for Orwellians, are political and economic sovereignty. Dominion over the populace. We the people are to render unto Caesar that which is Caesar's, and unto Yahweh whatever's left over.

---

[409] Occupycorporatism.com, *Peter Brabeck*, http://www.occupycorporatism.com/nestle-ceo-wealthy-people-access-water/

[410] Quotewise.com, *Charles Koch*, http://www.quoteswise.com/charles-koch-quotes-2.html

Manipulating the population via Republican Jesus is *how* Dominionists achieve control. Societal subjugation by means of fearing divine wrath, should they not comply with the twenty-first-century, GOP version of Christianity. It is not enough for Orwellians to have incomprehensive wealth or even direct influence over national policy. In fact, nothing will ever be enough. They are sociopaths, incapable of conceiving ever having enough to be satisfied.

Dominion. Mine!

I use the term "Orwellian" as an homage to the George Orwell masterpiece *1984*. It's an economic term used to describe the obscenely wealthy circumventing our economy and republic for their own self-interest. Orwell described a world of *perpetual war*, omnipresent government surveillance, and a manipulative media. The oligarchic, inner-party elite from Orwell's glimpse into the future foretold a political system where economic fascism became a euphemism for socialism. We hear that drivel today whenever any dullard on the right conflates the socialist principle of everyone having essentially the same amount of wealth with the extraction of capital out of our economy to favor an exclusive few. They really mean "the same level of poverty."

> *We cannot afford four more years of this misguided socialist policies from President Obama and his administration.*

—Rick "Pray for Rain" Perry[411], referring to the first four years under President Obama, where wealth inequality went in the opposite direction of socialism, as socialism

or:

---

[411] BrainyQuote.com, *Rick Perry*, http://www.brainyquote.com/quotes/quotes/r/rickperry553932.html

The idea that a congressman would be tainted by accepting money from private industry or private sources is essentially a socialist argument.

—Newt Gingrich[412], suggesting that the wealthy donate millions to political campaigns out of the kindness of their hearts and wouldn't care how the politicians they donate to vote any given piece of legislation because that would be dishonest

Only socialists would make such an accusation regarding the conflict of interest between decent, hard-working politicians and the millions of dollars they receive in donations. Right.

Amazingly the Gingrich-backing Super PAC "Winning Our Future" received approximately twenty million dollars from billionaire Sheldon Adelson alone. I'm sure Sheldon expected nothing in return for his investment. Did I say investment? I meant donation.

The thing is, lions care not for the opinions of sheep. Orwellian billionaires have no regard for America as a nation, but rather only as a labor force. Their patriotism extends no further than their ability to manipulate media, legislators, and those pesky voters so as to accommodate their interests. They don't give a flying fuck about red, white, and blue. They only care about green. Yet, Dominionists have the gall to package "patriotism" to the rest of us as an amalgamation of Glenn Beck revisionist history, Roger Ailes economics, Rush Limbaugh sociology, and Christian fundamentalism.

Freedom! Yay!

The post WWII America that many of us remember, and hope to have again, is in the hands of a few white-Anglo-Saxon Kim Jong Un's. Would-be dictators, corporate fascists who—as they garner more wealth and power—are becoming increasingly less concerned with disguising

412   Ibid., *Newt Gingrich*, http://www.brainyquote.com/quotes/quotes/n/newtgingri134434.html

their intention. But as long as I'm pretending that I'm both smarter, and better read than I actually am, I'll end with this:

> *The only wealth which you will keep forever is*
> *the wealth you have given away.*

—Marcus Aurelius[413]

You should try one of my mojitos.

Koch Whores

> *Jesus entered the temple courts and drove out all who were*
> *buying and selling there. He overturned the tables of the*
> *money changers and the benches of those selling doves.*

—Matthew 21:12[414]

The twenty-first-century GOP is a vicious cycle of Republican politicians being chosen by news-ertainers, who are funded by billionaires.

It does not take an extraordinary acumen to see that the "higher power" to which Republican politicians answer to is more likely big-money donors like the Koch brothers than Yahweh. As such, in the Christian Dominionist political world, there is no conflict of interest when candidates collude with their donors. That *is* their interest. So in keeping with the tea party ruse, the Dominionist "God-isms" conveniently accord the best interests of billionaire Republican financial donors who essentially employ the politicians who are financially beholden to them.

[413] BrainyQuote.com, *Marcus Aurelius*, http://www.brainyquote.com/quotes/quotes/m/marcusaure384872.html

[414] Holy Bible, *Matthew 22:12*, Holy Bible. New International Version ®, Copyright © 1973, 1978, 1984, 2011 by Biblica, Inc.®

And beholden they are. The tea party/GOP policy specifically caters to legislating on behalf of the wealthiest Americans, to help ease the widening financial gap between them and the rest of us. It's remarkable how many less-than-sane rationalizations can be made to accord a Jesus who condones a miser-like obsession with monetary copiousness. From legislators, to "conservative" judges, the capitulation to Dominionist interests are consistent.

From the state level:

Buddha didn't create us. Muhammad didn't create us. It's the God of the Holy Scriptures. They didn't bring the Koran over on the pilgrim ship. Let's get real, let's go back and learn our history. Let's stop playing games.

—Alabama Chief Justice Roy "Jesus or Die" Moore[415], explaining that the First Amendment only applies to Christians.

To the national level:

The reaction of people of faith to this tendency of democracy to obscure divine authority, should (be) the resolution to combat it as effectively as possible.

—Supreme Court Justice Antonin "Here to Enforce Biblical Law" Scalia[416]

---

[415] Patheos.com, *Justice Roy Moore*, http://www.patheos.com/blogs/ warrenthrockmorton/2014/05/10/alabama-chief-justice-roy-moore-says-first-amendment-only-protects-christians/

[416] Firstthings.com, *Justice Antonin Scalia*, http://www.firstthings.com/ article/2002/05/gods-justice-and-ours

To the process by which we elect the most powerful person on earth:

> *"We cannot survive as a republic if we do not become, once*
> *again, a God-centered nation that understands that our*
> *laws do not come from man, they come from God"*
>
> -2016 Presidential hopeful and a man who should
> never wear horizontal stripes, ever again, Mike
> Huckabee[417], in a 2015 interview on "Life Today".

It's sociologically fascinating to see how America's perception has been changed over the last thirty years. It's changed even more since the election of Barack Obama. The ravings of what was once the lunatic fringe is now spoken by Supreme Court justices and presidential candidates. Dominionist-funded tea party amateurs run for office everywhere in our nation, many without having the acumen to do their jobs properly.

Indeed, tea party members of Congress merely follow the Dominionist, twenty-first-century conservative playbook and move to the right whenever the line dance demands. And while tea-candidates have little chance of winning in some areas of the country, they have enough of a political presence to change the political discourse—and our legislation. Their influence is reflected in—among other things—the unabashed, contemptuous regard for the once-cherished church-state separation in our judicial process.

Yes, when billionaires fund candidates, they expect a return on their investments. And thanks to the Supreme Court, in state and local elections, through the lower courts, their tea-investments are paying massive dividends. To best understand the relationship between Christian Dominionism and Orwellians, one need only acknowledge who benefits from a "Christian nation." Who benefits from a proletariat addicted

---

[417] Talkingpointsmemo.com, *Mike Huckabee,* http://talkingpointsmemo.com/livewire/mike-huckabee-secular-theocracy

to Jesus? Religion is the oldest scam in history that the wealthy use to manipulate the masses.

It's remarkable that Jesus loving tea-folk fall for it.

Supper's Ready

Anyone whose name was not found written in the
book of life was thrown into the lake of fire.

—Revelation 20:15[418]

What many casual Christian Americans don't seem to realize—because fundamentalists rarely speak of this for fear of frightening would-be voters and donators away—is that the tenets of Christianity are such that Jesus Christ's return will usher in the destruction the world. That is one hell of an end game. This is the biblical story from the book of Revelation, written by Saint John the Divine, per his vision of the second coming of the messiah. It's about our New Testament hero descending from heaven, sorting through the earthly riff-raff, picking out the faithful few, and the rest can go fuck themselves and burn in a lake of fire. Terminator 2: Judgment Day.

Written approximately sixty years after the crucifixion, resurrection, ascension, and ensuing confusion; the book of Revelation is the last book of the Bible. It was omitted by Thomas Jefferson from *The Jefferson Bible,* as he considered it the ravings of a maniac, yet it is nonetheless a science-fiction masterpiece. Undeniably, *St. John the Insane* tells a spectacular tale of giant sea beasts, a seven-headed dragon, sky-riding, woe-dealing horsemen, lion-headed cavalry, a giant aerial birth, scorpion-tailed locusts, all culminating in a no-holds-barred steel-cage grudge match between Jesus and Satan.

---

[418] Holy Bible, *Revelation 20:15*, Holy Bible. New International Version ®, Copyright © 1973, 1978, 1984, 2011 by Biblica, Inc.®

And it's what fundamentalist Christians—many of whom have already been elected to public office—absolutely, positively believe will happen.

For thousands of years, religious nuts have believed that they were living in "end times." And twenty-first-century American Christian loons are no different. Ask any fundamentalist, born-again Christians you might know if they think that we are close to the end of the world. Inquire of tea-Christians—whose vote counts just as much as yours does—what they believe about St. John's psychotic hallucination. Hell, ask your typical Fox News viewer. The self-obsessed megalomania inherent in fundamentalist religiosity has allowed Christian zealots from every generation to believe that they are so star-spangled special that they were chosen to be on the court as the clock wound down.

Everybody wants to go to heaven, but nobody wants to die.

—Joe Louis[419]

Irrationality has been presented as normalcy for so long that it has become part of our everyday sociopolitical discussion. Americans barely care about crazy and stupid anymore. We have become so numb to nonsense that not many people took notice when, in late 2013, former Republican President George W. Bush flew to Israel to speak on behalf of a group—*the Messianic Jewish Bible Institute*—that hopes to convert enough Jews to Christianity that they can expedite the ushering in of end times. That's end times, as in the book of Revelation.

Right. Pass the potato chips.

Jews for Jesus makes about as much sense as *Dykes for Dicks* would. I'm not sure if the more casual Christians reading this are giving the "end times" concept the consideration that it's due. But by end times, these psychotic mental cases actually mean end times. Armageddon. The end of the world.

---

[419] BrainyQuote.com, *Joe Louis*, http://www.brainyquote.com/quotes/quotes/j/joelouis163459.html

The apocalypse. The zombie son of Yahweh returns. Everyone on Earth dies, and the Christian faithful ascend to heaven.

The vision of the MJBI is to bring Jewish people into a personal relationship of faith with Yeshua the Messiah, knowing their acceptance will eventually mean life from the dead (Romans 11:15) [420].

—From the home page of the MJBI website. In case you're wondering who "Yeshua" is, us Americans spell it "Jesus."

Astonishingly, a man who was leader of the free world for eight years thought that speaking at an event like this was a good idea. The Dominionists around him—be they on the pulpit, in public office, or in the media—were on board as well. It's about Jesus, so Republicans were all in. Indeed, one of the things that is often overlooked by people like me—when pointing out the erosion of church-state separation, the bigoted legislation, irrational hyperbole, convoluting of information, revisionist history, and denial of science—is that these very same Jesus-nuts look forward to the end of the world so that they can go to heaven and blow a postlife raspberry at the rest of us.

And these raving lunatics want the nuclear launch codes.

The Knot

Only Americans can hurt America.

—Dwight D. Eisenhower[421]

So here is another "big reveal" pertaining to the author of this book: I am a Republican. I doubt that many Republicans who read this book will believe

---

[420] Holy Bible, *Romans 11:15*, Holy Bible. New International Version ®, Copyright © 1973, 1978, 1984, 2011 by Biblica, Inc.®

[421] BrainyQuote.com, *Dwight Eisenhower,* http://www.brainyquote.com/quotes/quotes/d/dwightdei149089.html

it, but it's true. I just don't recognize the twenty-first-century version of the GOP as the Republican Party. Hardly anyone in the contemporaneous GOP is remotely reminiscent of the great Republican President Dwight David Eisenhower.

Surely, based upon his policies—when juxtaposed against similar ideas spoken today—the Supreme Commander of all the Allied Forces in WWII wouldn't even be granted the courtesy of being labeled a RINO. There is little doubt that Ike's presidential administration—viewed via the convoluted political interpretations of the conservative-industrial complex—would earn him the label of "socialist." Just check to see what the conservative political and media reactions are when someone in either party disparages the military-industrial complex, as Eisenhower did. It's laughable.

In truth, I don't know what Ted Cruz, Michele Bachman, Rick Santorum, Mitt Romney, Rand Paul, Scott Walker, Marco Rubio, Mike Huckabee, or Paul Ryan are. But they sure as shit aren't Republicans. Corporatists, oligarchs, and theocrats all apply at various times. But Republicans? Certainly not. That goes for evangelical preachers and conservative media as well. Yet the best phrase I've found to describe the Orwellian policies of the twenty-first-century conservative movement, is *Christian Dominionist*.

Science is the true theology.

—Thomas Paine[422]

Above all else, reason is the characteristic that our nation's founders collectively possessed. None were prone to discard facts derived from peer-reviewed evidence. Nor were they inclined to deny self-evident truths in favor of what they might have wanted truth to be.

The Founding Fathers of the United States of America were men of the Enlightenment, whose reverence was for the scientific method, not biblical

---

[422] Mind on Fire by Emerson., Thomas Paine, page 153.

superstition. So, as it applies to blind adherence to one's political party, there is nothing more American—or patriotic—than being rational. As such, any form of loyal, nationalistic dissent must operate from the premise of science and reason. Which is why crazy/stupid tea party affirmations are undeniably un-American.

Thus, American laws must reflect socioeconomic reason and scientific understanding, not the beliefs of an oligarchy or theocracy. If we are to amend the Constitution to reflect the century in which we live, via having garnered a better understanding of the world in which we live—as we did when we abolished slavery—we must do so according to sociological, economic, and scientific facts derived from peer-reviewed evidence ... not the twisted morality of Bronze Age rapists.

Democrats and Republicans are not different "teams." I—and others like me—did not leave the Republican Party. The Republican Party left us the day when Christian fundamentalism corrupted its ability to legislate.

Complex problems need to be solved. We can't wish them away. The political party one affiliates themselves with cannot—must not—be so important to any individual that it comes at the expense of the nation's ability to solve political perplexities. And when an entire political party and its media affiliates adopt the backward legislative policies of maniacal religious fundamentalists, then the premise that they operate from—on every political and socioeconomic issue—is at best, less-than-sane and not-too-bright. At worst, there is a malevolent intent to undermine the nation's best interests for those of an elite few.

Thus, seeking solutions to complex twenty-first-century economic, sociological, or political problems is not possible if the cognitive process of those whom we elect to solve these problems has been compromised.

Evolution is a bankrupt speculative philosophy, not a scientific fact. Only a spiritually bankrupt society could ever believe it. ... Only atheists could accept this Satanic theory.

—Televangelist Jimmy "Hey Sugartits, Have You Ever Gone for a Ride in a Limo Before?" Swaggart[423]

Creationists make it sound like a "theory" is something you dreamt up after being drunk all night.

—Author and professor of biochemistry Isaac Asimov[424]

The first step to recovery is realizing that there *is* a problem. Before we can hope to address the more difficult fiscal and civic tasks set before our nation, we need to address *who* is attempting to solve these problems on our behalf. That is priority number one. So if you're a self-identified Christian who hasn't been mentally subjugated into believing absurdities or denying scientific facts, then you should be able to realize that those who have, are not rational enough to lead our nation to recovery.

And in twenty-first-century America, such cognitive incompetents are called "tea party Republicans."

Certainly, the Democratic party is imperfect. At times, sensationally so. But the DNC is not overrun with religious lunatics seeking to usher in end times. Twenty-first-century Democrats do not deny science in favor of fairy tales. Nor, for that matter, do they make celebrities of lunatics, bigots, and morons. The DNC has a lot of problems, but an infestation of psychotic personalities is not one of them.

[423] BrainyQuote.com, *Jimmy Swaggart*, http://www.brainyquote.com/quotes/quotes/j/jimmyswagg144802.html

[424] Goodreads.com, *Isaac Asimov*, http://www.goodreads.com/author/quotes/16667.Isaac_Asimov

Boring, politically correct, and race-baiting, perhaps, but not *800-pound-savior-in-the-room* crazy.

Schism Method

Talk sense to a fool, and he calls you foolish.

—Greek tragedian Euripides[425]

Indeed, twenty-first-century Dominionism is manifested through Republican legislation and justified with biblical morality.

As such, all of the irrational, sociologically regressive, economically Orwellian and science-defying would-be statutes are pertinent to American Christianity. Indeed, everything I've mentioned in this book—culminating in the restoration of pre-Depression wealth division—came about because of the revival of Christian fundamentalism that has occurred in the United States. Without the mental incapacity that goes along with religiosity, none of the accompanying crazy and stupid could have been introduced into the legislative lexicon.

Frankly, we are dumber than we were a generation ago—and a lot dumber than we were a few generations ago. As a nation, our knowledge of math, history, and science has significantly regressed. The scholastic demands we once put on ourselves—requisite of all grade-school Americans—is condemned as "elitist" or even "blasphemy." Most of this country believes in angels, and few are scientifically literate. Thank you, Jesus.

If the evangelicals vote, they determine the election.

—Ted Haggard[426]

[425] BrainyQuote.com, *Euripedes,* http://www.brainyquote.com/quotes/quotes/e/euripides125384.html

[426] Seattletimes.com, *Ted Haggard,* http://seattletimes.com/html/nationworld/2003365311_jesuscamp08.html

But it gets worse. In tea/GOP circles, stupid has become the new cool. Like reality TV keeps dumbing-down America, so too does media-driven conservative politics. In fact, reality TV and conservative entertainment are eerily similar. How else could one explain the constant presence of irrational pontiffs on conservative TV and radio? It's like a Shmuck Dynasty audio loop.

The basis of religious fundamentalism—despite what those who profit from it may claim—is not faith. It is fear. If we were in a different time or a different place, Dominionists would use different myths and legends to dumb down the populace and drive fear into people's hearts. But we are in twenty-first-century America, so Yahweh and his self/son Jesus is the deity used to accomplish an Orwellian wealth and power partition.

As I sit here writing, there is a greater amount of wealth in fewer hands than at any time in American history. We also have a greater percentage of the population who believe that they have a personal relationship with a long-dead savior. There is a direct correlation between those two sociological dynamics. It translates into more money and power for an elite few, and Jesus for the rest of us.

Never underestimate the power of stupid people in large groups.

—George Carlin[427]

The guano psychosis has gotten so bad in Christian red states that the working-class poor have been convinced that raising their own wages and getting access to health care are against their own best interests. As it pertains to politics and legislation, Christianity is an arrogant assertion, made without humility by stymied intellects. Yet reviving Christianity in America is a sociological means to an end. The more religious a culture, the more amenable to subservience it becomes … hence, the more willing it is to make the rationalizations required in order for people to allow

---

[427] Goodreads.com, *George Carlin*, https://www.goodreads.com/quotes/335169-never-underestimate-the-power-of-stupid-people-in-large-groups

themselves to participate in the economic separation of the extremely wealthy from the working class.

I don't think any American would vote for someone who publically stated that he or she firmly believes that "Macbeth murdered King Duncan after a trio of witches gave him a prophecy" is a scientific and historically accurate event. No one would vote for that person because, to make such an assertion, one would have to be a combination of crazy and stupid. Therefore, that individual would have rightfully eliminated himself or herself from any real legislative consideration. Yet, twenty-first-century Republican voters are increasingly doing just that, only they substitute for the fiction of Shakespeare things like Noah's Ark.

When voting for Christian fundamentalists, the tea/GOP electorate routinely say to themselves, "Yeah, this guy/gal claims that the earth is six thousand years old. Nothing crazy or stupid about that … sure, I'll vote for them!"

In Christian evangelism, Orwellians have found the perfect delivery system to infect the minds of the populace with enough ignorance and incomprehension to mold them to their will. Indeed, Christian fundamentalism has not only taken control of the Republican Party and its electorate, it has woven its way through the American legislature, corrupted the lexicon, and managed to bring crazy and stupid into the national discourse. Christianity is merely the means by which Orwellian, economic elitists *obtain* financial and emotional control over a population, Dominionism is the means by which to *maintain* that control through legislation.

For the true Orwellian resides in the *top tier* of the economic 1 percent. To lump Foster Friess or the Koch brothers in with a wealthy construction contractor does not reflect the prolific wealth and power distribution in America. Even if said contractor has tens of millions of dollars. For he or she would be further removed from the Orwellian economic stratosphere than a person who scrubs toilets would be from them.

Perception is not reality. Reality is reality. So if you perceive through the lens of Christianity, then what you believe to be socioeconomic reality is fuck-nut false.

Beam Me Up, Scotty

What I'm about to tell you is true. Anything you didn't do for one of the least important of these, you didn't do for me.

—Jesus Christ, Matthew 25:45[428]

It has been my sincerest wish to illustrate how, first and foremost, religion inhibits our ability to perceive. It permits us to settle for inaccurate answers. And, thus, it allows us to be manipulated.

For if one's religious convictions are absolute, despite the absence of any evidence, then how can Christians debate with any other theist whose beliefs vary from their own? How can a Christian claim that Joseph Smith or the Reverend Sun Myung Moon are not the true messenger of God, rather than Jesus? Mormons and Moonies are just as resolute in their beliefs as Christians are. The same lack of any valid evidence exists with every faith.

And when religion and politics co-mingle, everyone's ability to perceive, or pursue happiness, becomes compromised. Which is why I implore Christians of more casual faith to indulge in a little introspection. Twenty-first-century American Christianity accompanies some un-Christian legislation. Dark-Age fear has pervaded the nation's sensibilities.

Most Christian Americans are decent people who do not abide the cruelty and lack of empathy of their fundamentalist brethren. Yet many allow the umbrella of Christianity to assume a sociopolitical affiliation where none

---

[428] Holy Bible, *Matthew 25:45*, Holy Bible. New International Version ®, Copyright © 1973, 1978, 1984, 2011 by Biblica, Inc.®

is deserved. Decent people from various religions and cultures throughout time, and all over the word—including Christian Americans—follow *the golden rule.*

But tea party Republican voters have gone from this:

Do to others as you want them to do to you.

—Luke 6:31[429]

to this:

You get nothing! You lose! Good day, sir!

—Willy Wonka[430]

So you can cut food stamps to the poor and hungry. You can make fiscal cuts to education. You can deny unemployment insurance to people who have lost their jobs. You can be against policies that help people get access to health care. You can vote for those who want to privatize Medicare, Medicaid, and Social Security. You can allow corporations to pollute our drinking water with little, if any repercussion. You can deport foreigners. You can execute prisoners.

But if you do, you are not just a lousy Christian. You are an immoral person.

Approximately 40 percent of American children live in poverty. That is an appalling fact that should not be acceptable to any American, regardless of religion or political association. Even worse, the ability to escape poverty is becoming increasingly difficult. The Christian/tea/GOP is not only

---

[429] Ibid., *Luke 6:31.*

[430] Willy Wonka and the Chocolate Factory (1971), *Willy Wonka,* http://www. imdb.com/title/tt0067992/quotes

exacerbating this condition through legislation, they are complicit in siphoning capital away from people who need it most and giving it to those who need it least.

Overcoming poverty is not a task of charity; it is an act of justice. Like slavery and Apartheid, poverty is not natural. It is man-made and it can be overcome and eradicated by the actions of human beings.

—Nelson Mandela[431]

We have escaped the Dark Ages, and I think that it's fair to say that most of us don't want to return there. Thus, every human being has the right to food, shelter, clothing, education, health care, and clean water. But in twenty-first-century America, there is an ethical disconnect concerning fundamental human rights and applied legislation.

None of this is a condemnation of an economic system that financially rewards hard work and ingenuity. It is rather a factual statement about the immorality of a nation that permits such widespread poverty alongside generational wealth. Empathy and compassion for our fellow human beings is a moral prerequisite. As such, morals are not strictly a Christian— or for that matter, religious—phenomenon. And most definitely, neither are morals politically specific.

Most Americans understand why no one in this day and age should ever go hungry. In the twenty-first century, we have the ability to cure diseases that previously meant a long, miserable death sentence. But Christian politics has impeded our ethical incentive to have those cures accessible to people who need them. Christian Americans understand that cultural, ethnic, and gender biases are detestable, yet they vote for those who abide them. Most Americans believe that violence against women and gays has to be stopped, yet the GOP electorate and the conservative media industry are apathetic to intolerant discourse.

---

[431] Goodreads.com, *Nelson Mandela,* http://www.goodreads.com/ quotes/136955-overcoming-poverty-is-not-a-task-of-charity-it-is

Moreover, the "American dream" is such that generational wealth and poverty are contrary to its premise. The United States of America was never intended to be an oligarchy. And some might refer to fighting against the Dominionist Christian socioeconomic injustices, and the Orwellian monetary and power structure in America as a moral imperative.

That is, providing Christianity hasn't impaired their morals.

ABOUT ME AND THIS BOOK ...

For most of my adult life, I've been a construction worker in New York City. I entered the electrical apprenticeship when I was twenty years old, and since then, my duties have ranged from going for coffee to foreman. If there are any life skills that high-rise construction prepares you for, it's a capacity to spot bullshit from a mile away and an ability to cope via the use of colorful metaphors.

Needless to say, I am not an academic. Although I went to school at night in order to earn a bachelor's degree, for integrity's sake, I had to write this book in a blue-collar context. That is my unique perspective as it applies to the topics I've addressed within these pages. There are a lot of really smart atheists who write books, but I bet that not many of them have been in a bar fight.

Where it concerns skepticism, reason, and sociology, I have the privilege of standing on the shoulders of intellectual giants. However, Richard Dawkins is an evolutionary biologist; Sam Harris is a neuroscientist; Daniel Dennett is a cognitive scientist; and Christopher Hitchens was ... a unique genius. Yet if I endeavored to write in the vein of most books authored by atheists, I would fail miserably. I gotta be me, even if "me" is sometimes an asshole.

As such, I'll provide very few original thoughts about politics or the ridiculousness of religious fundamentalism within these pages. Indeed, what can I say about American Christianity that those before me have not already said? The thing is, the verbiage, viewpoints, and architecture of my affirmations will *all* be unique. I bet that I can use the term "jizz guzzler" more effectively than most atheist academics, and I've been told that I can be mildly amusing in an intestinal flu kind of way.

Not that anyone cares, but I was born in Queens, New York as a part of an upper-middle-class family. I'm on my second marriage, and this time I seem to have gotten it right. I am madly, hopelessly in love with my wife. As a fifty-year-old self-indulgent narcissist, I am fortunate to still have terrific hair.

I wrote this book because—having read a shitload of books about politics, and gods—I felt that it needed to be written. Before now, this kind of book didn't exist. I also wrote it because I wanted to make a few bucks as a means to psychologically compensate for my thirty-inch inseam and to have the means to fly first class. And I'd be lying if I didn't admit that it was a whole lot of fun.

R.W.